Jimmy Hoffa Called My Mom a Bitch!
Profiles in Stupidity

Jason Vines

Published by Waldorf Publishing
2140 Hall Johnson Road
#102-345
Grapevine, Texas 76051
www.WaldorfPublishing.com

Jimmy Hoffa Called My Mom a Bitch!
Profiles in Stupidity

ISBN: 9781943274260

Library of Congress Control Number: 2015941171

Copyright © 2015

Printed in Canada

Foreword by Henry Payne

Henry Payne is *The Detroit News* auto critic, an award-winning syndicated editorial cartoonist, and opinion writer. A 30-year newspaper veteran, lifetime motor head and active race car driver, Payne is a Pulitzer-Prize-nominated cartoonist and has published three books.

I first spoke to Jason Vines in 2005. Jason who?

He and his auto pals were recreating "The Steakout" and he wanted me to cartoon the program cover. The Steak-what? It was Detroit's version of Washington, DC's "Gridiron Dinner" – an off-the-record evening between journalists and industry execs (autos in Detroit; government in DC) so they could share a meal, a few laughs, and generally get to know each other beyond the pressure-cooker of daily deadlines. I had moved to Detroit from DC to become *The Detroit News* political cartoonist a few years before. A veteran of a half-dozen Gridiron dinners and a couple of program illustrations, I thought I knew the drill.

Until I talked with Vines.

This hilarious, profane, politically-incorrect, auto communications veep was an American original. Admired in the industry for his handling of product crises like flipping Ford Explorers, the outspoken Vines' legend would grow in the next few years with over-the-top Detroit Auto Show-stoppers like the 2008 cattle drive launching the new Dodge Ram pickup (look it up). I was about to get my initiation into Vines' World.
We brainstormed, sketched ideas, and laughed. A lot. A friendship was born. Unlike the cramped, stuffy Gridiron dinners (because nothing in D.C. is ever really off-the-record), the truly off-the-record Steakout was wildly un-PC. I could tell you some of the jokes, but then I'd have to kill you. Suffice to say, it was funny, profane, and utterly inappropriate - just like its host. I laughed so hard I had tears running down my face.

I would draw three more Steakout programs for the standup-comedian-turned-auto PR man. But I would also learn that Jason was more than a funnyman who knew where every skeleton in town was buried. He had a heart the size of a basketball. He introduced me to Forgotten Harvest, one of many charities that he worked with to raise money for the needy. In one evening late in 2005, he and I would team on a cartoon that we auctioned off, bringing $5K to the food rescue charity.

So when I created *The Michigan View* - a funny, un-PC, opinionated, commentary publication for *The Detroit News* in 2010, one of the first people I turned to as a columnist was Jason Vines. He jumped at the opportunity.

MIView would become a nationally-known publication in no small part thanks to high profile contributors like Jason. He took the column title "Wisecracker" and made his mark almost immediately by coining the phrase "Masturgate" to describe the scandal of the illiterate (honestly) president of the Detroit School Board who resigned after (um) unzipping in front of a Detroit superintendent (still not making this up).

Now you know why Detroit is such a great news town. "Masturgate" ruffled feathers, rolled eyes, and brought us a flood of attention. Vintage Vines, in other words. The PR whiz's second career as columnist was born.

In the four years he wrote for me at MIView and the Detroit News Politics Blog, Brother Vines was a must-read for his sense-of-humor and keen insights as a longtime auto and Detroit insider. And he did it without ever seeing a dime (like many on the Internet, alas). For this Foreword, then, I am happy to return the favor.

Herewith, the very best of The Wisecracker and beyond. Enjoy.

Henry Payne's cover art for the 2005 Detroit Press Club Steakout just two days after former Mayor Kwame Kilpatrick was jailed for perjury in the infamous "sexting" scandal.

Dedication

I dedicate this book to my mom: Peggy Jean. I love you.

Table of Contents

The Intro to Stupidity   1
Jimmy Hoffa Called My Mom a What? September 6, 2011

Chapter One: Stupid Perverts   7
Masturgate June 19, 2010
Globe Al Warming Gets Rubbed the Wrong Way June 29, 2010
A Swiss Miss and Masturgate at It Again July 12, 2010
Just When You Thought it Was Safe to Go Back in the Pew September 28, 2010
Mathis: Touch My Junk. Please! November 22, 2010
Masturgate Exonerated January 18, 2011
The New Weiner – Mobile June 1, 2011
No Hiding the Weiner June 13, 2011
Pop Goes the Weiner June 16, 2011
Fired Superintendent Hits Masturgate Jackpot October 14, 2011

Chapter Two: Stupid Criminals   18
Kwame Kilpatrick's Baghdad Bob June 28, 2010
Book 'em, Danno August 15, 2010
Kwamecare Could Save Obamacare March 25, 2011
Detroit DHS: Reclining, er, Denying the Hungry May 18, 2011
Three Men and a Bong: The Kwame Kilpatrick Story August 1, 2011
Professor Kwame the Philanderer August 8, 2011
Kwame Wants Norwegian Justice August 26, 2012
Panty Bomber: Deck the Balls September 16, 2011
With Assassinated Cops, Al Sharpton and Mayor de Blasio Guilty as "Charged" December 20, 2014
Artist Indicted for Making Kayak in Image of Her Va-Jay-Jay December 24, 2014

Chapter Three: Stupid People   30
Chipping Away at a New Cold War July 9, 2010
The Chrysler Doobie Brothers: Taking It to the Streets (or the Park) September 23, 2010
Obama Takes a Hit on Chrysler's Doobie Brothers September 29, 2010
62 Miles per Gallon? What're They Smoking? October 4, 2010

Smart is as Smart Does February 16, 2011
Stupid People of the Week: Mormons and Idiots March 6, 2011
Stupid People of the Week: People Who Paid to See Charlie Sheen's "Show" April 4, 2011
No-No Geronimo May 10, 2011
Black-on-Black Ethnic Intimidation? WTF? May 18, 2011
I Did Know Jack June 3, 2011
Squawk Like an Egyptian November 28, 2011
Stupid Person of the Week...and It's Only Thursday and It's Killing Me February 2, 2012
Stupid People of the Week: Uncle Joe Takes the Gold August 20, 2012
Stupid Person of the Week: Welcome Back McCotter June 3, 2012
PETA Jumps the Shark...Again! September 30, 2011
The NAACP Spits a Lugar May 20, 2012
The Yin and the Yang of a Totally Screwed-up Country August 21, 2012
Stupid Quotes of the Decade September 24, 2012
Petraeus: The Mrs. Will "Cut It off" November 11, 2012
Starbucks Liars and "Happy" Idiots at the United Nations March 23, 2015
Stupid People of the Week: It's a Tie Between Hillary's People and the U of M April 9, 2015
"Rights" vs. "Right" May 4, 2015

Chapter Four: Stupid White House   57
Obama, Iowa, and the G Spot August 18, 2011
Obama: The "I" of Hurricane Irene August 29, 2011
Super Soak the Rich: Plouffe Goes the Weasel September 26, 2011
Obama and Holder: Take This Photo ID and Shove It! December 13, 2011
Obama: Bombs Away from Russkies March 27, 2012
Obama's Supreme Temper Tantrum April 3, 2012
Biden Takes One for the Team May 1, 2012
Obama Re-election Campaign Begins; No S--- Sherlock! May 6, 2012
The Lawlessness of Team Obama July 2, 2012
The Lawlessness of Team Obama: Take Two July 15, 2012
Hillary to Obama: Take the VP Job and Shove It! August 19, 2012
Kick Ass: The Debate October 4, 2012
Obama's U.S. Flag Burning Stimulus Plan October 23, 2012
The "I" of the Storm: Again, Obama October 28, 2012
Obama: Hurricane Sandy Is a Breath of Fresh Air October 29, 2012

Chris Matthews: 2012 Election Proves White Americans hate Obama more than al Qaeda October 30, 2012
The Accidental Voter – Scary November 2, 2012
Obama: Eye the Prize, Finally November 19, Chapt2012
Obama's First Major PR Blunder March 11, 2013
Obama Gets Outraged Over "Some" Kids' Deaths April 18, 2013
Obama: Legacy or Bust April 15, 2013
The White House's "New" Dictionary April 28, 2013
The "Stand Up" Administration May 14, 2013
Administration Scandals et al.: "I Love to Count!" May 18, 2013
Even Obama's PR Machine is Blowing It June 1, 2013
Back "to" the USSR June 16, 2013
Secretary Kerry: Welcome to Liar's Gulch July 9, 2013
Pressure Cooker Bombs from Our President July 19, 2013
President Obama: The World's Rodeo Clown August 18, 2013
Obama: Inflictor-in-Chief October 5, 2013
Uncle Joe and #FreeCommunityCollege: Stupid Is as Stupid Does January 28, 2015
White House Should Hire Baghdad Bob; at Least He Was Entertaining January 29, 2015
Queen Elizabeth: Obama Advisor February 1, 2015
A Look Back at the Most Lawless Week of the Obama Administration March 2, 2015
Hillary Clinton: Liar, Liar, Pantsuit on Fire March 9, 2015
"Some Democrats" Slam @HillaryClinton in Sexist Rant in @nytimes March 12, 2015

Chapter Five: Stupid Democrats   111
Do as I Say, Not as I Do June 15, 2010
Clinton Is Back - Hide Your Daughters October 25, 2010
Democratic Cheeseheads Raise a Stink February 17, 2011
Dems Need a Course in Dirty Tricks April 18, 2011
Warren Mayor's Stunt Is Getting Old May 15, 2011
The Vagina Stupidity June 17, 2012
Long Johnson a Political Weiner August 5, 2012
Eva Longoria and Me August 27, 2012
Dems Find Jesus September 5, 2012
The Brothers Levin: Disgrace Under Fire July 1, 2013

Chapter Six: Stupid Republicans   121
Romney Fumbles While Newt Scores "Double Dipping" January 23, 2011
Mitt-Stake…Pure and Simple April 9, 2011
Michael Bloomberg: Tone Deaf May 3, 2011
The Donald: Firing on All Meats May 15, 2011
The Great GOP Slugfest August 7. 2011
Ron Paul Channels Dukakis October 2, 2011
Perry's 6-6-6 Plan October 9, 2011
Cain (Hart) Trouble October 31, 2011
Romney, Gingrich: Dumb and Dumber January 25, 2012
Is Granny on the Pill? February 20, 2012
Nice Rack Newt! February 21, 2012
Santorum Projectile Hurls His Way into Michigan February 27, 2012
The GOP Needs to Take a Pill and Get Over It March 3, 2012
Romney is no Dick, Nixon July 6, 2012
Romney's Gaffes in London vs. Obama's Gaffes in the Universe July 29, 2012
Mitt: Fire Someone! September 18, 2012
Tubby Submarined Romney November 7, 2012
2012: The Lowlight December 20, 2012
Conservatives: Remain Calm! May 26, 2013
Tea Party: Tweedle dee and Tweedle dumb June 19, 2013

Chapter Seven: Stupid Policies   146
Taco Bell "Runs" for the Border January 25, 2010
Gored While Fishing in Los Cabos December 28, 2010
Live From Israel January 15, 2011
Detroit Gets its NOJO Back March 30, 2011
Nightmare (for the Greenies) on Woodward Avenue August 19, 2011
Department of Energy Secretary Chu is Re-Volting March 12, 2012
Chu Chu on the Tracks Again March 20, 2012
Summa Chu Laude March 20, 2012
The Big, "Good" Wolf Lobby April 24, 2013
Textual Healing? April 21, 2012
Eric Holder Finally Cares for U.S. March 6, 2012
Obama Down on the Farm…Kids April 26, 2012
Courage? May 5, 2013
Abortion: Taking It to the Streets July 9, 2013

IRS, NSA, and Justice: The Real Vamps and Zombies! June 23, 2013
Anthony Weiner Not the "Nuttiest" Person in NY After All August 13, 2013
Al Gore's Nightmare September 17, 2013
Takata and NHTSA: Dumb and Dumber December 15, 2014
Sometimes, It Hertz December 16, 2014
The Cuban "Situation" From My Outraged Cuban Friend 52 Years "Off the Boat" December 18, 2014
Mitt and Putin ONE; Obama and Hillary ZERO January 30, 2015
Operation OverLOAD: No Caliphate Left Behind February 16, 2015
Bibi Wins — NetanYAHOO! March 17, 2015
The Real Enemy of Autonomous Cars: The Tax Man Near You March 19, 2015
My Friend Has ALS and You Can Help #FDAhope4ALS March 29, 2015
Wi-Fi Ya Doing That to Me? April, 19, 2015
The Home Depot: You Can Do It. They Can Help…in CODE April 20, 2015

Chapter Eight: Stupid Washington   188
DC Is Nuttier Than Chinese Chicken Salad January 29, 2012
Washington Weakly: Truants and Killers February 5, 2012
Washington Weakly: Where the Rubbers Meet the Campus February 12, 2012
Detroit City Council Loses "Stupidest" Crown June 14, 2012
Sanity Strikes Washington, D.C. No Kidding September 12, 2013
Washington Redskins: What's in a Name? September 15, 2013

Chapter Nine: Stupid Dictators   196
Kim Jong "Ill" is Now Kim Jong Dead December 19, 2011
North Korea: Not a Wet Eye in the Place December 28, 2011
North Korean BBQed Rocket April 12, 2012
Chavez Is Dead. Long Stay Dead Chavez. March 5, 2013
Hugo Get an Air Freshener March 20, 2013

Chapter Ten: Stupid Media   200
The NY Mosque Is Greek to Me! September 7, 2010
The Whine Albom February 21, 2011
More Bubbly from Albom's "Whine" Cellar March 14, 2011

NewsCorpse July 20, 2011
Free Copy of *The New York Times*: I Want My Money Back September 19, 2011
MSM Pre-"Occupied" with "Grassroots" Nature of Protests October 11, 2011
Cain "Most Racist" in Campaign October 12, 2011
Black Night; Pathetic Morning for Journalism July 22, 2012
The Bitchings of Eastwood September 3, 2012
Dying Wrong April 8, 2013
The Left's Tragedy of the Boston Bombing April 21, 2013
Blame It on the Intern: It Worked for Bubba Clinton July 15, 2013
Read This Column and Then Shut the F--- Up! September 29, 2013
Saw *American Sniper* and My Wife Wants "to Kick Michael Moore's Ass" January 27, 2015

Chapter Eleven: Stupid Occupiers   225
Occupiers Throw Homeless to the Curb November 2, 2011
OWS to Homeless: Leggo My Eggo November 13, 2011
Raid on Insipid: The Occupiers November 21, 2011

Chapter Twelve: Stupid Atheists   230
God Checks Out of Iowa September 15, 2010
Atheists Get Cross July 28, 2011
Atheists Storm Washington for a "Reason" March 25, 2012
Earth to Vegans: You're Killing Me April 23, 2013
Chicago's "Jesus Free" School Zone November 3, 2013

Chapter Thirteen: Stupid Christians   237
Florida Pulpit Fiction September 8, 2010
Praise Be to the Holy Powerball! November 15, 2010
Return of The Three Miscue-teers March 6, 2011
Reverend Terry Jones: PR Master April 26, 2011
Reverend Terry Jones pulls a Charlie Sheen April 29, 2011
The Reverend Jesse Jackson: Open Mouth, Insert Foot May 2, 2011
Betting the Farm on Us Buying the Farm May 21, 2011
Reverend Jesse Jackson Shakedown Artist: R.I.P. March 25, 2013
Christ as a Liberal Crutch April 1, 2013
Reverend Al Sharpton's Prayers Answered July 14, 2013

Chapter Fourteen: Stupid Sports Figures   252
University of Michigan Hiring Assange as Football Coach? December 7, 2010
Ban Tobacco in Baseball? Why Stop There? October 19, 2011
Akin "Akin" to Penn State's Ex-President August 23, 2012
Pennsylvania Gov. Tom Corb-idiot January 3, 2013
Is the Whole World Juicing? March 17, 2013
A Twisted Tale in Happy Valley Gets More Twisted January 17, 2015
Super Bowl Announcer Al Michaels Is a Fugitive January 31, 2015
The "Possible" Pete Carroll-Reggie Bush Pre-Game Call February 1, 2015
The Brady "Hunch" May 7, 2015

Chapter Fifteen: Stupid Predictions (on my part)   262
Obama Gets Nailed by *The Washington Post* June 10, 2011
A Little Town Called Hope…in Iowa October 7, 2012
The Tour de Mitt October 20, 2012
Bring on the Hanging Chad October 23, 2012
Iowa: Obama's Field of Screams October 28, 2012

Chapter Sixteen: Finally   269
Energy September 26, 2012
I Want to "Live Life Backwards" January 10, 2015

Author Bio: 273
Acknowledgments: 275
Reference Pages: 276

The Intro to Stupidity

"Would you like one or two lumps with your tea?"

Politicians and other public figures often say and do things that are egotistical, hysterical, mind-numbing, hypocritical, and bizarre. And sometimes, they reach levels of stupidity that are nothing short of what the young people like to say today ad nauseam: amazing! (The burrito bowl at Chipotle is amazing! The pumpkin spice latte at Starbucks is amazing! You get my drift.)

In the late spring of 2010, long-time *Detroit News* editorial cartoonist Henry Payne called me and asked if I wanted to be a part of a new venture connected with the newspaper. Payne was starting a political blog for the newspaper and was calling it *The Michigan View* (it would later be melded into the actual website of the *Detroit News* as the "Politics Blog"). It was to be a conservative take on the political follies in Detroit, the state of Michigan, in our nation's nutty capital of Washington, D.C., and across our great country and the world.

My assignment—my quest according to Henry—was to bring some humor and satire to the website, and Henry gave me carte blanche – write whatever you want, whenever you want. Henry offered me a stellar pay package of zero dinero, so I jumped at the offer, and over the next few years pumped out a few hundred columns about the scandals of Detroit's city government and now-incarcerated former Mayor Kwame Kilpatrick, the follies of the Left, the self-inflicted wounds of the Right, and more hypocrisies and stupidity at the local, state, and national political levels and in the media than you could shake a stick at. My column came under the heading, "The Wisecracker." (Notice "Wisecracker" is one word and not two. After all, it was a Detroit news organization and with me being a white dude, "Wise Cracker" would go over like a pregnant pole-vaulter.)

My first big break came early in my "career" as a columnist for the *Detroit News* when the president of the board of Detroit Public Schools (DPS), Otis Mathis, decided to let his fingers do the, er, walking. Mathis had been in the news in prior months when *Detroit News* columnist Laura Berman spilled the beans that the top politician connected with Detroit's dysfunctional public school system was illiterate. Read that last sentence slowly. Mathis had, decades earlier, successfully sued Detroit's Wayne State University in order to get his bachelor's degree despite the fact he could not do the course work due to his illiteracy. It was a shameful example of social promotion, but the real shame was years away after Mathis somehow landed the DPS board president's job.

The shame? In June of 2010, Mathis was accused of fondling himself in front of a female superintendent on several occasions and announced his resignation after admitting his "handy" work. He later tried to rescind said resignation, claiming he suffered from an undisclosed illness that led to his public "shaking hands with the unemployed." Ahem. I coined the term "Masturgate" for the scandal in my column, and the rest is, well, hysterical. The life and times of the "Mad Hander" is chronicled in the first chapter of this book, Stupid Perverts, which also includes my favorite column during my tenure with the politics blog—"Globe Al Warming Gets Rubbed the Wrong Way." Oh yes, there are several "Profiles in Stupidity" concerning former Vice President Al Gore.

So, why the title of this book, "Jimmy Hoffa Called My Mom a Bitch"? Early in 2011, something very unfunny happened in Tucson, Arizona, when several people were gunned down by a sicko. One of the victims that was badly injured was Arizona Congresswoman Gabby Giffords. At a memorial service days later, President Obama attended and gave what I believe was the best speech of his tenure, in which he called for "a new era of civility in politics." His words were moving and seemed real. Well, for at least that day. The "new era of civility" would soon vaporize, thanks in great part to Mr. Obama himself.

Fast-forward eight months to Detroit, Michigan, and the annual Labor Day rally for union members, one and all. On stage were President Obama and the grand master of the rally, Teamsters President James P. Hoffa, Jr., the famous son of the infamous Jimmy Hoffa, who some suggest has been enjoying retirement since 1975 in the end zone concrete of Giants Stadium in East Rutherford, New Jersey. Hoffa Jr. decided that before he introduced the President of the United States, he would personally see that the "new era of civility in politics" was toast. Here's how Real Clear Politics reported the scene:

Teamsters President Jimmy Hoffa had some profane, combative words for Republicans while warming up the crowd for President Obama in Detroit, Michigan, on Monday.

"We got to keep an eye on the battle that we face: The war on workers. And you see it everywhere, it is the Tea Party. And you know, there is only one way to beat and win that war. The one thing about working people is we like a good fight. And you know what? They've got a war, they got a war with us and there's only going to be one winner. It's going to be the workers of Michigan, and America. We're going to win that war," Jimmy Hoffa said to a heavily union crowd.

"President Obama, this is your army. We are ready to march. Let's take these sons of bitches out and give America back to America where we belong," Hoffa added.

Obama addressed the crowd shortly after Hoffa (and said he was "proud" of Hoffa).

Immediately below is The Wisecracker's take on Hoffa's Labor Day 2011 rant concerning "The Day That Civility Died." It is just one example of the "Profiles of Stupidity" that make up this book, which I have shared with readers of The Michigan View, later *The Detroit News'* Politics Blog, and recently, on my own blog at whatdidjesusdrive.wordpress.com.

Jimmy Hoffa Called My Mom a What? September 6, 2011

Am I mad that James Hoffa Jr. called my dear mother the B-word? I am, after all, her son and I am a conservative Republican and love the Tea Party. So, therefore, if Jimmy wants his buddies to "take these sons of bitches out" then I guess I am a target and Momma Wisecracker is a "you know what" in his eyes.

4

Ah, that new order of civility called for by our President. That same President who tries to pull the lowest form of partisan politics and demands a full session of Congress for him to speak to at the exact same time of the first major Republican presidential debate. He said he wanted to go back to the unifying spirit of 9/11, but I guess September 5th didn't count.

Back to Jimmy (Hoffa). Am I mad? Not really, because what everybody is focusing on—the use of SOB and "take out"—are probably uttered by union "strongmen" like Hoffa and the AFL-CIO's Richard Trumka on a daily basis. No, I'm disappointed in his sentence construction. "Let's take these sons of bitches out and give America back to America where we belong." The phrase "give America back" should have been followed by some form of "to whom." Like, give America "back to the little people." Or give America back "to hard-working men and women." What he said, in the end, while widely-covered, was nonsensical.

What was equally silly was Aretha Franklin warming up the crowd singing "Chain of Fools." Considering Obama's dreadful economic results, the failure of the stimulus and increasingly awful poll numbers, "Down by the Lazy River" or "I Can't Get No (Satisfaction)" would have been less heinous choices. Chain of Fools? Holy hits Batman, you just can't make up this stuff!

Stranded up here in Northern Lower Peninsula Michigan, I was once again forced this morning to listen to liberal talk radio. Yes, yes, the infamous Stephanie Miller Show. Her guest hosts "shockingly" blamed FOX News for "editing" Hoffa's words. "He was urging the crowd to vote," they protested. The rest of the three-hour set included the following "civil" morsels from the leftists, who at least once every half-hour importantly reminded the audience that they were gay:

"Rick Perry is a wacko."

"Michelle Bachmann is a Stepford wife. Whenever she talks about guns, I want to go out and get one."

"Dick Cheney is evil. He is Darth Vader."

"The Tea Party has a large contingent of mouth breathers."

"America is run by corporations and white men."

"The Postal Service's problems are George Bush's fault."

I will admit, it is a bit entertaining to listen to them, but it's also a bit depressing how angry they are about everything. But what makes them insanely mad is that no one is paying attention to their anger. The real anger is not left or right, not liberal nor tea partier. No, it is everywhere.

Case in point: Finally, at 10 a.m. I was granted a reprieve from their hate-stained rhetoric with a break for ABC Radio News. Egad! Horrible news for Obama with his lowest approval numbers ever. But just seconds later, ABC was snatching victory from the jaws of defeat for Mr. Obama. "The Republican Congressional numbers are even lower than the President's."

Whew. That was close. And the liberals buy the spin. Only problem is, it's phony. Our nation votes for the President. States vote for their representatives, so a "national poll" on the Republican-held Congress as a whole is something they should "take out."

Chapter One: Stupid Perverts

"ANTHONY WEINER'S RUNNING FOR OFFICE AGAIN."

Masturgate: June 19, 2010

Otis, my man! I gotta hand it to him (sorry, cheap laugh, and more to come)—the former (maybe not) President of the Detroit Public Schools Board, Otis Mathis, has given new meaning to that old tune "Shama Lama Ding Dong!" The scandal—I call it Masturgate—is the latest in the wacky happenings at the Detroit Public School Board (Remain calm! All is well!). Now I get why he had trouble writing coherently. He couldn't see what he was writing because—as our mothers told us at a young age—"Do the deed and you will go blind." Now it all makes sense.

But wait, Otis now has an excuse. He needs medical treatment so that it doesn't happen again. Are hand amputations covered by Blue Cross/Blue Shield?

For the DPS Board, the job at hand is to make this story go flaccid. But, just when you thought Masturgate couldn't possibly get any more bizarre, a fellow DPS Board member jumps the shark. Reverend David Murray—yes, a minister—said he supports the 55-year-old Handy Man and says he shouldn't quit. Said Murray: "It happens to a lot of young men. They engage in behavior they feel is harmless, and it's offensive to certain people."

Young men? Otis "love to love me baby" Mathis is 55 years old! Offensive to certain people? The only "certain people" that wouldn't be offended are Larry Flynt and the late Bob "Hogan" Crane.

Could we be rushing to judgment on the Mad Hander?

"He then rezipped and unzipped his pants again, again placing the hand with the handkerchief inside the zipper again," said the female superintendent making the claims about Mathis. Maybe, just maybe, Mathis was practicing some sort of magic trick. Everybody loves magic tricks, especially superintendents.

If nothing else, this whole embarrassment reminds me of the precious words of the late, great Rodney Dangerfield. "Was I afraid when I first had sex? Of course, I was. I was alone."

Globe Al Warming Gets Rubbed the Wrong Way: June 29, 2010

In a story that makes former DPS President Otis "Masturgate" Mathis look like a slacker, former Vice President, Academy Award winner, and Nobel laureate (they give these things away like Chiclets these days), Albert Arnold Gore is alleged to have sexually assaulted a female masseuse in the Hotel Lucia in Portland, Oregon, four years ago.

Supposedly, when describing the type of massage he wanted from the masseuse, Gore indicated that he wanted work on his "adductor muscles." I have now learned that the adductor muscles are on the insides of your thighs. In all my life, I have never asked for a female to massage my "adductor muscles" for fear that she would not understand that I indeed wanted my inner thighs rubbed and would flee the room thinking I was too weird to be around.

Gore also allegedly asked the masseuse to work on his abdomen, which, considering the last photo I saw of him would be full-time employment.

Gore, apparently realizing the abdomen work would take longer than the current Afghan War, grabbed the masseuse's hand and shoved it onto the South Wing of the White House (sorry), crying out "there."

From "there," the story gets weird, as—according to my very unreliable sources—just as the masseuse was ready to escape from her hell-on-earth situation, Otis Mathis jumped into the room and snapped the Vice Pervert's chief-of-staff with a rolled-up handkerchief and, um, er, oh wait, let me wake up from this bad dream.

So, the masseuse temporarily gets out of the clutches of the Al-atollah Comeontoyou, at which point he turns on the charm, offering her brandy and condoms stored in the "treat box" supplied by the hotel. Remind me never to go trick-or-treating at the Hotel Lucia.

Gore then allegedly maneuvered Magic Fingers into his bedroom in order to show her his "iPod docking station." (I'm gonna use that line on my wife tonight and promise to share the results.) Upon docking, Gore allegedly forced his ginormous body on top of the masseuse in what can only be described as "Earth in the Balance."

I guess all's well that ends well because she escaped from the seismic event. She later told her "liberal" friends of the ordeal, who told her to "just suck it up; otherwise the world's going to be destroyed from global warming." No. It was a marriage that was destroyed by The Goracle.

A Swiss Miss and Masturgate at it Again: July 12, 2010

Perverts seem to be everywhere in the news these days, don't they? "Roaming" Polanski is now free, thanks to those "gutsy Swiss." Think about their decision to free an admitted and convicted rapist of a 13-year-old girl back in the 1970s the next time you want to buy an expensive watch, some chocolate, or whatever the heck the Swiss make.

Not to be outdone by the exploits of Polanski, Otis "Masturgate" Mathis is back in the news, just when you thought it was safe to let your kids read the newspaper. The media says that the former Detroit Public Schools board prez may have had his "hand" in the Synagro cookie jar of bribery. If true, the Mad Hander has definitely been letting his fingers do the walking everywhere he goes. But why would the president of a school board need bribes from a corrupt sludge hauler? Incredibly unreliable sources have given the Wisecracker an alleged transcript of the wiretapped phone conversation between Mathis and (now convicted) Synagro moneyman, Rayford Jackson.

Rayford: Hello! Dammit Riddle, I said don't call on this number!

Mathis: Rayford, Otis Mathis here.

Rayford: Oh, my bad. Otis, my man!

Mathis: Hear through the grapevine you're "dancing in the streets" spreading some of that Synagro money around, and I want my loot, too.

Rayford: That booty is for Detroit City Council, not the DPS! Are you nuts?

Mathis: (Long, dramatic pause)

10

Rayford: Otis, you still there? Otis? Otis?

Mathis: Sorry, Rayford, I got distracted just then. I think I'd be happy with five large, brother.

Rayford: Beat it, Otis. (Click)

Just When You Thought It Was Safe to Go Back in the Pew: September 28, 2010

You've heard the Wisecracker rant from time to time about the liberal media seeming to hate Christianity while, at the same time, begging for tolerance of all other religions including Paris Hilton Worship. Christianity somehow survived the mini-church nutcase in Florida who wanted to barbecue the Quran. But just when you thought it was safe to go back in the pews, a Georgia minister is being sued for "luring" four young men into sexual relationships.

The good minister, Bishop Eddie Long, may very well be totally innocent, and this is nothing more than a horrible smear campaign. But his words the other day in front of his ginormous congregation—around ten thousand (yikes! Where do they park?)—were troubling, to say the least, and pure, unadulterated (oops, sorry — my bad) fodder for the Christianity haters.

"I feel like David against Goliath. But I got five rocks and I haven't thrown one yet," the minister extolled the cheering masses.

If he is truly innocent, then he should cry foul from the mountaintop. But, if we find out in the end that he did do what he is accused of doing to those very young men, then this David vs. Goliath theme will truly seem, well, sick. After all, if you are the leader of a 10,000-member church, and you are hitting on young, fragile teenage boys, you are, in fact, Goliath. Not David.

Bishop Long's other words give even more pause: "I have never in my life portrayed myself as a perfect man," he said. Uh-oh, sounds a lot like the start of the Eliot Spitzer press conference when he finally admitted he was Client No. 9.

Oh, things get worse the more you read. The bishop is a father of four and is an outspoken opponent of gay marriage – the Left's proof that Christians are intolerant, homophobic bigots. If these allegations are true, Bishop Long gets to add "hypocrite" to his resume.

When Long spoke to his flock Sunday, he did not address the nasty allegations directly, deciding rather to talk about the "painful" and "difficult" times he was experiencing. Sounds like a page out of the Bill Clinton playbook.

Is he a guilty, sick hypocrite, or is he a terribly wronged man of the cloth? That may very well depend on what the definition of "is" is.

Mathis: Touch My Junk. Please! November 22, 2010

Former Detroit Public School Board President Otis "Masturgate" Mathis is back in the news. According to the Wisecracker's incredibly unreliable—but talkative—sources, the Mad Hander was arrested by Metro Detroit Airport police this afternoon after he attempted to go through security more than a dozen times.

One TSA official, who did not want to be identified, said Mathis "wasn't even flying. He just kept going into the security line demanding a full body pat-down, saying there was something very dangerous in his boxers that was about to go off."

The official said Mathis tried a variety of disguises in order to move through the line time after time. "Hell, the fifth or sixth time, he came in as a nun. With a mustache. It was sorta scary." According to the TSA official, around the tenth attempt, Mathis reportedly began shouting, "Touch my junk, touch my junk, you won't know 'til ya touch my junk." Mathis even recorded his antics on his cell phone camera. But on the twelfth attempt, Mathis apparently went too far. Disguised as a TSA agent, his plan was thwarted when a crack agent noticed that Mathis had actually misspelled "TSA" on his bogus uniform. He was subsequently booked on an "impersonating an officer charge" and "erroneous spelling of a three-letter moniker."

Masturgate Exonerated: January 18, 2011

Finally, we have news of a definitive malady, which caused former Detroit Public Schools (DPS) Board President Otis "Masturgate" Mathis to do the Shama-lama-ding-dong in the presence of female DPS staffers until his resignation and later indictment. According to a just-released report out of Reuters in London, "A mysterious syndrome in which men come down with a flu-like illness after an orgasm may be caused by an allergy to semen."

The researchers discovering this phenomenon, Dutch scientists (yeah, go figure) have called it post orgasmic illness syndrome or POIS. The condition rears its ugly head post-event, with flu-like symptoms such as feverishness, runny nose, extreme fatigue, and burning eyes.

In the case of Mathis, it can also lead to blindness and bad grammar. Symptoms can last for up to a week. (Warning: if conditions last more than one week, please consult your doctor as this may be a sign of, um, er, wait, wrong problem.)

Marcel Waldinger, a professor of sexual psychopharmacology at Utrecht University in the Netherlands, suggests that men with POIS have an allergy to their own semen. In a study of thirty-three men, Waldinger performed "a standard skin-prick allergy test using a diluted form of their own semen." (Note to Editor Henry Payne: Hope I got the sequence of that quote right!) All told, twenty-nine, or 88 percent of the unlucky suckers had a positive skin reaction indicating an autoimmune response or allergy.

According to sources close to Mathis (but not too close), he will soon be asking the judge to throw out his conviction based on the Dutch findings and is asking for reinstatement on the DPS Board. Reached for comment, Mathis texted the Wisecracker saying that he now wants his good name back as soon as he returns from "The Neverlands."

The New Weiner – Mobile: June 1, 2011

"I can't say with certitude." Those were the weasel words invoked by New York Congressman Anthony Weiner (giggle, giggle, snort) when asked whether a photo of a man's wedding tackle sent out on his Twitter account to a West Coast coed was, in fact, a photo of his chief of staff.

In a spooky interview on CBS, Weiner begged the reporter that the main point to be made was that he did not send the tweet. He was the victim of a hacking prankster. Or is that a packing huckster? His condescending remarks on how this incident should be reported were eerie to hear.

Victim or liar, we will know probably sooner than later. But that's not the issue here. The real issue is two-fold. One, if there is a chance that it is a photo of Weiner's, um, er, thingamajig, the question is not how it got out, so to speak, but rather why it ever existed. Who takes a photo of their crotch besides Tommy Lee and Pamela Anderson? Since he can't say "with certitude" that the crotch in question is not his, a logical person comes to the conclusion that Mr. Weiner has captured his likeness on at least one occasion or more. "Ah, here's me and my John Thomas at Mt. Rushmore. And here's a beauty of me and the little Weiner at the Grand Canyon."

Second, if you can't say with "certitude" that a photo of a crotch on your Twitter account is or is not your crotch, you're not paying attention or you're lying. Shoot nine crotches and mine, and I can pick mine out of a police lineup. And so can every male on the planet. Perhaps we dudes are dirt-blind and can't remember important dates, but we know our crotches like the back of our hand. Ahem.

Fess up, Mr. Weiner. Victim or liar, you have certainly been caught with your pants down. Literally.

No Hiding the Weiner: June 13, 2011

Anthony Weiner needs to be taken to the cleaners. Literally, as well as figuratively. The most watched man in America, with cameras trying to follow his every move, Congressman Weiner decided on Saturday that it was time to walk to the cleaners to get his clothes laundered. From the photo, I couldn't tell if he had some of those famous undies in tow along with some dirty shirts. Regardless, you'd think that a guy under such public scrutiny and scorn would find a less public way to take care of his dirty business.

Now, you wouldn't want his wife to have to do the dirty deed. The media and paparazzi would love to get in her face. That would be wrong of Weiner, as she is a victim of Weinergate. But couldn't he ask a buddy to come over, grab his clothes and walk to the cleaners undetected?

Weiner: Yo, Angelo, it's Anthony Weiner. Hey, buddy, I need a favor. Could yous come over to my place and take my dirty clothes to the cleaners?

Angelo: Sure, anything for my friend. How much you got?

Weiner: Ten shirts and three pair of briefs.

Angelo: (Click)

Apparently, I was wrong. But it is apparent that the Weiner Tweeter craves any and all attention he can get, even if it is horrible. He may be seeking counsel for some kind of sex addiction but why is he constantly getting in front of cameras? (Note to Anthony: all men are addicted to sex, and no amount of counseling can help. What ya think they are going to give you? An anti-Cialis pill to "stop that special moment?")

It is as clear as the nose on his face that Anthony Weiner is addicted to attention for attention's sake. This guy makes Paris Hilton look like a rookie. So, what's next? I sure hope it's not Weiner getting out of a NY cab going full commando. Ugh.

Pop Goes the Weiner: June 16, 2011

Stick a fork in the Weiner. He's done, at least politically. The pressure on Weiner had mounted for weeks. There was nary a single Democratic supporter for Weiner. When President Obama FINALLY suggested "if he was Weiner", he would quit, you knew it was just a matter of time for Weiner to finally shrink from his goofy "I won't resign" claim. Funny how it took the Prez two painful weeks to weigh in on Weinergate, yet it took all of two seconds for him to comment on the Cambridge, Massachusetts cops acting "stupidly" some time ago.

And when a porn star throws you under the bus, well, it's time to throw in the towel that dangles from your waist in the Congressional men's locker room. Guess there is nothing left for Weiner except to go home, lick his wounds and wait for the eventual call from CNN offering him a seat alongside Eliot Spitzer.

Picture that.

Fired Superintendent Hits Masturgate Jackpot: October 14, 2011

The Masturgate Scandal is back in the news, further soiling the Detroit Public School (DPS) system and its leaders. Former Superintendent, Teresa Gueyser, has agreed to a whopping $650,000 settlement for the lawsuit she filed against the district after she was terminated following her report that then-DPS Board President Otis "Shama-Lama-Ding-Dong" Mathis fondled himself in front of her.

What's wacky in the latest episode of this sordid affair is the reaction to the settlement by those supposedly trying to rebuild the DPS. Chris White, founder of the Coalition to Restore Hope to DPS, all but blamed Otis's "actions" on former emergency manager Robert Bobb. "The incident with Mathis and her may not have been averted…I'm not letting Otis off the hook—he pleaded guilty—but this was all part of who had academic control," White said.

16

What? The battle over academic control of the DPS between Bobb and the Board caused Mathis to take matters into his own hand?

Not to be outdone, DPS spokesman Steve Wasko offered up this gem: "Neither the settlement nor the payment establish liability but are merely a compromise of a disputed claim."

Translation: We literally and figuratively got caught with our pants down.

I guess a bird in the hand is worth a lot more than two in the bush.

Chapter Two: Stupid Criminals

Kwame Kilpatrick's Baghdad Bob: June 28, 2010

You know that insurance commercial where the duck is in the barbershop listening to Yogi Berra make absolutely no sense and finally walks out shaking his head screaming "AFLAC"? I'm starting to do that every time I read or hear a quote from former Detroit Mayor Kwame Kilpatrick's PR guy, Mike Paul, or his new lawyer, Arnold Reed.

When nineteen federal indictments for fraud and tax evasion pistol-whipped the Textaholic Kwamester on June 23, Paul offered up this gem: "Where is the corruption, payoffs, and bribes everyone expected the FBI to find attached to former Mayor Kilpatrick?" Let's see Mr. Paul, last time I checked, mail and wire fraud were corrupt behavior, and tapping into a charity for personal gain is a payoff—to yourself. Oh, the FBI was short on bribery? Give it a week or so and they'll bat three-for-three.

Mr. Paul has implied that he is representing Kwame for free. With statements like this, Kilpatrick is definitely getting his money's worth.

Not to be outdone, lawyer Reed—who believes the citizens in the grand jury were acting as an arm of the U.S. Attorney's Office—tried to top Mr. Paul with this beaut: "A federal grand jury would indict an empty glass of water." Last time I checked, an empty glass of water is just a GLASS.

Clearly jealous of Mr. Paul's lead on the Stupid Quote Meter and getting desperate, Reed then planted his head deeply in the southern hemisphere of his body and said of the indictments: "What this is not, is any indication that Kwame Kilpatrick is guilty of any crime."

These guys make Baghdad Bob look like Walter Cronkite. All I can say is "AFLAC!"

Book 'em, Danno: August 15, 2010

It's that time of the year when one of the cruelest crime enterprises gets back on the field. No, I'm not talking about University of Michigan football. (Go Spartans, and this year, only crack the heads of your

19

opponents ON THE FIELD!) The blood-sucking, felonious crime family I'm talking about is comprised of the nation's college textbook publishers, the dealers that sell them to our kids (also known as campus bookstores) and the universities and professors that are nothing but shills and accomplices.

I was in the publishing world for a short stint. It is brutal. Today, most publishers are losing their shirts as Amazon, Wal-Mart and others continue to drive down the retail price of books, sometimes actually selling them below cost. Publishers are screaming while authors are crying. A new book for $9.95!?

But not in the world of college textbooks. $9.95? $19.95? Oh no, no, no. Try anywhere from 75-to-200 bucks a freaking book. Why not buy used? All well and good, UNLESS the professor who was using the book last year "decides" to use a different one, rendering last year's model worthless.

But Wisecracker, you're not suggesting the Profs game the system for personal gain? As sure as (ex-Detroit Mayor's father and partner in crime) Bernard Kilpatrick will skip his next deposition, I am. As sure as (convicted Detroit City Councilwoman) Monica Conyers finally being escorted to prison will have the highest local news ratings in Detroit history, I am. As sure as Otis "Masturgate" Mathis's hands, well—er—okay, you get the picture.

But what about those wonderful authors (read: professors) who toil to bring enlightenment to our college children in between their bar-hopping and attempts to qualify for a medical marijuana certificate? They make their OWN textbooks obsolete within a few years by "writing" revised versions with about as much new material as an Andrew Dice Clay standup routine.

But oh, it's all gonna change in a heartbeat when college textbooks become e-books. Seventy-five bucks? Try 15. Want to revise it to milk the system again? Good luck. Changing a few words here or there is super simple and cheap in the digital world. And what does the future hold for those campus bookstores (read: the universities) once they can no longer milk our kids (actually, us parents)?

Good luck developing a new monopoly selling NoDoz, condoms, and sweatshirts. What did Obama's nutty preacher say? Oh yeah, the chickens have come home to roost.

Kwamecare Could Save Obamacare: March 25, 2011

America this month celebrated the one-year anniversary of the passage of Obamacare with a collective hurl as the truly devastating financial impact of this canard became clearer. With each new "revised" estimate showing huge cost overruns and the key Obama aide on health care admitting to Congress they double-counted some "savings" (oops!), the situation looks dire.

Until now. Until Kwame Kilpatrick.

The former mayor of Detroit—now known as Area 714K in the hoosegow—is suing the telecommunications company in Mississippi that literally let the cat out of the sack, er bag, when they released the now-infamous text messages that brought down His Honor and His Lover, Christine Beatty. Kwame was exposed as a liar, liar, pants on fire. And with at least one other affair on those texts, those pants must have been red-hot.

Kilpatrick believes the illegal release of his personal messages—albeit on a city-issued device—has caused him to suffer from post-traumatic stress disorder (PTSD), and that he is depressed and hopeless. The latter we can all agree with, considering his painful court testimony over the past two years and his constant excuse that he did all of this for his family. (Kinda sounds like the protesting teachers in Wisconsin and now Michigan saying they are protesting for "the kids." Oh right, Kwame was a teacher before he was a criminal.)

21

The good news for Kilpatrick is that he has a note from his doctor proving that he is indeed a victim of PTSD. Kilpatrick is stressed and emotionally drained when he thinks about being away from his family and children, according to the diagnosis of Dr. Norman Miller of East Lansing. Miller blames Kilpatrick's stress disorder on "the unlawful release of his personal text messages." (Wow, not only is Miller a shrink, but he's a legal expert, as well. Two, two, two mints in one!)

Dr. Miller told the court that Kilpatrick has frequent headaches, backaches, and stomach problems. But here's the problem: Miller never spoke to the Kwamester until after he'd made the diagnosis. What kind of doctoring is this you ask?

It's called "Kwamecare." It's the answer to the threat of financial ruin with Obamacare. Gone would be those pesky MRIs and other costly tests doctors think they need to perform to find out what is actually wrong with the patient. Blood tests? Phooey! A stool sample? Stick it! It's all a waste of money. In fact, with Kwamecare, the doctor may never have to see the patient. The cost-saving bonanza would be monumental.

I always knew that Kwame's troubles would eventually be a godsend. And now his "comeback" may save the entire nation.

KK: Thx. LOL. C u soon.

Detroit DHS: Reclining, er, Denying the Hungry: May 18, 2011

Boy, will the corruption and malfeasance in Detroit government ever end? Former Mayor Kwame Kilpatrick and many of his gang are behind bars for shaking down businesses. It's one thing to shake down a viable business because they, in theory, get business out of it. But now it appears that members of Detroit's Department of Human Services, including the head honcho, have literally taken food out of the mouths of the city's most vulnerable, funneling grant money expressly intended to feed and clothe the poor for office furniture at the DHS.

And not just for a Detroit Public Library-approved $2,000 chair or two, but $200,000 in office furniture! On top of that, the non-profit to which the $2 million in grant money was given to help the poor—Clark and Associates—spent another couple hundred thousand or so on overtime for their workers.

So what's a measly 400 Gs the poor didn't get? Detroit's problems are so big it's a drop in the bucket, right?

I have had the honor of being on the Board and working with Forgotten Harvest for more than half a decade. Their twenty-nine refrigerated trucks travel more than two thousand miles every day throughout the metro area, rescuing perfectly good meat, dairy, bread, and vegetables from Kroger, Meijer, Sam's Club, Costco, Busch's, and other generous retailers and wholesale food companies who charge nothing for their offerings. That good food makes its way the same day to Capuchin Kitchen, the Salvation Army, and other food shelters and churches. This year, they will feed our most vulnerable neighbors twenty million meals. That's million with an MMMMM.

Forgotten Harvest does not charge the recipients for the food and relies on individual and corporate donations to pay for the staff, the diesel fuel, and the maintenance. Incredibly, Forgotten Harvest provides five meals for EVERY dollar they raise.

So what would the money allegedly purloined by the DHS leadership and Clark and Associates for furniture and overtime pay do for the hungry poor? It's simple math: $400,000 times five equals two million meals.

If he finds them guilty of this heinous indecency, Detroit Mayor Bing promises to fire all those involved in the DHS. I assume he has no prevue over the Clark and Associates clowns. For the shameful involved, I guess your view on helping the poor literally depends on where, or rather, on what you sit.

Help the real heroes. Go to forgottenharvest.org or Gleaners Community Food Bank of Southeastern Michigan at gcfb.org and donate a few bucks. If you're not in Metro Detroit, there is a similar organization close to you. The need has never been greater. Your donation won't buy much furniture, but it will feed a hungry kid. These organizations don't "couch" their response.

Three Men and a Bong: The Kwame Kilpatrick Story: August 1, 2011

It is obvious that two men close to former Detroit Mayor Kwame Kilpatrick have applied for -- and received -- their medical marijuana cards, judging by their recent statements, at least.

Khary Kimani Turner, who co-wrote Kwame's soon-to-be-released Auto-Lie-Ography, offered up this beauty: "You may still hate Kwame Kilpatrick, or you may not, but that's not the point. The point is facilitating understanding."

Facilitating understanding? We ALL understand. He cheated, he lied, he got busted. Then he cheated and lied about his finances and went to prison. And that was all before the Feds started "facilitating" their own understanding.

Turner must have been sharing a Bob Marley with Kwame when they came up with this line in the book, commenting on Barack Obama's 2008 election night victory while Kilpatrick was incarcerated: "I was robbed of diplomacy on American history's biggest political night." Exhale. I admit, Obama's election was historically a big deal, but I still believe the signing of the Declaration of Independence tops it on the American history greatest hits chart. And how do you get "robbed of diplomacy anyway"? Liquor stores and gas stations get robbed. And Water Departments and non-profits get robbed, as Kilpatrick and his enterprise know. But diplomacy? I've heard of it being hijacked but never robbed.

Not to be outdone in the weed-induced wacky comments department, former Kilpatrick publicist and unintentional stand-up comedian, Mike Paul, offered up two gems recently. Commenting on Kwame's political career opportunities, Paul believes it will not be in Detroit. "His stage is a national one now," said the chucklehead. By national, does he mean a federal prison? And on Kwame's potential as a public speaker, Paul offered up this stellar line: "His is a global story."

Global? Perhaps the only thing global in this sad saga is the fact that there is a pretty good chance that's Kwame's loot is scattered around the globe. I get the feeling we will hear more of this hilarious banter in the coming days and weeks. So, light up another doobie, brothers.

Professor Kwame the Philanderer: August 8, 2011

So, the ex-con-perhaps-soon-to-be con and former mayor, Kwame Kilpatrick, has put out his shingle and has landed his first gig as a motivational speaker for a group of young African-American college students. The only problem is he couldn't have picked a more inappropriate place to start if he wants to put his past behind him.

Kwame will soon undress, um, er, I mean address students at Philander Smith College in Arkansas. Philander? As in philandered, philandering, and philanders? Come on, this is too easy!

Perhaps a lying crook, but no one ever accused him of being a big dummy. Are you telling me that Kwame didn't stop for a second when he got the offer and say: "Hmmm, need the money, but I think I'd better start at another school."

Kwame Wants Norwegian Justice: August 26, 2012

The Wisecracker's unapologetically pitiful sources have confirmed that former Detroit Mayor Kwame Kilpatrick's lawyers will file a motion in federal court today asking the judge to move the criminal proceedings from Detroit to Oslo, Norway. The surprise move comes on the heels of the slap-on-the-wrist sentence received by confessed mass murderer Anders Behring Breivik.

Breivik, you may recall, went on a bombing and shooting spree 13 months ago in Norway, killing 77 people and injuring 200 others. His sentence: "preventative detention" of at least 10 years and a maximum of 21 years. At the maximum, that's roughly three months and one week behind bars for each life he extinguished. Way to throw down the hammer, Norway. You make the Swedes look downright ruthless.

The Kwamester faces 20 years or so for screwing the citizens of Detroit throughout his now-disgraced reign of graft, corruption, and sexting. However, the crazed Norwegian killer could actually serve less time in the hoosegow. This has upset the former mayor.

"WTF?" said Kilpatrick in a text. "This cr8z, fish-eatin, RW nut job crkr whax 77 n I goin sleepn on my back longr than him. It's racism. No way! NORWAY!"

The Democratic National Committee has come to Kilpatrick's defense. Commenting on the former mayor's plight, DNC Chairwoman Debbie Wasserman Schultz, called Kilpatrick's possible incarceration an outrage:

"Mitt Romney wants right-wing extremists like Breivik to freely massacre Muslims; especially Muslim women. It's just a part of his war on women. Where is Governor Romney's outrage? He's probably too busy writing a "legitimate rape" Wikipedia with Congressman Todd Akin or checking his offshore banking account on-line. I guess we should expect this type of behavior from this felonious, out-of-touch, cancer-causing birther and his grandma-killing sidekick."

When asked about Wasserman-Schultz's comments, Kilpatrick replied: "Women—can't text with 'em, can't text without 'em."

Vice President Joe Biden waded into the issue. "I told you the Republicans are gonna put 'ya'll' back in chains, and they're starting with Kwame."

Panty Bomber: Deck the Balls: September 16, 2011

And on the Monday after the Seventh Day, God created Irony. And he said it was hilarious.

So, too, with panty bomb terror suspect and court jester, Umar Farouk Abdulmutallab. In court proceedings in Detroit, we find that hours after this radical Islamist punk lit his Johnson on fire in a failed attempt to blow up a plane full of innocent passengers as it was landing in Detroit, nurses attending to his self-inflicted wounds provided the ultimate and most ironic insult.

As you may remember, Abdulmutallab, which is Nigerian for "Great Balls of Fire," decided to carry out his jihad on Christmas Day 2009. The self-professed al Qaeda operative apparently became "testy" in the emergency room at the University of Michigan Hospital where Christmas tunes filled the air as nurses tended his burned right thigh, hands, and genitals. He demanded the infidel's holiday music be stopped. I don't know about you, but I wouldn't be demanding anything when a nurse has got you by the, um, er, you know.

The nurses refused his demand, and the Wisecracker's seriously unreliable sources say that the FBI got "Great Balls of Fire" to finally crack by playing a continuous loop of "Grandma Got Run Over By a Reindeer."

With Assassinated Cops, Al Sharpton and Mayor de Blasio Guilty as "Charged": December 20, 2014

There are no roving bands of police officers protesting in the streets today. No Asian-Americans or Latinos setting cars on fire, breaking store windows, looting, or exercising in very violent "civil disobedience." Yet, two (now three) cops were murdered in the last twenty-four hours in this country. Not sure about the third, but the two in New York—one Asian-American and one Latino Man in Blue—were shot in an alleged

27

"payback" for the deaths of two African-American individuals, Ferguson's Michael Brown and Staten Island's Eric Garner.

The two NY cops were not shot in a gun battle. Neither was asking the gunman to move off the street (after robbing a liquor store) or to stop selling cigarettes illegally. No, these "rogue" cops were sitting in their squad car, according to some reports, eating their lunch. Then, a piece of crap decided to "eat their lunch" after earlier posting on the Internet that "we" should take out two cops for every single black person shot in this country by police.

According to NYPD Commissioner Bill Bratton, "They were, quite simply, assassinated—targeted for their uniform. They were ambushed and murdered."

Police officers represent three-tenths of 1 percent of our population, so I think they should "organize" as the "Three-tenths of One Percent" movement. Maybe these cops—all of them—should "Occupy" the parks in their representative cities, not bathe for weeks, urinate in public, rape cohorts, and smoke a lot of pot in protest of the killings of their peers.

Nope, they won't. They will just get up every day and protect you, me, law-abiding citizens, and a lot of people that don't deserve a lick of protection.

Race hustler (the Reverend—Ha!) Al Sharpton came out with a confused apology for the NY cop killings, but it was too lame and too LATE. Sharpton needs to (besides pay his back taxes) man-up and resign, along with NY Mayor de Blasio, and move to Cuba; get the hell out of our airspace. The Castros would love both of these clowns.

The NY cops said this blood is on de Blasio's hands. They are right. He indeed put a target on the backs of police in his city, perhaps the country. But, the blood is all over Sharpton's "body of work."

Artist Indicted for Making Kayak in Image of Her Va-Jay-Jay.
Strange but True Story: December 24, 2014

It's getting weird in the Land of the Rising Sun. Japanese officials have indicted a local artist for "distributing obscene data." It's a "crime" that could cost the young woman $21K and land her in the hoosegow for a couple of years.

So, what is obscene about what Megumi Igarishi is "distributing?" Well, apparently, she had the inspired idea to create a useable kayak out of a 3-D image of her, ahem, Va-Jay-Jay. Igarishi is, of course, not the first "artist" to include her "special unit" in her "artwork." Remember Madonna infamously talking at length about the "wind beneath her waist" in her late-'80s book, "Sex"?

If Megumi snatches victory from the jaws of defeat, beats the charges, and is successful in building her "boat," I wonder what she will name it. "Chicken of the Sea"? Just wondering.

The world seems to get weirder by the second.

Source: *Japan Times*

Chapter Three: Stupid People

Chipping Away at a New Cold War: July 9, 2010

Now that the spy swap with the Russkies is over, the Obama Administration needs to turn its sights to another and perhaps more dangerous group of creepy commies from the former Soviet Union, who have infiltrated suburban America. I'm talking about those young men who hang around car washes and want to fix the alleged chips in your car's windshield for free.

Creepy factor number one is that they're all cut from the same cloth: five foot six, buzz-cut hair, blue jean shorts, wife-beater shirts, and shades of Deliverance. Creepy factor number two is that their M.O. is eerily similar, obviously due to training in the same Siberian camp. You pull into the car wash and wait for the attendant to take your money when out of nowhere the Chipski arrives. He does not make eye contact with you. He begins staring at your windshield as if it is a Picasso in an art gallery, wondering if it is flawed. He then pulls out a marker and draws several circles on the glass for no apparent reason. Finally, he speaks probably the only English the KGB has taught him and his ilk: "You have chips in your windshield and I can fix for free."

Those clever Russians: Fix my car for free while they undoubtedly attach bugs on my car to follow my every move. Only I was too smart for these Russkie spies. When the offer was made for the free service, I responded: "Can you do it in less than five minutes, 'cuz I'm in a big hurry?"

His answer: "Nyet."

The Chrysler Doobie Brothers: Taking It to the Streets (or the Park): September 23, 2010

So, a bunch of autoworkers at Chrysler's Jefferson North Assembly Plant in Detroit—home of the new, most excellent Jeep Grand Cherokee—got busted by the local FOX channel for partying during their noon break. The story makes it to FOX News nationwide and across the media in general. There is genuine outrage! This is a company the American taxpayers bailed out! This is a company the American taxpayers bailed out that was given to Italian automaker Fiat for the grand total of zero dollars!

And how do "they" reward us? By drinking cold ones during lunch and smoking (though, obviously, "medical marijuana" to meditate the obvious humbling trauma of being rescued by taxpayers and being forced to work for Italians, led by a brilliant CEO that wears heavy wool sweaters to work every day during the hottest summer on record in Michigan. CEO Sergio, we need to talk, dude.)

The outrage of this story is all over the conservative talk shows and FOX. Don't get me wrong—I love FOX News, and my kids and relatives hate me for it. But FOX and everybody else are missing the real outrage here. Blue-collars at many, many companies start their mornings with a "shot and beer or two" before punching the clock. Executives and managers routinely take a client or prospect to lunch and have a cocktail or several (hopefully not too many before they drive back to work).

No, the real outrage for taxpayers in the case of the partying Chrysler "nooners" was played out on the video camera of the local FOX affiliate. As the reporter approached these brain surgeons, you saw them scramble into their rides to make a hasty retreat from the cameras. Many left in a Ram pickup while others hastily packed themselves into their Chrysler ride.

But one slid into a fairly new Ford Mustang. There is the outrage for American taxpayers! We bailed all of you Chrysler workers out of insolvency and yet you—an employee—drive a Ford?! A non-bailed out Ford? You cannot even back your own company when you purchase your wheels? Want a hot ride? Buy a Challenger or a Charger, you mouth-breather.

The workers will probably be fired. But in this economy, I hope the idiotic partiers are given a second chance, though on serious company probation. They are fathers and possibly grandfathers. This economy sucks, and I would hate for their families to suffer from their stupidity. Give them two strikes.

The Ford Mustang owner, a Chrysler employee, should be fired and possibly stoned. Oh wait, he probably was.

Obama Takes a Hit on Chrysler's Doobie Brothers: September 29, 2010

So, almost all of the Doobie Brothers at Chrysler's Jefferson North Assembly Plant are given the heave-ho in response to the "worldwide" outrage over their lunch break partying. Said one onlooker: "Taxpayers bailed these $%#@!*$!#kers out, and they pay us back by getting stoned on the job!"

I told my priest to wash out his mouth with soap.

So now, the real question is: What would Brian Boitano do? Check that—the real question, is what are President Bob King and his UAW going to do? As usual in this space, incredibly unreliable sources to the Wisecracker have uncovered the transcript of a phone conversation between the UAW leader and President Barack "Whose Ass to Kick" Obama.

Obama: Hi Bob, it's Barack.

Bob: Hello, your Holiness.

Barack: Couple of things we need to talk about.

Bob: Sure, your Godlikeness.

Barack: Hold on a second. Gotta adjust the teleprompter. There we go. First, I want you to know that when I saw the "F the UAW" quote from Rahm Emanuel in Steven Rattner's book about the auto industry bailout—um, er, rescue—I decided it was Rahm's ass I needed to kick. So I did, and he's being exiled back to Chicago.

Bob: Thank you, your Awesomeness!

Barack: Second, we need to talk about those party animals at the Chrysler plant that just got fired.

Bob: Oh, don't worry about that, your Excellency. We'll have the grievance papers filed in no time. After all, that's what a union does to protect its members. Besides, there is no proof that it was pot that they were smoking. May have just been rolling their own. And how about the hypocrisy where a management fat cat can go to lunch and suck down a couple of martinis, return to work, and write himself a huge bonus check. Trust me, Mr. President, this is a slam-dunk.

Barack: That's just it. I can't have you do that. The majority of Americans want these losers fired.

Bob: Since when did you start listening to the American people?

Barack: Listen Bob, look what I have done for you in the short time I have been supreme leader. While trying to drive this economy out of George Bush's ditch, I personally saved two car companies and secured your members' pension benefits by totally screwing those fat cat white-collar retirees at Delphi. So, on this Chrysler firing issue, I'm ordering you to stand down because this is—as my nutty Vice President would say—a big f-ing deal.

Bob: But what do I say to my members?

Barack: Tell the Doobie Brothers at Chrysler I'll hire them and put them in charge of the next Beer Summit.

Bob: But they have no experience in government.

Barack: Then take it from me. They'll be perfect.

62 Miles per Gallon? What're They Smoking? October 4, 2010

According to the Wisecracker's cadre of incredibly unreliable sources, moments after calling UAW President Bob King and ordering him not to file grievances on behalf of Chrysler's fired Doobie Brothers, President Barack "Whose Ass to Kick" Obama called the UAW's finest.

He invited them to the White House last Thursday to tell them personally: He felt their pain. Indeed—again, according to my usual shaky sources—the Prez was sharing a brew (left over from his infamous White House Beer Summit when he prevented WWIII between the Harvard faculty and the Cambridge police department) with his new band of down-and-out Chrysler brothers, when one of the invitees whipped out a reefer and offered The Commander-in-Cool a drag. In an attempt to showcase his street cred, the Prez did not refuse.

One Chrysler Doobie Brother—protected from identification by the Wisecracker, unless I am asked nicely—said: "Wow, dude, it was like, you know, serial."

You mean surreal?

"Yeah, whatever, man. Anyway, the President of the frickin' (the Wisecracker has edited this part) US of A handles the frickin' Bob Marley like a real pro and then gives it to me, man. We're like, you know, partying with the 'Commando and Chief' and then he says, 'Hey fellas, watch this.' The next thing we know, the Big Guy is on the speakerphone with the head Nazi, who says how much fuel economy the car companies gotta meet."

The Wisecracker at this point informed his Doobie Brother source that the President was probably calling the head of the National Highway Traffic Safety Administration—that's NHTSA, not NAZI.

"Yeah, whatever, Wisecracker dude. Anyways, he gets this guy on the phone and tells him to jack up the fuel economy standard to like sixty-two mpg or so. Then the Nazi guy asks the President if he is smoking something. And we all, like, look at each other and then out the window and then a couple of guys in our group start kinda choking as they hold back their laughs. One of my buddies actually has beer comin' outta his nose. So the President hangs up on the Nazi dude and then he orders like fourteen pizzas and a keg, he has a ping pong table wheeled into his office, and we all play beer pong until his nasty wife comes in and starts yelling at him for bringing junk food into the White House. And the rest, man, is historic."

You mean, history, don't you?

"Whatever, man. Whatever."

Smart Is as Smart Does: February 16, 2011

The shortest verse in the Bible is John 11:35—"Jesus wept." Succinct and to the point, redundantly speaking. On a much less biblical scale, the shortest summation of an auto brand for the U.S. market is "Smart isn't." Those words were not uttered when Daimler and Roger Penske recently parted ways regarding the distribution of Smart cars in the USA. Nope, those words are more than a decade old.

Back when Tom Stallkamp was the head honcho of Chrysler, in the early days of the DaimlerChrysler merger of equals (gulp), he was at a meeting in Stuttgart with the joint company's top brass. The newly created venture was still basking in the glory of phenomenal press clippings that were masking the growing turmoil within Chrysler's operations. The discussion item was the global marketing of the newly envisioned Smart car. Stallkamp, never one to mince words, blurted out that now infamous line, "Smart isn't." The pithy and now prophetic half-a-liner was not received well by Stallkamp's German superiors, um, er, colleagues. In fact, it went over like a pregnant pole-vaulter.

But what's a Smart-Alek remark among friends? Months later, Stallkamp was given the ziggy (oh, and a boatload of cash), but the ziggy nonetheless. Years later, the car finally made it to the U.S. shores, with an unveiling at the Detroit Athletic Club, hosted by Dieter Zetsche and his newly signed distributor, The Roger (Penske). All was right in the world. The car was going to take the States by storm.

Indeed, it did. Like Katrina. Almost everyone that wanted one bought their Smart car in the first few months after it went on sale. From then on, sales started to decline week after week, month after month. Even the incredible business acumen of Roger Penske and his team couldn't get this dog to hunt.

No doubt, Stallkamp is chuckling to himself, realizing how "Smart" he was back then. Move over, Edsel. Step aside, Aztec. You've been replaced by a "Smart Decision."

Stupid People of the Week: Mormons and Idiots: March 6, 2011

Okay, kids, it's time for the Wisecracker's irregular "Stupid People of the Week Award." And hold on to yourself: Charlie Sheen shockingly did not make the finals. Neither did those nutty Wisconsin Democrats who are calling the protests in Cheeseland, "America's Egypt." The latter is weaker, sillier, and more contrived than it is stupid.

The two winners for their actions and words last week took different paths in winning the much-coveted prize, "The Cracker." First, give it up for PETA, those wacky animal rights activists, who protested a donkey basketball fundraiser at Redford Union High School just outside the city limits of Motown. You may remember, PETA is that grounded group that several years ago protested dairy farmers treatment of milk cows by taking out full page ads in college newspapers, urging students to boycott milk, and instead, consume alcohol with the catchy line "Got Beer?" Mothers Against Drunk Driving had a field day blasting PETA for their recklessness and stupidity.

This time, PETA decided to put its head up the "ass" controversy at Redford Union. Claiming the bright lights of the gymnasium were cruel to the beasts was just one claim, but not the dumbest. No, that would be the claims that this practice was cruel due to the work and travel schedule for the donkeys, and the ultimate "humiliation" the donkeys were suffering. Regardless, the fundraiser went off without a hitch, and there were no reports of any of the beasts of burden breaking down, sobbing, and putting themselves in the fetal position. Nope, no donkeys "Going Charlie Sheen" in front of the cameras and on Twitter.

Winner number two are those geniuses at Brigham Young University who kicked a talented sophomore, Brandon Davies, off of the basketball team for having pre-marital sex with his girlfriend. Not suspend him for a couple of games. No. Not whack his, well, er, never mind, you know. He had clearly violated the "code" of the school.

Hmmm. As the Church Lady would say, "Isn't that special."

Brigham Young University, a top-notch school by all accounts, was founded as Brigham Young Academy by, oh yeah, Brigham Young. Mr. Young succeeded his boss, Joseph Smith, who was killed by an angry mob while leading his Mormon followers to the Promised Land via Keokuk, Iowa. Before his untimely and violent death, good ol' Joe told his flock that the Lord had personally commanded him to take virgins "hundredfold in this world" in order to "multiply and replenish the Earth" so "they may bear the souls of men."

Isn't that convenient? Kinda like the 77 virgins in heaven promised to the 9/11 terrorists, later accurately translated into 77 golden raisins, not babes, for the thugs. Imagine their disappointment, and aren't ya kinda surprised how hot heaven is, boys?

Anyway, Joe decided 33 wives was a solid and godly-like number. One of them was 14 years old when he carried her over the threshold. It is kind of funny that the god that personally told Joe to wed and wed often wasn't around when the mob tore his body to shreds.

Enter Brigham Young. Taking up where Smith left off, Young founded Salt Lake City and was very proud of that until he was told "ain't no fish" in the Great Salt Lake. Something he "could have known yesterday!" He also started the Mormon Tabernacle Choir, which later became the Utah Jazz, I think. Sorry, lost my place. Brigham Young had many loyal followers, especially his estimated 55 wives. To be fair to the late Young-ster, not all of his reported 55 wives were (gently now) "doing the Brandon Davies" with him. When Congress completely outlawed polygamy, many of Young's polygamist followers cowardly went into hiding in Illinois with Wisconsin Democratic legislators, I'm pretty sure.

So, in the end, a bright, young basketball star gets booted for sinful sex by a school conceived by a booty-monger and with the nickname, get this, The Cougars. Gotta hold your nose on this one.

Final note: to those that are disappointed the comments by the Westboro Baptist Church nut jobs after their free speech victory at the Supreme Court didn't warrant a "Stupid People of the Week Award," relax. If you caught their lawyer's comments on Chris Wallace's FOX show Sunday (she called President Obama the Anti-Christ if you missed it), you realized their protected hate speech is beyond stupid. It's really, really sick and twisted. And all supposedly in the name of God. Which god would that be? Joseph Smith's?

Stupid People of the Week: People Who Paid to See Charlie Sheen's "Show": April 4, 2011

It's time to hand out a few more "Crackers," the cherished award given out from time-to-time to those occupying space on our planet without so much as a clue. The envelope, please.

Our first Cracker recipient is actually a group award for the 4,700 supremely stupid people who took money out of their wallets and gave it to Charlie Sheen for his train wreck at the Fox Theater in Detroit last Saturday. Many in this illustrious group of dorks had the gall to cry for a refund after the "show" was over. Ask for a refund of your high school education. You obviously learned nothing.

Our second Cracker goes to another group—the 700 or so Sheen followers who actually stayed to the bitter end of Charlie's money grab. What were they expecting? Did they think Charlie was going to share with them the meaning of life? How the world was created? If there is an afterlife? Wednesday's Powerball numbers?

Cracker number three goes to the management of the Fox Theater, who used this lovely venue to make Detroit a laughing stock with the kick-off to the "Lamest Show on Earth." Shame on you. What's next? Dr. Kevorkian on stage doing live assisted suicides. (Oops, sorry about the oxymoron.) Fire these people, (Fox owner) Mike Ilitch.

Our final Cracker goes to two state Democratic Michigan lawmakers who want the motorcycle helmet law thrown out. "It's a personal liberty thing," said Rep. Richard LeBlanc of Westland. Not to be outdone in the stupidity race, Sen. John Gleason, a non-motorcyclist, threw his support to the helmet-less ones after consulting motorcycle enthusiasts. "What I've been told is that they can hear and see better without a helmet," Gleason said. "Most of the accidents that occur are cars hitting bikes, and it gives them a better defense." (Say that last line really slow three times to get the full-stupidity effect.)

Helmet-free bikers are only putting their own lives in danger, right? Okay, I'm all for personal liberty. So, let's make seatbelt use optional. Let everyone who wants to smoke pot do so. (Oops, already there. My bad.) But, because I am getting low on Cracker awards, LeBlanc and Gleason will have to split their trophy. Kind of like a head does in a motorcycle accident without a helmet.

No-No Geronimo: May 10, 2011

News item: A local Native American organization is offering counseling to anyone who feels offended or hurt by the use of "Geronimo" as the code name for the recent U.S. operation that killed Osama bin Laden.

"Geronimo's name shouldn't be used in a context like that," said Nickole Fox, director of health education at American Indian Health & Family Services, which is offering the counseling. "He's a hero among a lot of Native people. It's disrespectful to use his name like that."

Are you kidding? And counseling? But wait Wisecracker, how would you feel if your Irish ethnicity was used in confirming the death of the most sinister terrorist in modern history?

"Command, this is Navy Seal Six. There's a hole in the eye of the Potato. I repeat, there's a hole in the eye of the Potato."

Okay, Ms. Fox, you got your name mentioned in a news article. As former President Bush would say, "Mission Accomplished." Oh darn, I bet I just offended everyone who works in a mission.

Black-on-Black Ethnic Intimidation? WTF? May 18, 2011
Stupid things on the walls of bathrooms and the Internet are all over the news.

In Birmingham, Michigan, an African-American student at predominantly-white Seaholm High School (where two of my kids graduated) is being indicted on ethnic intimidation charges after he allegedly admitted to scrawling death threats to African-American students, including himself, on the walls of a restroom. If the kid is guilty, the real question is why this charge?

If you report a thief in your home and file an insurance claim, and the police determine you "stole" your own stuff, you are charged with filing a false police report and insurance fraud, not theft. Similarly, if you accuse someone (say a Duke Lacrosse team) of rape, and it is proven you just made it all up, you are not in turn charged with rape against yourself. So, how is it that an African-American can write death threats against African-American students, including himself, and have it be ethnic intimidation? Shouldn't the real charge be one of two things or both: perpetuating a hoax, and/or the more serious, producing death threats?

According to reports, the Seaholm administration has handled the whole affair with class, as have the students. The media, of course, continue to point out that of the 1,250 students at Seaholm, only 70 are

African-American. That's code that surely there must be racism inherent within the school.

Which makes me wonder: if those death threats were made against white students in equally foul language—"gonna kill these five crackers tonight"—and it was determined that the perpetrator was himself or herself white, would that person face ethnic intimidation charges? Hmm?

I Did Know Jack: June 3, 2011

In a rich irony, Dr. Jack Kevorkian—aka Dr. Death—died this week. On his own.

I did know Jack. About halfway through Dr. Jack Kevorkian's assisted suicide exploits, I gained the uncanny ability to predict the day the next victim or beneficiary—depending on your opinion—would buy the farm. I got so good at this I usually beat the media reports by hours. Did I have a gift? Was the Wisecracker all-knowing?

Nope. But like any seasoned PR professional, I had a corporate American Express, um, er, I mean I had a great contact. Early in my PR career at Chrysler, I was in charge of Technology PR, promoting the Chrysler electric minivan. The head of the program was Bob Davis, a wonderfully friendly engineer in the final days of his career.

I was in Bob's office every morning and was always greeted with a fresh cup of coffee and a brilliant smile from his secretary, Margo. But I would soon learn that Margo had a job on the side, and she'd always call her boss to request a day off when she was moonlighting.

See, Margo was Dr. Death's sister and his assisted suicide assistant (ASA). Whenever I showed up in Bob's office and Sister Death wasn't in, I would ask Bob if she had called in that morning for a day off. If the answer was yes, I would return to my office and boldly predict that another one was going to bite the dust. I finally had to fess up to my source, worried that I could be implicated in the adventures that eventually sent Jack to the hoosegow.

I got to meet Kevorkian several times after he got out of prison and relayed my story of his sister. He chuckled a bit and recalled what a sweetheart she was.

So that's how Jack Kevorkian touched my, er, life.

Squawk Like an Egyptian: November 28, 2011

It's the question we're not supposed to ask in this politically correct world. We didn't dare to ask it last year, nor this week. Until now. Why in the hell were those college kids – captured and supposedly tortured by Egyptian police – in the street mess in Cairo, Egypt, in the first place? And, last year, why in the hell were young Americans "hiking" near the Iranian border.

My mom always said, "Nothing good happens after midnight." Well, in this day and age, nothing good happens in a Cairo riot, Iran, or Occupy Whatever.

The Iranian "hikers'" act of stupidity cost the taxpayers a cool million in ransom money. How much it cost us to retrieve the dunderheads from Egypt is not being told. They claim they were not throwing Molotov cocktails at police prior to their detention. It is obvious they were slamming some sort of cocktails to be there in the first place.

I think these kids have watched too many episodes of Storm Chasers. The one kid from Missouri, rescued from the gulag in Cairo, was quoted as saying that while in captivity, "a thousand things were going through my mind." If that's true, then a "thousand things" were going through his posterior end.

Stupid Person of the Week...and It's Only Thursday (and It's Killing Me): February 2, 2012

With two full days still remaining in the week, St. Clair Shores' Joseph Gentz has snatched victory from the jaws of defeat and has won the prized Wisecracker "Stupid Person of the Week" award.

43

If you have followed the sad and bizarre murder of marketing executive Jane Bashara of Grosse Pointe Park, Michigan, Gentz is familiar to you. He was the man who voluntarily appeared at the Grosse Pointe Park police station Tuesday at 4 a.m. and confessed to his role in the killing. Some sources say he claims he was paid to kill Bashara by her husband, Robert Bashara.

"I'm not going to take the fall for this," Gentz told police, according to the source.

Um, you admitted you murdered someone, Joe. You are going to take the "fall" for this—and the winters, springs, and summers—in a federal pen for the rest of your miserable life.

Good grief. Enjoy the award; you earned it.

Stupid People of the Week: Uncle Joe Takes the Gold: August 20, 2012

Wow, what a week of stupidity! And the winners of the completely un-prestigious Wisecracker "Stupid People of the Week" medals, or "Crackers," go to:

GOLD: Vice President Joe "Ya'll" Biden. A no-brainer, but there I go being redundant. What is it with Democratic pols that make them assume when campaigning south of the Mason-Dixie line you must adopt a southern accent? President Obama does it. Hillary Clinton did it during the 2008 campaign. For Biden, the real problem with his "chains" reference was not that it was the wrong choice of words to support his metaphor (the common liberal pundit defense). The real problem is that he meant every word he said. The fact that the nation's first black governor, Virginia's Doug Wilder, slammed Biden for his racist rant made Biden's stupid comment even, um, er, stupider. Thus, our gold medal.

SILVER: The GOP talking heads non-stop blasting of Biden's stupid remark. The drumbeat following Biden's folly even extended—albeit with a heavy dose of excuses—into the MSM. This encouraged talk of dumping

Biden from the ticket and adding Hillary. This would be extremely bad for Romney and Ryan. In fact, I do not believe Republicans can beat any ticket with a Clinton on it—despite Obama's horrible record. According to reports, Obama top aide Valerie Jarrett offered the job to Hillary, who declined. Thankfully for the GOP, Hillary (and Bubba) hate Obama and will do the least they can to help him win. So, shut up about making this nightmare reality.

BRONZE: Republican Senator John McCain. (Read that again, slowly.) He went on camera to suggest Biden be axed in favor of Hillary. This, of course, allowed the stumbling and bumbling White House press secretary Jay Carney to actually say something comprehensible: "I have great admiration for and respect for and a long relationship with Senator John McCain, but one place I would not go for advice on vice presidential running mates is to Senator McCain." Ouch.

SCRAP IRON: Any media outlet that lets Democratic talking heads get away with the line that Romney/Ryan want to "end Medicare as we know it." Why? Medicare "as we know it" is going bankrupt! Unfortunately, I don't have enough awards to hand out as this line is embraced daily on every MSM outlet.

LEAD: President Barack "I got Bin Laden" Obama and his "walk softly and stick-to-it" approach to foreign policy. When the Russkies threw three female dissidents in jail for harmlessly protesting Genghis Putin, the White House tweeted something along the lines of: "We are kinda ticked." Meanwhile, his backhand to Israel over the past three-plus years has put the Jewish State in the unenviable position of striking Iran's nuke program before the Israelis are victims of a second holocaust. Oh wait: according to Iranian Nutjob Marmaduke Ahmadinejad, the Holocaust never happened. My bad.

Stupid Person of the Week: Welcome Back McCotter: June 3, 2012

The champagne had been sufficiently chilled, the foil wrap daintily torn off, and the harrowing wire cage removed as New York Mayor Bloomberg readied his team to celebrate being named the Wisecracker's "Stupid Person of the Week." Like the Masters, it is an honor "like no other." His stellar performance earlier in the week of proclaiming that no New Yorker could ever again purchase more than 16 ounces of any sugary beverage—unless, of course, they decide to buy multiple 16 ounce fat-inducing beverages—was ridiculed from the Daily Show to main street as the dumbest, most nanny-state thing people had ever heard. (Note: where were the greenies complaining about the added landfill garbage due to more Styrofoam and paper cups?) As they pulled out the glasses for the victory toast, the worst possible thing happened: someone did something even stupider.

Enter Thaddeus McCotter, Michigan congressman and rockmeister. McCotter, known as a pretty hip dude and funky policy wonk, was a long shot in the presidential race when he entered last year. While he promised little chance to win, the line was he was probably the smartest politician and only "real" individual in the race. Down to earth, funny, and smart as hell.

His presidential fortunes had the half-life of a mayfly, and so we thought this episode was over. But then, McCotter and his staff forgot the little things necessary to keep his current job as a Michigan congressman and scrambled at the last minute to acquire (perhaps illegally, Doh!) the necessary signatures to get on the Michigan ballot. Fire yourself; fire your incompetent staff. You, Thaddeus, are winner of the "Stupid Person of the Week."

As judge and jury for this fabulous award, this week's nominees made the decision hard and required several shots of tequila. Besides Bloomberg, other nominees included Massachusetts' senatorial candidate,

46

Elizabeth Warren, who stumbled with her Native American Indian heritage. Sorry, she didn't stumble: she outright lied and then blasted her foe Scott Brown in bogus outrage. And, of course, our fabulous President, who went against a measure to stop abortions based solely on gender, thus killing potential baby girls. Yikes, I thought Romney was leading the war on women. Silly me.

Congressman McCotter: Enjoy your "Cracker," your "Stupid Person of the Week" award. It was close, but you earned it, you moron.

PETA Jumps the Shark...Again! September 30, 2011

Just when you thought it was safe to go back in the water, those wacky PETA people are at it again. This time the Perverts for the Everyday Torture of Americans are trying to take advantage of a young Florida man's brush with "death by shark" by posting a billboard that reads: "Payback is Hell...Go Vegan" and features a shark with the bloody leg of a tasty human jutting out of its mouth. How classy.

So PETA is once again putting human life at the bottom of the food chain. But it is apparent that PETA gets more and more loony and less and less influential with each nutty stunt they pull.

In my days as an automotive spokesman, I had many a run-in with PETA. The first was during their campaign against using live pigs in crash testing. To be honest, as an Iowa native, I too found it wrong to use pigs to predict human injury in car crashes, unless, of course, right after the crash you threw ol' Floyd on a spit and loaded him with tangy BBQ sauce. Mmm, Mmm, Good! I asked our engineers at Chrysler if we used pigs in testing. Sheepishly, they said "no" as Chrysler did not have the scientists skilled in determining the correlation between swine and human injury. So, they relied on data purchased from those blood-thirsty mad scientists at GM. One engineer told me: "If we used pigs, all we could tell you after the crash was that there was, indeed, a dead pig sticking out of the dash of that Volare."

A few years ago, while protesting dairy farmers for having the "udder" audacity of torturing cows by "stealing" their milk, PETA ran ads in college newspapers with the tagline "Got Beer?" Yes-indeedy, PETA was hoping our young folk would abandon brain-developing milk for alcohol. It was a great move for all of two seconds until Mothers Against Drunk Driving placed their large boot up PETA's posterior. With their stupidity, those of us who had faced PETA protests in the past thought that finally the whack jobs had figuratively jumped the shark of credibility.

So, now a young man is mauled by a real shark, and PETA thinks it's pretty cool.

Ashley Byrne, a PETA spokesperson, said she and her merry band of mosquito-protecting morons are still trying to find the best billboard spot that would give maximum exposure at the best rates for their handy work. "With the shark attack in the news, we thought it'd be a good time to remind people that sharks are not the world's biggest predator—we are," she told FOX News. "People have the choice to be kind every time they sit down to a meal," she continued. "We hope the billboard will lead to Floridians choosing a healthy vegan diet."

For me, it's Surf and Turf tonight.

The NAACP Spits a Lugar: May 20, 2012

The National Association for the Advancement of Colored People (NAACP) has weighed into the same-sex marriage debate saying its support of "marriage equality is deeply rooted in the Fourteenth Amendment of the U.S. Constitution and equal protection of all people." According to *The Washington Post*, the NAACP "now presents itself as a counterbalance to the influence of the traditionally socially conservative black church." That's a nice way of saying the NAACP is turning its back to the values of the majority of people it says it represents.

According to a 2010 study by the Pew Forum on Religion and Public Life, 47 percent of Americans support legalization of same-sex marriage, but only 39 percent of blacks do, and only 33 percent of black Protestants do. A more recent Washington Post Kaiser Family Foundation poll found similar numbers. Is the NAACP pulling a Richard Lugar here? We know what ignoring his constituency did for the long-time Indiana Senator, who earlier this month, got trounced in a Republican primary.

NAACP President Benjamin Todd Jealous, of course, decided to inject race into the same-sex marriage debate. That is what they always do, even if homosexuality, according to its supporters, is color blind. Said Jealous: "The well-funded right wing organizations who are attempting to split our community are no friend to civil rights, and they will not succeed."

Ah, the classic cry: conservatives are rich, white, racists, and bigots. And homophobes. But then what are the blacks against same-sex marriage? Confused? Brainwashed by the Church? And Mr. Jealous, please get your historical facts straight on which political party tried its best to stop the civil rights movement in the 1960s.

How do we know that the NAACP's endorsement has absolutely nothing to do with same-sex marriage and everything to do with getting America's first black President re-elected? Let's jump into the Time Travel Hot Tub Machine and go way, way back to 2008. At the time, then-candidate Obama clearly stated that he believed that the institution of marriage was only between one man and one woman. This, of course, was contrary to his earlier support for same-sex marriage while an Illinois state senator. He had obviously "evolved" on the issue, angering many on the Left. What do you think the NAACP would have done if GOP candidate John McCain had come out in support of same-sex marriage? Certainly not what they did last week in Washington, D.C.

Hypocrisy never sleeps.

The Yin and the Yang of a Totally Screwed-up Country: August 21, 2012

It seems damned if you do; damned if you don't.

Horrible droughts/Fewer tornados: After a record tornado season last year, tornados in the "Belt" are way down because there is a lack of thunderstorms that spawn them. The burned corn crop, in particular, is going to make those politicians shamefully promoting ethanol eat their own votes soon, as food and gas prices continue to rise. Talk about a twister of an issue.

9/11 cross rises/Atheists meltdown: The eerie broken wreckage that rose out of the 9/11 disaster as a symbol of survival is reportedly causing headaches and other forms of anxiety (hopefully, chronic diarrhea) to the American Atheists supposedly physically "sickened" by the inclusion of this symbol on the 9/11 memorial site in NY. The Wisecracker says: "Let them eat Imodium."

Quit Smoking/Freak out and kill yourself: Chantix became the wonder drug for smoking cessation. Only problem was folks on it had wicked dreams and some killed themselves. (Note: the Wisecracker was on Chantix for a few weeks, and to this day, cannot get the Barney Frank/Roseanne Barr nightmare out of my mind.)

Missouri GOP Congressman and Senate Candidate Todd Akin/Singer Clay Aikin: One, the latter, got screwed out of victory on both American Idol and Celebrity Apprentice, despite clearly winning over Reuben Studdard and Arsenio Hall, respectively. The former screwed the entire Republican Party for being an idol onto himself and his stupid "rape" comment, and in the end, will end up a Celebrity Former Congressman.

Stupid Quotes of the Decade: September 24, 2012

It is utterly amazing that some of the truly stupidest quotes of the decade have come in the last few days. Consider the following gems:

"Israel is a nuclear-armed fake regime shielded by the U.S."

Iranian President and Holocaust-Denier Mahmud Ahmadinejad, September 24, 2012

Israel is…"One of our closest allies in the region."

Barack Obama, President and Chief Appeaser of the United States, September 23, 2012

Wow. Comparative stupid quotes:

"Knowing that I met my soul mate (his Argentinean lover)…I am going to try and work out my marriage with my wife."

Former South Carolina Governor, Republican Mark Sanford

"F-you," said Sanford's wife.

"F-yous," said actor Joe Pesci in almost all of his films with the exception of *Lethal Weapon*.

Whatever.

Petraeus: The Mrs. Will "Cut It Off": November 11, 2012

Back in the early '90s when we first lived in Virginia, working for the Big Three (remember that dinosaur of a term) lobbying group led by Andy Card, the "story of the century" was when Lorena Bobbitt used her Ginsu knife to separate her husband John Bobbitt's John Thomas from his body. John Thomas and John got back together—sort of—and helped spark his brilliant, yet brief stint in the porn industry. I never saw it as I hate slasher films.

So, why bring up an almost 20-year-old story, Wisecracker? According to media reports, General David Petraeus has told friends he "cut off" his affair with his biographer lover. Ouch. Perhaps it was a preemptive strike, knowing that Mrs. General Petraeus was lying in wait. Or, is it laying? My bad.

Petraeus, it appears, was busted thanks to an email threat from his lover to another woman that resembled Glenn Close's character in the movie, *Fatal Attraction*. Despite the Benghazi-growing-scandal, Petraeus's future was limitless. Now, like John Bobbitt before him, he is scouring the side roads of Northern Virginia, looking for his "special purpose."

To repeat a classic men's urinal joke: Don't look here. The joke is in your hands. General-ly.

Starbucks Liars and "Happy" Idiots at the United Nations: March 23, 2015

Liars and celebs speaking out on subjects they apparently know nothing about capped the news as we entered a new week of chaos in the world. Let's start with the liars and, unfortunately, they are people in my craft – PR people thrown to the wolves by an incredibly shallow, self-absorbed, and overly-caffeinated CEO.

I am talking about, of course, the debacle at Starbucks created by CEO Howard "I know nothing other than lattes" Schultz. The kazillionaire thought it would be moving, inspirational, and just-plain-enlightened if he convinced his "partners" to engage in discussions with customers about "race relations in America" as they prepared the overpriced coffee drinks. Starbucks printed "Race Together" on cups in hopes that customers eager to throw away four or five bucks on a beverage would happily wish to engage in race relations discussions with a minimum wage "partner" whom undoubtedly spent much of their higher education studying the issues of the past three hundred years.

I went to a Starbucks, hoping for the engagement. I wanted to find out if the coffee technician knew that the fight for slavery, the Jim Crow shame, and the fight against the civil rights revolution of the 1960s was led by Democrats, not Republicans. I was ready to point out that Jews in America stood by Black America to give them equal rights over the objection of Democrats in the U.S. House, the U.S. Senate, state legislatures, and racist Democratic governors, only to have our first black President, twice elected, recently show nothing but disdain and contempt for the Jewish state of Israel and its leaders. I wanted to find out if these

52

newly-called-to-action-race-relations-discussers, working on my
cappuccino (venti, of course), knew that the former hallowed Democratic
dean of the Senate, the late Robert Byrd, was a former KKK grand wizard.

I got squat. Just my four-dollar drink. No discussion, just a "Jason"
when my beverage was complete. Deflated, I left, got in my car, and drove
away. This morning, I found that the $40 million a year or so CEO Schultz
had abandoned his pathetic attempt at "civil discourse." He, apparently,
was not ready for the pushback for his silly stunt, and he tucked his tail
between his, ahem, and mercifully ended his stupidity.

Then, the worst thing happened. A spokesperson for Starbucks stated
that the program had not been discontinued—nay, nay, nay—but was
merely "concluded as planned." After a week? Shut up, liar. You
disgraced yourself, your company, and the craft of PR. Nobody bought it.
Nobody. If you wish to stop covering your bosses' moronic behavior and
want to continue lying for a living, quickly send your resume to the State
Department, Hillary Clinton's campaign, or Team Obama. You have
gained the necessary "spin doctor" credentials to fit in with any of these
places quite nicely, and perhaps, thrive. But don't buy a mirror for your
apartment as you may have a hard time looking at yourself. But, then
again, maybe you won't have a problem after all, considering your recent
track record.

Finally, on to celebs speaking out of their paper a—holes. Pharrell
Williams brought his "Happy" message to 1,300 kids at the United
Nations saying that "happiness was a birthright," and that "happy" people
will focus on Climate Change. Williams, of course, is "happy" that his
annoying song has made him millions. I just wonder: would he be "happy"
to know that the United Nations' Human Rights Council includes such
stellar "happy" places for the "little guys and gals" as China, Cuba,
Russia, and Venezuela? I guess "happiness" is "bliss." And blind.

Happy now, Pharrell? Grow up, get informed, and maybe your next
cute song will be called "Pissed."

53

Stupid People of the Week: It's a Tie Between Hillary's People and the U of M: April 9, 2015

Most times there is a clear and present winner for "Stupid Person of the Week." It appears there is a tie. First up for the honor: Hillary Clinton's staff, cohorts, supporters, or the eerie "Super Supporters" are telling everyone (read: Conservatives) that it is SO WRONG to refer to said Hillary—the presumed Anointed One For 2016—by her, um, first name.

Calling Hillary Clinton simply "Hillary" is so wrong on so many levels, don't cha know. (I don't know why I just slipped into Northern Minnesota lingo, but what the hay der.) It is SEXIST. It is BIGOTED. It is RACIST. (Oh, wait, Hillary is whiter-than-white). DAMN!! Hillary, ahem, Mrs. Clinton, deserves much more respect for her past positions. What positions? Like when she spearheaded the first attempt at national health care—the precursor to ObamaCare—in which she proudly embraced the program's name of HillaryCare. Maybe she wants to forget that really bad episode. For that, I do give her credit.

But is it so bad to call a potential or announced presidential candidate by their first name? We called the former leader of American forces against the Nazis by his frickin' nickname (Ike). We referred to JFK as "Jack." We called Carter the "idiot." (Oh, sorry, recalling Sunday dinners.) We called Reagan "Dutch," we called Bill Clinton "the President who has a human cigar humidor," and the left-wing media called Dubya "kind of slow." (Actually, some called him retarded, but you can't use that term any more as it is wrong on so many levels). Oh, the names we have for our fearless leaders.

But, we can't call Hillary, "Hillary." Google "Hillary Clinton 2008 campaign posters" and you will see all kinds of "just HILLARY" artwork. Go figure.

Second up: those geniuses at the University of Michigan were finally saved by their new football godsend, Jim Harbaugh. The U of Ahem was going to show the epic classic "American Sniper" on campus until a handful of students protested. Their protest: it might offend Muslim students. True, the film shows the hero, Chris Kyle, smoking a lot of Islamic jihadists. Most Americans loved this movie. The film was fantastic, although it was not a testament to our war-mongering. It showed the bitterness of war. But the U of M puked on themselves and then had to walk back their spinelessness and approve the airing of the film. Why? Mainly because their new multi-million dollar football coach called the administration a bunch of lightweights.

Those that say universities should be more about academics than sports should take heed: the academicians had their collective heads up their you-know-where while the "dumb" football coach was thinking clearly. And, had some guts.

I think I will forever call Harbaugh "Jim." Just as I will call Mrs. Clinton, "Hillary."

"Rights" vs. "Right": May 4, 2015
There is a difference between having a "right" and doing the "right" thing.

Feisal Abdul Rauf, the Islamic cleric, had the "right" to build a new Community Center two blocks from the hallowed ground of the World Trade Center's Ground Zero, if his group had legally obtained the property from Burlington Coat Factory. But it wasn't the "right" thing to do. Eventually Rauf did the right thing and opted for a different location. Whew.

A few years ago, open (hand gun) carry advocates had the "right" to bring their fire arms to a family–centered three day, open air festival in Royal Oak, Michigan (Arts, Beats and Eats sponsored by Ford Motor Company). But, it wasn't the right thing to do.

Now we know some boneheads in Garland, Texas, decided to throw a "Muhammad Cartoon Contest." Thanks to our First Amendment free speech guarantee under the U.S. Constitution, the organizers had every right to celebrate their "art." (Personally, I am always scouring the pages of my local newspaper looking for cartoon festivals making fun of the Muslim prophet. Not!) But, it wasn't the right thing to do. Sure, the alleged Muslim criminals that decided to open fire at the event were 100 percent wrong. I am thankful that the cops took little time in giving them a one-way ticket to Hell, and sure, if they are indeed Islamic jihadists, they might have tried to attack a day care center sooner or later for all we know. But why do we have to take our First Amendment rights and use them as gasoline on a fire.

Sure, I am a hypocrite when it comes to the First Amendment. If I saw someone burning our flag, I would accept their right to do so...and then I would promptly go up to the perpetrator and spit a massive lung oyster in their face and accept the consequences of my actions.

Back to Garland, Texas: Luckily, no innocent victims were harmed. Had that not been the case, the blood would have been on the terrorists and the event organizers as the latter did not know the difference between "rights" and what is "right."

Chapter Four: Stupid White House

"TWO INCHES OR TWO FEET? WHAT DIFFERENCE DOES IT MAKE, SENATOR?!"

(Caution: This section of stupidity includes "All the Presidents' Men and Women," including the Department of Justice (Ha!), the IRS, and those wacky, fun-loving Pinocchios at the State Department, as well as the presumptive Democrat candidate hoping to make the White House her home again in early 2017.)

Obama, Iowa, and the G Spot: August 18, 2011

The President went to Iowa. And he spoke their language. NOT. Mr. Obama went to the most famous of the fly-over states and tried—repeat, tried—to talk like a Hawkeye. He did so by adopting a Sarah Palin technique of dropping Gs. He said are "you havin'" and are "ya doin'" and the infamous "goin'."

Only problem for the Campaigner-in-Chief was that people from Iowa don't talk like that. Perhaps news to our President and perhaps many others, Iowa has the finest public school system in the country year after year. We—I was born and grew up in Iowa—know the G spot when it comes to vocabulary. It's having, doing, and going. Please.

Did the MSM pick up on Obama's vernacular? Of course, not. But just imagine Texas Governor Rick Perry losing his Texas accent and adopting a Yooper (Upper Peninsula of Michigan) lingo on a campaign trip to Marquette, Michigan.

Perry: Hey der. The Federal Government is really spendy, don't ya know. Der caboose of da moose is loose, there, don't ya know there.

Audience member: Belch.

Perry: There ya go, I agree, don't ya know there.

The MSM would slay Perry for such a transgression. But Obama's fake Iowan lingo is all too typical as his legacy grows uglier by the day. Reagan was derided for being an actor that became President. Obama is clearly a President that has become an actor. Is this Iowa? No, it's Hollywood. Can't wait for his next performance in Martha's Vineyard. "Hello, Miff and Buffy, damnation the Cape is chilly."

Obama: The "I" of Hurricane Irene: August 29, 2011

President Obama "boldly" ended his much-criticized vacation on Martha's Vineyard in order to lead the efforts of the East Coast surviving Hurricane Irene. But claiming you are "giving up" your luxury sabbatical in the midst of an oncoming storm is a bit like the caption of that classic cartoon where two friends are in line at a bank just as the tellers and customers are being robbed by armed bandits: "Hey Bob, here's that $100 I owe you."

What became swiftly apparent was that Obama was injecting himself into the "I" of the storm for two reasons: to avoid any further damage his trip to the Cape had done in rendering him tone deaf and to heed the words of his ol' buddy Rahm Emanuel—take advantage of every crisis. Being a hero on the latter would be yet another way to show what an utter failure George W. Bush had been. Remember that little Katrina thing?

Obama saw the opportunity for a one-two punch on his predecessor. Earlier in the day, we got to hear the President's pre-recorded weekly radio address in which he called on Americans to "reclaim that spirit of unity that followed 9/11." Seconds later, in that same address, he said the country is still fighting al Qaeda, while "ending the war in Iraq, pulling back troops from Afghanistan, and emerging from the worst economic crisis in our lifetime." Uh, that, of course, is Obama-code for "Blame Bush." So much for that "spirit of unity."

Immediately, Obama went live to airwaves, teleprompter locked-and-loaded, warning people to get off beaches they had already left. He then went down the laundry list of all he and his team were doing, all the while hyping the severity of Irene. Tragically, more than a dozen died in the storm, but Irene didn't come close to the dire predictions. Had this been the only Obama citing or reference during the storm, it would not have garnered any attention. However, with each live FEMA briefing, the first few minutes, regardless of the speaker, were dedicated to how much

59

President Obama and his team were doing for the country. It was if it had been scripted. Duh.

Super Soak the Rich: Plouffe Goes the Weasel: September 26, 2011

This past Sunday, I joined my Palestinian brothers in that time-honored ritual of throwing one's shoes at the television set in protest. They, of course, were protesting the appearance of Bibi "Have You Schooled an American President Lately" Netanyahu at the U.N. I, meanwhile, was listening to Chris Wallace's interview with White House Senior Advisor David "Silent L" Plouffe on the evil FOX Network.

"Absent tax reform, the President believes the right way to get our fiscal house in order is ask the wealthy to pay their fair share," Plouffe spewed.

Thank God I had my flip-flops on as my sandal harmlessly bounced off of Plouffe's pie hole on the screen.

When Wallace pointed out those who fall into the wealthiest 10 percent pay 70 percent of the country's taxes, Plouffe took control of the interview and firmly planted his head in the southern hemisphere of his body with this gem: "The American people are screaming out, saying it's unfair that the wealthiest, the largest corporations, who can afford the best attorneys, the best accountants, take advantage of these special tax treatments that lobbyists have—along with lawmakers—cooked into the books here. ... Again, they make a ton of money."

Splat! The shoe on the other foot had been launched, violently bouncing off the screen and careening toward my dog, temporarily interrupting his normal routine of doing what dogs do best…because they can. Hmmm.

Barefooted, I wondered aloud how the White House thought it could get away with this class warfare crap. I mean, facts are facts. The numbers aren't there for manipulating. They are what they are and they come from the IRS— – the Infernal Rectum Squeezers—a group that knows a thing or two about extracting every penny they can from our paychecks and wallets. (Ever been audited? I have. It takes away more of your dignity than a colonoscopy by a female doctor.)

According to the IRS, in the last tax year available (2008) and the last year of W's reign of terror, the top 1 percent of the earners—the filthy rich SOBs Jimmy Hoffa believes we need to take out—paid 38 percent of all the income taxes paid to the Federal Government. The top 5 percent—including the slightly-less-filthy-rich, but still dirty scumbags—paid 59 percent of all Fed income taxes. And finally—to the number Chris Wallace shared with Plouffe-Daddy—the top 10 percent, including those wealthy bastards like me who have the gall to make an Adjusted Gross Income of $113,799 or higher, paid 70 percent of all federal income taxes.

But wait, Cracker! I just bet the rich were paying a lot less than they paid when W first got into office in 2001. Wrong again Plouffe-ster! For the tax year 2001, the top 1 percent paid a "mere" 34 percent of all federal income taxes while the top 10 percent paid a miserly 65 percent of the tax bill. The lesson: Like everything else, blame it on Bush.

Obama and Holder: Take This Photo ID and Shove It! December 13, 2011

When I go to the airport tomorrow, I think I will leave my ID at home. Apparently, the Obama Administration doesn't believe I need to carry it, or so I gather from their actions on illegal immigration and voting.

As you know, the Justice Department's suits against Arizona, South Carolina, Alabama, and Utah for ironically enforcing the federal anti-immigration laws in their states are appearing before the Supremes next year. The Obama Administration doesn't believe it's fair to ask for ID from a potential illegal immigrant detained for some potential offense like say speeding, robbery, rape, or murder.

61

The other place the Administration believes photo IDs should be off-limits is at the voting booth. A dozen of those pesky red states in our union have had the audacity to tighten rules requiring voters to present state-issued photo identification at the polls, while four blue states had the requirements vetoed by their Democratic governors. The ACLU has called these ID requirements "an assault on our democracy" and an attempt to depress minority vote. Huh?

What keeps a minority from getting a state-issued photo ID? Think, Wisecracker, think. Oh yeah, maybe the fact the person is an illegal immigrant or a felon or wanted by authorities. By the way, the same reasons a "non-minority" may choose not to get a state-issued photo ID.

Attorney General Eric "Fast and Furious" Holder is leading the efforts on both issues. On December 12th, Holder told a reporter: "We are a better nation now than we were because more people are involved in the electoral process." That's code once again for we were a shameful, arrogant, and racist nation until Obama and his gang came along to fundamentally change our country.

Holder added this gem: "The beauty of this nation, the strength of this nation, is its diversity, and when we try to exclude people from being involved in the process…we weaken the fabric of this country."

Please. According to CBS News, "illegal immigrants are just 7 percent of Arizona's population but make up nearly 15 percent of the state's prison population. They represent 14 percent of all inmates jailed for manslaughter and murder, and 24 percent of inmates on drug charges—troubling to many Arizonans—even if the overall crime rate is down."

Mr. Holder, give your "fabric" speech to the families of those murder victims. Oh, and do your job and enforce the laws of our land instead of wasting our tax money fighting them. As you mocked Chairman Issa the other day in the House hearing: Have you no shame?

Obama: Bombs Away from Russkies: March 27, 2012

Washington is aghast that President Obama was caught on a hot mike telling outgoing Russian faux President Dmitry "Can I buy a vowel" Medvedev that he'll have "more flexibility" to deal with U.S.-Russkie relations once he gets reelected in November. How Mr. Obama could be any more "flexible" with our frienemies in Moscow is a real knee-slapper. Let's see, he withdrew our missile defense systems from Eastern Europe, scaring the bejeezus out of our friends there. And, he remained quiet when the Russians joined the Chinese in thwarting sanctions against a Syrian government killing its own people by the thousands.

On that hot mike, he also told Medvedev to tell incoming President Vladimir Putin that he needed some "space." Wait a minute: didn't we already give up our space program to the Soviets, um, er, Russians?

What is telling about President Obama's open-mike gaffe is his attitude of appeasement toward our former Cold War enemy. Back in 1984, President Reagan famously had his own open-mike gaffe when he said: "My fellow Americans, I'm pleased to tell you today that I've signed legislation that will outlaw Russia forever. We begin bombing in five minutes." Nope, the Gipper was in no mood for appeasement, even if he was joking. Sort of.

Maybe Obama was channeling ol' Ronnie when he was whispering sweet somethings in Medvedev's ear: "My fellow comrades, I'm pleased to tell you today that I've signed legislation that will outlaw our aggressive behavior towards Russia forever. We begin dismantling all of our bombs in five minutes."

Finally, it appears that *The Washington Post* editors were asleep at the switch this week. In a front page story covering the Supreme Court arguments over Obamacare, Post reporter Eli Saslow threw out this beauty: "When it comes to a divisive President's most divisive piece of legislation, public opinion leaves little room for middle ground." Whoa,

hold the phone, Chuck! The Post is calling Obama a "divisive President."
How did that make it into print?

Obama's Supreme Temper Tantrum: April 3, 2012

If you are a parent or a John McEnroe fan, you know a good temper
tantrum when you see one. They are rarely planned; they just happen and
the more spontaneous, typically, the more volatile. Unless, of course, you
are the President of the United States or maniac chef Gordon Ramsay.
What we witnessed in Washington Monday was a planned,
choreographed, and sad temper tantrum regarding the fate of Obamacare
as the Supreme Court deliberated its future.

The Washington Post tried its damnedest to portray Mr. Obama's
hissy fit as somehow presidential with the headline, "Obama Confident
Supreme Court Will Uphold Health-Care Law." A couple hundred miles
north, *The Wall Street Journal* actually called it what it was: "Obama
Warns Supreme Court." Funny, the guts of both stories, including the
myriad barbs by the President aimed at Roberts, Alito, Scalia, and
Thomas, were largely identical despite the completely different takes on a
headline. Can't we all just edit along?

"For years, what we've heard is the biggest problem on the bench was
judicial activism or the lack of judicial restraint, that an unelected group of
people would somehow overturn a duly constituted and passed law," said
the President. "And, I'm pretty confident that this court will recognize that
and not take that step."

No, you aren't; thus the temper tantrum. Hell to the Court! Notice Mr.
Obama's choice of words: a "duly constituted" law obviously means it's
constitutional, right? And I have never heard anyone reference the highest
court in our land as "an unelected group of people."

Mr. Obama also whined that it "would be an unprecedented,
extraordinary step" for the court to overturn "a law that was passed by a
strong majority of a democratically-elected Congress." First and foremost,

64

the real "unprecedented, extraordinary step" IS Obamacare. Furthermore, the size of a Congressional minority has absolutely no constitutional bearing. Oh, and that "strong majority" was actually a nail-biter in the Senate—thanks to the "Louisiana Purchase" and Ben Nelson's and Bart Stupak's deals—and only passed the House 219-212 with not a single Republican voting in favor.

It is interesting that since this supposed slam dunk for the Administration clanked off the back rim countless times thanks to a shaky point guard – a formerly revered Solicitor General – Obama and his defenders, like *The Washington Post*, have followed an almost identical script in distributing the blame for Obamacare's defeat. Check that: it is an identical script and the major storylines are as follows: "Constitutional" means anything Obama and the Democrats in the House and Senate concoct. After all, Mr. Obama taught Constitutional Law, so he should know, don't ya think.

Biden Takes One for the Team: May 1, 2012

According to a report in the UK's *Telegraph* newspaper, Vice President Joe Biden admitted that he advised Barack Obama against Osama bin Laden's take down, arguing that the administration needed more information before deploying the Navy SEALs. I think the whole thing is a canard to make BHO look tougher. I imagine the conversation this way:

Obama: Joe, now that Bin Laden is six feet under, I need you to say you were against the raid so that I look like a stud.

Biden: Why do I have to look like a wimp?

Obama: Because elections have consequences and I won.

Biden: But WE won.

Obama: Joe, there is no "I" in "we"—therefore, I cannot use it.

Biden: Wait a minute, there is an "I" in "Oui."

Obama: Joe, you've been reading too much soft porn. Stop it.

65

Biden: But this is really a big f****** deal. Why do I have to take the fall?

Obama: If it makes you feel better for doing this, I am authorizing the Surgeon General to give you fifty more hair plugs.

Biden: Sweet.

Obama Re-election Campaign Begins; No S--- Sherlock! May 6, 2012

President Obama "finally" kicked off his re-election campaign in my new home state of Virginia, with a rally in front of 10,000 well-wishers. Well, actually, it was a group of mostly college students who don't have and can't get jobs. Ironically, the inaugural campaign event was held at Virginia Commonwealth University. Common wealth: isn't that Obama's plan for a redistribution of wealth?

Coincidental with Obama's campaign "beginning," was news that unemployment ticked down to just 8.1 percent. Heck, even the President's official spokespaper—*The Washington Post*—had to admit on page one Sunday that unemployment had declined "only because the labor force shrank as discouraged Americans gave up looking for work." Hope and Change? How about Dope and Clang.

No, no, no. The Wisecracker is not calling our President a dope. That reference is reserved for VP Joe Biden. If the President's approval ratings, coupled with the economy, don't improve by August, plan on the "Dope" getting the ziggy in favor of Hillary, despite her debacle with the asylum-seeking Chinese "Sexy Specs "dude, which gives new meaning to "the blind leading the blind."

So, all the pundits now believe that Virginia is the bell-weather state to determine the November election. The formerly traditional red state went big for Obama in 2008 and has had an influx of immigrant minorities over the past decade. (Mrs. Wisecracker is an English-as-a-Second-Language Tutor and she is working overtime as a volunteer. Oh yeah, ya think if I moved to France I could get French lessons for free? America! What a country!)

Anyway, talking to the cheering crowd in Virginia, the President claimed that "his work was unfinished." My only thought was: what in the hell does this country look like when he is finished? Historical note: Jeffrey Dahmer made the same claim in his murder trial.

The later event for Obama at Ohio State University featured a less-than-full arena in a sign that "The One" just might be losing some of his enthusiastic core. On second thought, it was a Saturday, and most Buckeyes are in jail on the weekends. My bad. There, as in Virginia, he threw out his campaign's new line about Romney: that he was a "rubber stamp" for the radical Republican Congress. By that he means radicals like Paul Ryan, who defied Washington by actually presenting a budget and a way out of the entitlement train wreck our children face.

The Lawlessness of Team Obama: July 2, 2012

You've gotta give the Obama Administration kudos in one area: consistency. Actually, consistently turning their back on the laws of the land. The latest example is the U.S. Attorney in Washington, D.C.'s decision not to prosecute AG Eric Holder for his criminal contempt of Congress, even after a bi-partisan vote of their resolution. Instead of following the law, Team Obama decided to fan the flames with charges of racism. That's right, Holder is the victim here, despite the fact we have a dead border agent, and who knows how many dead Mexicans thanks to Fast and Furious.

Uphold the law and deport youngish illegal immigrants; some 800,000 of them we know about? Nope, Obama all but grants them amnesty and a path to citizenship despite the fact that he had earlier stated it would be unlawful for him to do so. We don't need no stinking laws because it was just another form of, you guessed it, racism.

Prosecute Black Panthers practicing the most blatant form of voter intimidation many of us have ever seen in our lifetime? Nada. Reward Arizona for upholding federal laws against illegal immigration? No, and instead, sue the state, win suit with the Supreme Court, and then flip Arizona the bird. Make sure people voting are actually who they say they are by demanding a photo I.D.? No way you racists! After all, the citizens you teabaggers are targeting don't need a photo I.D. to cash a check, take a flight, or visit the White House or the Justice Department. Right? Sheesh.

The Lawlessness of Team Obama: Take Two: July 15, 2012

The Obama Administration is breaking the laws of the land at such breakneck speed it would make Tricky Dick Nixon, even Al Capone, blush. The latest examples, both last week, were the crime of slander against Mitt Romney and defying a nearly two-decades-old law crafted by Bubba Clinton and a bi-partisan Congress concerning welfare reform.

The slander against Romney was further evidence that: one, President Obama has never had a job that remotely touched business; and two, his campaign is desperately seeking to discuss anything other than his record as President. Not his criminal record, but rather his record of non-accomplishment, particularly in terms of the economy.

Actually, his behavior and actions have made it hard to differentiate between those two records. Romney's firm, like so many private equity companies, buy or invest in troubled firms that would otherwise eventually "buy the farm" and fix them, saving the company and jobs. Yes, many times that includes outsourcing sectors of the company that are uncompetitive (sometimes the very reason the company was on the verge of death in the first place.) Obama and his team don't seem to get this.

Luckily, we have two prime examples of outsourcing that were the creation of Team Obama: Fisker Motors and Chrysler. In Fisker's case, they got loads of U.S. taxpayer money (officially bazillions) and are building a high-end sports car in Finland. They're not finished vehicles. They're Finnish vehicles. At Chrysler, the whole company, minus a few thousand dealers and employees who got the ziggy, was outsourced to Italian automaker Fiat. Just like private equity often does, Obama's efforts, using outsourcing, has come with mixed results. Fisker has pretty much been a basket case since day one and is threatening not to build vehicles in the U.S. as promised once it got the dough. The Chrysler results, led by St. Sergio Marchionne, have been marvelous, and the company is on solid footing again saving tens of thousands of jobs and the communities their facilities serve.

Calling Romney a felon for allowing the firm he helped create, Bain, to do this same thing after he left to save the Olympics and then go into politics, was so slanderous that the liberal bastion *Washington Post* took only four hours to publish an article calling the charges by Team Obama a lie—not stretching the truth and not an exaggeration. A lie. Bammo Obama!

Last week's other crime was against the 51 percent of us Americans that pay taxes. With an official policy directive, Obama negated Clinton's 1996 bipartisan welfare reform by flushing away the federal requirement that in order to get a welfare check you either work or train for work. In a *Washington Examiner* Sunday editorial: "according to the Congressional Research Service, those requirements are 'mandatory' and cannot be waived, even though some other parts of the law can." Unless you're Obama, who, for the sake of truthfulness, should change his campaign slogan from "Moving Forward" to "Laws are meant to be broken."

Too harsh? Try this gem: "The President does not have power under the Constitution to unilaterally authorize a military attack in a situation that does not involve an actual or imminent threat to our nation." Those words were freshman U.S. Senator Barack Obama's in his criticism of George W. Bush. As President, he did not practice what he preached when Libya blew up.

On CBS Sunday morning, Obama complained about his inability to
"change" Washington. Oh, Mr. President, you have indeed changed
Washington AND our country as your Administration's crime spree
continues.

**Hillary to Obama: Take the VP Job and Shove It! August 19,
2012**

It is rumored here in Washington, D.C., that Obama top aide, Valerie
Jarrett, recently met for lunch with Secretary of State Hillary Clinton,
offering her the VP spot on the 2012 Democratic ticket. Thanks to the
Wisecracker's breathtakingly unreliable sources in the bowels of the
White House (redundant), I have received a recording of that meeting:

Jarrett: Hey, Hill!

Clinton: Hi, Val!

Jarrett: Let me cut to the chase. We have to dump Joe Biden before he
does even more damage.

Clinton: Ya'll need to put him in chains. (Hearty laughter)

Jarrett: Ya'll?

Clinton: It's okay, I'm from Arkansas. Isn't it funny that we might
elect a Mormon because the Vice President is a Moron?

Jarrett: Hillary, this is serious business. With you on the ticket, we'll
crush Romney and Ryan and you will be perfectly situated to become
President in 2016.

(Hillary's phone rings.)

Clinton: I'm so sorry; it's the Philanderer-in-Chief. I've got to take
this. Yes, Bill, I'm working. What is it?

Bubba: Whoa-doggie! Gotta take the job, honey! I can smell the
White House cookin' already; the bowling alley; the White House theater
and Air Force One. I can get to D.C. in a couple hours and we can
announce this puppy! People will freak seeing me, um, er, us in the Rose
Garden!

70

Clinton: Bill, don't get your panties in a bunch.

Bubba: Actually, I don't have any on right now if you know what I mean.

Clinton: Please, Bill, I am at lunch. Anyway, there's no way I can do this. We talked about it, Bill. Remember when Obama accused you of being a racist and how much that hurt after all you have done for minorities in this country? Hell, Bill, they called you America's First Black President!

Bubba: Yeah, I remember, but...

Clinton: That's a big but, and if anyone knows a big but, it's you. Remember the discussion we had about how much we hate the President and the Gardener-in-Chief?

Bubba: Yeah, but...

Clinton: No buts, Bill! How about the time he called himself the fourth best President of all time. You remember what you did when you heard that?

Bubba: If I recall, I barfed up a Big Mac, a hot apple pie, and a large frozen Coke.

Clinton: And a Happy Meal. Drop this, and here's what I will do for you honey. I'm going to have your office in New York completely redone as an exact mirror image of the Oval Office. I'll even buy you one of those walk-in cigar humidors like Rush Limbaugh has.

Bubba: Wow. You do love me, after all, don't ya, Hill?

Clinton: Gotta go, Bill; I've got a bigger fish to fry. (Click) Sorry, Val. Thanks, but no thanks.

Jarrett: But Hillary, we can't win without you!

Clinton: I know. Isn't that special?

Kick Ass: The Debate: October 4, 2012

I have often been asked by CEOs for a joke to start their speech and I have always warned them: if an opening joke bombs, the rest of your speech is on life-support. So was the case with the first presidential debate.

An ever-cocky Barack Obama began the night with a joke about his 20th anniversary. Unfortunately for him, it went over like a pregnant pole-vaulter. I did not hear a single laugh. To add salt to the wound, Mitt Romney—who until recently had been in a witness protection program—started his night with this zinger: "Congratulations to you, Mr. President, on your anniversary. I'm sure this was the most romantic place you could imagine—here with me." It brought down the house and then some. It showed Romney's respect for the Office by referring to Obama as Mr. President, and it set Romney on a course that can only be described as an old-fashioned "ass kicking."

Those are not my words, but rather those of my next door neighbor here in Old Town Alexandria, Virginia. She's a classic lib, annoyed at all of my GOP campaign signs in my miniscule front yard, including a five foot Romney/Ryan sign. But, I always fix stuff for her, be it a leaky toilet, a broken door, trimming her marijuana plants, whatever. She texted me an hour before the debate: "Can I come over and watch the debate with you guys?" Sure, I replied. The next text was "can we watch it on CNN?" I replied my Direct TV dish only gets FOX so live with it.

She arrived with a nice bottle of wine in tow and joined us for the debate. She thought it was funny that I had decided to count the number of times Obama said "ah" or "um"—the twin sisters of LUS (lying, uncertainty, or stupidity). At the end of the debate, the count was forty-nine. I looked over to our friend and asked her what she thought. She replied: "Obama got his ass kicked." Nuff said.

Obama's U.S. Flag Burning Stimulus Plan: October 23, 2012

Wow, President Obama finally may have a stimulus program that actually creates (or saves) U.S. jobs. As U.S. flags burn in the Muslim strongholds of Egypt, Libya, Indonesia, Pakistan, and, um, Australia, there is certainly a prime market for replacement flags. And contrary to claims led by Ohio's embattled Democratic Senator Sherrod Brown that a boatload of U.S. flags are imported from China, about 94 percent of our flags are made here.

According to James Giraudo, owner of Pacific Coast Flag in Sacramento, California, and President of the National Independent Flag Dealers Association, U.S. flag makers produce between $50 and $60 million worth of Old Glories annually. We import less than $4 million worth of American flags, and yes, most of those ironically come from Communist China.

So, it appears Obama's '09 Apology Tour and "Leading from Behind" foreign policy in the region is having a "War Dividend' for American workers who produce the cotton, thread, and dye and those that dutifully stitch our flag together and ship them to the Middle East as fuel for the protests. Literally.

And who knows, maybe Americans will get tired of seeing our flag burned in countries for which we send billions of taxpayer dollars only to see the red, white, and blue go up in flames amid chants of "Death to America, and will go out and purchase a new flag and fly it proudly. Some, sadly, will prefer to fly the new "Obamanation" of our flag for his campaign purposes. (Yet another sick and twisted issue coming out of their camp.)

Osama bin Laden is dead, and the U.S. Flag Industry is Alive. Great job, Mr. President.

The "I" of the Storm: Again, Obama: October 28, 2012

Watch the coverage as Hurricane Sandy rips up Delaware, New Jersey, and New York; along with my home in the Washington, D.C. area. Count how many times the MSM compares President Obama's response to that of George W. during Katrina. If you want to play a beer-drinking game and you pick Katrina as your word, please don't drive.

Perhaps, this is the "October Surprise" Obama thought had eluded him. First, it was a supposed "deal" with a nuke-happy Iran. That fizzled faster than a Korean ballistic missile. Then pathetic ambulance chaser, Gloria Allred, tried to punk Mitt Romney with yet another bogus "war on women" claim. Dud Scud. So now, Obama is counting on the Almighty to save his faltering campaign of Dope and Clang.

Obama has canceled campaign events due to the storm—akin to Georgetown Law School's Sandra Fluke passing on a romp in the sack with free contraceptives. To be fair, Presidents should be involved in natural disasters affecting a ginormous percentage of the American population. But, this won't be about involvement. It will be purely about politics.

So watch the news over the coming days and count the times Katrina and Bush's "failures" are mentioned. Oh, the other best choice in "word drinking poker" will be "I."

Obama: Hurricane Sandy Is a Breath of Fresh Air: October 29, 2012

Alexandria, Virginia: At the edge of Hurricane Sandy, the wind howls, and the rain continues to pour—all day and night—in greater Washington, D.C. Hopefully the damage will be minimal and those in harm's way will be safe in Jersey, Delaware, and New York.

Here in Northern Virginia, this is "the storm of the century." Funny, the century is only 12 years old. Washingtonians treat tough weather like Armageddon. You cannot find any bottled water anywhere. Batteries are

in short supply. And finding a flashlight at the Lowe's or Home Depot?
Ha. It's as if we've been told the sun will extinguish itself tomorrow or
"Dancing with the Stars" is being cancelled. The people here act like
Mayans on steroids.

By Wednesday, trees will be down, along with power lines…and the
sun will come out.

There are some positives about the storm:

• All of Donald Trump's holdings in Atlantic City are literally under
water so he can stop trying to interject himself into the presidential race.

• Barack Obama actually faced the White House media instead of
those pesky "reporters" at MTV.

• "Romnesia" was not mentioned today. (Shoot, I just mentioned it.)

• New Jersey Governor Chris Christie got to go on the air and
confirm that some people in his state are "stupid."

• And finally, we were not forced for the first day in months, to
listen to David Axelrod "ah, er, and um" his way through a painful
explanation for the debacle in Libya or other silly excuses for the present
administration.

Obama campaign officials are already touting the line that Hurricane
Sandy will help their guy. After all, it was an earlier Sandy—Sandra
Fluke—that helped create his bogus charge about Romney's "war on
women." I wonder how many folks right now in the hurricane zone are
saying, "Ya know, honey, as I saw our car float down the river in our
street, I realized that Obama really deserves four more years."

Yeah, right, that's the ticket.

Chris Matthews: '12 Election Proves White Americans Hate Obama More than al Qaeda: October 30, 2012

This is the most important presidential election of my lifetime. That is
not a hyperbole. My first presidential election was in 1980, and like a

typical stupid college kid, I voted for John Anderson if I remember correctly. Call it the "Fog of Weed."

Why the most important? We cannot get anything done in Washington due to a complete stalemate in Congress. If Obama is re-elected, that stalemate will become stifling as the House we have today will undoubtedly look nearly identical the day after the election. That will lead the President to exert his arrogance and play chicken with Congress to show them that, in his words, "elections have consequences, and I won."

Then, as if a child throwing a temper tantrum, Obama will indeed take us over the financial cliff to punish the Republicans (ironically, the only group that has offered any solutions over the past four years). He will blame them for the sequester and the subsequent enormous spending cuts and job losses and how he wished he had another choice. He will claim he had no choice, but the fact is, his administration created the sequester as a political ploy and strapped this bomb to Obama to detonate on the American people, especially those who are connected to our military complex. Unemployment in the swing state of Virginia will soar close to 20 percent, Team Obama predicts. (Note to my fellow Virginians as I channel Chris Christie: Virginians, don't be stupid!)

The Divider-in-Chief doubled-down on derisive and racial politics, especially during the final two months of the campaign. The AP helped along this narrative with a "survey" last week that "proved" white Americans had become more racist between 2008—when they proudly voted for the black guy who didn't speak with a "Negro dialect" (thank you, Harry Reid) and helped Obama over the goal line—and today. The survey MUST be true because MSM nut job Chris "shiver up my leg" Matthews claimed that "racial hatred" solely motivates Romney voters. "They hate Obama. They want him out of the White House more than they want to destroy al Qaeda," Matthews screamed.

Matthews, in his twisted mind, might have a point: if Obama wins, winning the war on terrorism is a pipe dream. Another Apology Tour will do even less than the first. The nuclear-intent Iranians will add another shift to its centrifuge line and will edge even closer to the annihilation of Israel or perhaps World War III. Whose side will the Russians be on or will they remain "flexible"? Gas prices will go up again to unprecedented heights, and we WILL fall into another Great Recession.

Watch the stock market the day after the election is called. If Obama wins, a historic dive. Romney prevails, a historic rise. Actually, watch the stock markets around the world. If Obama wins, he won't look like the "World's President" anymore.

Simply put: The economic viability of the U.S. for our children and grandchildren, our national security, and perhaps the recoverability of the global economy is at stake. Hopefully, voters in this country are following the trend towards Romney, as witnessed in the polls showing women casting aside the drivel of Sandra Fluke and remembering that they write the checks to pay the bills for their families with fewer dollars than they had four years ago.

This is our country. This is our country on Obama's past four miserable years of bad policies and excuse after excuse; the latest not just playing the race card, but now the whole deck. Any questions?

The Accidental Obama Voter – Scary: November 2, 2012

As usual, my wife is a better human being than me. For those that know me, and her, that goes without saying. But, she blew it.

In our little spot of the earth in Old Town Alexandria—the only liberal burg of Virginia just outside of Washington, D.C.—we have a ginormous front yard. It's 20 feet by 10 feet. Actually, in this town, I am almost a rancher. I have used my ranch to promote Republican candidates from city council runners, to George Allen for Senate, to Mitt. I have more signs in my little yard than anyone in Old Town. It is pathetic. It is so

77

cool. Two weeks ago, the "civil" Libs stole my really big Romney sign. Hope they strained a groin muscle getting it out. It was anchored.

Back to my wife. Yesterday, a foreign woman of color (the Dem's term) came to our front door thinking—due to my signs—it was an early voting place. My wife turned her away. What? Me, oh crap on a crutch, I would have invited her in and shown her the voting booth—my TV on the FOX channel—and had her hit the "O" button on the remote for "Obama" and then "OK" and paid for her bus ticket home.

Voter fraud: Maybe. Bus ticket: $4.00. Saving our country one inane voter at a time: Priceless.

Obama: Eye the Prize, Finally: November 19, 2012

Democrats and the MSM (sorry for my redundancy) barked every time President Obama's "apology tour" was mentioned during the campaign. All the liberal "fact checkers" screamed that it wasn't an apology tour in the least, despite the fact that it was exactly that and more. More? A Nobel Peace Prize for Mr. Obama for, um, showing up. Remember.

The President could have been a class act and declined the prize, saying something like "let me earn this," but, alas, he grabbed the unearned award and spiked it; an early sign of his overwhelming arrogance. Three years later, he called himself the fourth best President behind Washington, Lincoln, and FDR.

My point? The Middle East is on fire. Literally. A truly "Nobel" Obama would cancel his shopping trip to irrelevant Burma and Cambodia and head east; actually west from where he is now. So far, Obama has merely offered verbal support for Israel, saying that any country should be able to defend itself against rocket attacks. Talk about a big "duh."

Mr. President, don't let your position on this issue "evolve." Come up with a coherent policy. Get over there and use your bully pulpit to the max. Clamp down on weapons-providing and soon-to-be-nuclear Iran, and stand tall with Israel ("one of our closest allies in the region"—your words). Then, send a clear message to Assad to get the hell out of Syria, and demand that Russia and China stop aiding and abetting terrorist states when they vote in the UN Security Council. In other words: Create a new world order. And, finally, earn that Nobel Peace Prize you were given almost four years ago for nothing.

Or, take the easy route and save Hostess from bankruptcy. At least that way, you will be a hero to kids and fat people as the world burns.

Obama's First Major PR Blunder: March 11, 2013

Washington, D.C. is atwitter this morning as a new dawn is here—four years of utter gridlock have evaporated thanks to President Obama's decision to reach across the aisle and "work" with Republicans. Of course, Mr. Obama did not want to be in this position, but was forced to by the first real PR blunder of his presidency—a blunder the result of his arrogance and taking the American people for granted.

Mr. Obama believed his re-election was a mandate to finish the job of "fundamentally changing America." Sure, he slapped the Republicans around and got his way for new taxes on the rich to avoid the fiscal cliff. The GOP was in tatters, but that wasn't enough for the President. Like Nixon in 1972, he wanted it all—including the death of the GOP as we know it. It was, in a word, greed.

Mr. Obama believed he had the final nail for his opponents' coffins—the coming sequester that would be so destructive to this country that Republicans would surely cave in and give him more ability to tax and spend. If nothing else, the sequester would help further demonize the GOP and Mr. Obama would have Nancy Pelosi as House Speaker for his final two years.

But then, someone in the GOP delegation called one of those testosterone drug companies that advertise constantly on FOX News, ordered a boatload of the magic pills, and made all of his colleagues take a daily dose—even the women. Magically, the GOP grew a big set of, ahem, they developed a spine. Finally.

"We already gave you your tax hike, so take a hike," they seemed to tell the President.

"How dare they?" Obama shot back. "Elections have consequences, and I won. This sequester is a bad idea by Congress, and it will kill our recovery."

"Stick it, Mr. President," they barked as their spines grew stronger. "Besides, the sequester was your idea."

"That is simply not true." (A common Obama response when confronted with the truth.)

"Mr. Obama is right," wept the MSM.

"No, Mr. Obama is wrong," said the legendary Bob Woodward, who, by the way, looks nothing like Robert Redford.

This sent Team Obama into a panic. "What do we do?" his minions asked.

"Spread fear across the land," he barked. "Make stuff up. Scare granny and all the little kids."

To be sure, Mr. Obama did his part: campaign stop after campaign stop, fear and loathing and lies too numerous to keep track of. The GOP held firm, and the day of reckoning came in like a lion and went out like a lamb. Air travelers went unaffected, planes didn't crash, janitors cleaned the Capitol and teachers kept their jobs. For once, the American people were not buying what Mr. Obama was selling. Incensed, the President channeled the Wicked Witch of the West and decided to get Dorothy "and her little dog, too." The little dog was those kids from Waverly, Iowa, that had tickets to a White House tour—"had" being the key word. Mr. Obama had placed the proverbial cherry on his PR Disaster Cake.

Enter last week, Mr. Obama the Charmer. "Steaks are on the house my Republican friends!"

It is not certain that the GOP is buying what Mr. Obama is selling now. After all, there's a four-year history of this President bashing his foes unrelentingly. While Mr. Obama plays nice (actually "presidential" for once), his big-money advocacy group (his former campaign team) is keeping the bashing up on a daily basis and DNC Chairwoman Debbie Wasserman Schultz says the GOP "continue to root for our economy to not be going in the right direction."

Finally, two predictions out of this whole affair: Mr. Obama will approve the Keystone Pipeline in hopes of softening up the GOP, but will then prove to be a Trojan horse when he sees the Republicans will not yield on closing tax loopholes unless tax rates are reduced. Thus, the gridlock will continue.

Obama Gets Outraged Over "Some" Kids' Deaths: April 18, 2013

Our President has a hard time keeping his outrage consistent over the deaths of innocent young people. When the Senate failed to pass new gun control legislation, a key component of his much sought-after legacy (remember, it's all about him despite his protestations), the President had a hissy fit in the Rose Garden in front of his familiar props throughout the gun control debate: the grieving parents of the Sandy Hook victims. Mr. Obama's outburst included calling his opponents the L-word that is supposedly verboten in Washington politics: "The gun lobby and its allies willfully lied about the bill," Mr. Obama screamed. Remember the outrage when Congressman Wilson shouted "You Lie" during the State of the Union presidential address?

Yes, indeed, the President was throwing a temper tantrum because his legacy train had been derailed and was doing so in front of people who, just months ago, had buried their little treasures, and would most likely re-live their horror every day for the rest of their lives.

When the bombs went off in Boston killing three, including an eight-year-old boy, Mr. Obama's outrage was clearly more under control as initially he would not describe the bombing as a "terrorist" attack. When asked what would keep the President from calling it such immediately after an obvious-to-everyone terrorist attack (regardless from right-wing or left-wing nut jobs or straight from Hell), longtime Obama advisor David Axelrod told MSNBC: "I'm sure what was going through the President's mind is—we really don't know who did this—it was Tax Day." What?

And, of course, Mr. Obama is outrage-free over the alleged murders by the abortionist in Philadelphia, currently on trial finally covered by some of the MSM after they were shamed into showing up. (*The Washington Post* eventually agreed to cover the trial after initially balking, calling it a "local crime story." Of course, that logic makes the Sandy Hook and Aurora massacres, the Oklahoma City bombing, and Jeffrey Dahmer's cannibalism-spree "local crime stories.") There will be no outrage on Mr. Obama's part unless he has "evolved" on the subject of what Dr. Kermit Gosnell had been up to in his house of horrors in the City of Brotherly Love: botching abortions and then all-but decapitating the live-birth babies (one so big he told a co-worker the six-pound baby was "big enough to walk me to the bus stop").

Just wondering: do all abortion doctors offer this type of side-splitting humor as they carry on their duties?

Partial-term (what pro-abortionists call them) or late-term abortions (what they really are) of these young, innocent lives apparently have never really bothered Mr. Obama, nor the First Lady. While Mr. Obama was running for the U.S. Senate seat in Illinois in 2004, Mrs. Obama sent out a fundraising letter, which read:

"We have all been concerned lately with the rise of conservatism in this country, especially as it relates to women. You've read the alarming news about the Justice Department's request for hospitals to turn over the private medical records of dozens of patients. This cynical ploy is designed to intimidate a group of physicians and force them to drop their lawsuit seeking to have the so-called partial birth abortion ban ruled unconstitutional.

"The fact remains, with no provision to protect the health of the mother, this ban on a legitimate medical procedure is clearly unconstitutional and must be overturned."

When Mrs. Obama's letter resurfaced in the 2008 presidential contest, Mr. Obama's handlers pooh-poohed it as just an example of Mr. Obama's firm belief in a woman's right to choose.

Wow.

Protecting the Second Amendment of the Constitution is what President Obama referred to as a "Shameful day for Washington." But banning the killing of babies capable of surviving outside the womb (Mrs. Obama's "legitimate medical procedure") is "clearly unconstitutional." Mr. and Mrs. Obama's lack of outrage in this arena is clearly outrageous.

Obama: Legacy or Bust: April 15, 2013

According to headlines in *The Washington Post* and most other MSM, President Obama is working full-time on his "legacy." He's not working on getting unemployed people "working," or reducing the deficit and debt that will soon strangle our children's future, or fixing Social Security before it goes belly up.

When I read mention of Mr. Obama's legacy push, it reminded me of a night in Tokyo about fourteen years ago. I was in Carlos Ghosn's office at Nissan headquarters. Mr. Ghosn had recently been given the reigns of Nissan after the take-over by Renault. Nissan was a mess—probably more bankrupt than GM and Chrysler were in 2009. Mr. Ghosn had a reputation as a ruthless cost-cutter. (Actually, he was just really good at restructuring companies for their survival.) Ghosn's reputation produced a nickname he wasn't all that fond of: Le Cost Killer. Ghosn asked me, "How can I get a better nickname?" Mustering up as much professionalism as I could, I laughed and then added, "You can't give yourself a nickname!" Ghosn immediately realized the futility of his request and subsequently went to work saving Nissan and literally changing Japan, Inc. Within a year, he was a comic book hero in Japan (really) and had a new nickname bestowed upon him—7/11, as in he worked so tirelessly to save the company.

You see, Mr. Ghosn earned his nickname and will earn his legacy by his actions. That is why Mr. Obama's full-court press on his "legacy" is so patently pathetic.

You would have thought that Mr. Obama's legacy would be in pretty decent shape by now. After all, he moved America away from its dependency on foreign oil by wisely investing billions of taxpayer dollars into wind, solar, and battery energy and saying no to those greedy, earth killers that wanted to put the Keystone pipeline through the heart of America. Oh snap, that didn't work so well. Oh, wait—he transformed our health care system so that everybody would get coverage and the average American family would save $2,500 a year. The air in that legacy balloon escaped as soon as his bean counters actually did the math and realized a ginormous increase in insurance premiums would be hitting everyone.

Paranoid that a proud legacy was slipping away, our fearless Leader from Behind donned his community organizer cape and left his Washington, D.C. office to tap into his 4G Network—Guns, Gays, immiGration and Greedy rich people. In Connecticut, he exploited the pain for the families who'd lost their loved ones in the horrific Sandy Hook school tragedy. He pleaded for his gun control ideas, constantly invoking the theme of "if we can save just one more life, we should do it" to an adoring press that up until last Friday had ignored the murder trial of a Philadelphia abortionist accused of killing seven babies who had escaped his butchery in the womb, only to have their lives extinguished with the snip of a scissors.

On gay marriage, Mr. Obama famously "evolved" when it made perfect political sense. Maybe this was the "change" candidate Obama was really talking about in 2008.

On immigration, Mr. Obama has all but tried to scuttle the bipartisan progress being worked out by the Senate's Gang of Eight by hinting that securing the border could not be a trigger to begin legalizing the 11 million or so illegal aliens—oops, forgot my AP Style Book for a second—eleven million or so "undocumented Democrats" (as Jay Leno put it.) Thankfully, we will probably get a bipartisan immigration reform agreement despite our President.

Finally, the fourth key to Mr. Obama's legacy push: pounding the fat cats into submission. The Divider-in-Chief convinced his Republican enemies to punish the rich to avoid the fiscal cliff months ago. Now, he figures what's good for the goose is even more satisfying the second time around, throwing another $1 billion in new taxes onto the rich in his tardy-by-two-months budget submitted last week. There is even talk coming out of the White House that Mr. Obama wants to tax those scoundrels who have saved "too much" money in their legal 401K accounts. He's gone from "you didn't build that" to "you didn't save that."

In Connecticut, Mr. Obama scoffed at those claiming all of his motives were political. "It's not about me," he pleaded. Oh yes, Mr. President, everything you do and say is all about you…and your precious legacy.

The White House's "New" Dictionary: April 28, 2013

As the immigration "reform" debate continues plodding along in Washington, the White House, thanks to my usual cadre of shaky sources, is preparing a first-ever edition of "talking points" for new entries to our shores. Knowing that those who come to the U.S. through legal means oftentimes have been well-versed in our English language, the Obama

Administration believes these folks need a "reset" as to what things really mean.

I obtained a very early galley of the talking points in a dumpster behind a McDonald's on Connecticut Avenue two blocks from the White House, so its authenticity is beyond reproach. Kinda. Thankfully, the 2,000-page volume included a foreword by President Obama—including proposed edits—I share as an exclusive.

"Dear immigrant fellow Earthling:

"Welcome to America. We are proud you decided this was the best place in the world to start a new life, despite the significant shortcomings of our nation over time. In contrast to those not following the proper-yet-ridiculously-arduous protocol to entering the United States, it is highly likely that you have a great propensity for the English language, probably dating back to your earliest years in your homeland's education system.

"Unfortunately, it is highly probable your English lessons were based on what ~~we~~ I refer to as 'Old English.' I apologize in advance because, well, that is what I want all Americans to do: apologize. This is why it is somewhat important that you thoroughly read the attached document which will help you to better understand our culture. If you are short on time, I have condensed the most important elements below, which you should be able to digest in a few minutes.

"Abortion is NOT about ending a pregnancy or 'killing an unborn child' as many of our less-than-stable residents spout on FOX News while cleaning their guns. Abortion IS a 'woman's health issue.'

"Obamacare IS the greatest health care reform of all time (You will love it, especially if you have trouble getting a job right away). It is NOT the socialization of medicine and a false promise for reducing the costs of healthcare in this country. Also note that a 'train wreck' is, just as you learned, a wreck of a Choo-choo train and has nothing to do with Obamacare as claimed by a recent ~~Republican~~ damned, Senator Baucas, who helped me craft it.

"A 'game changer' is not what happens when you set a 'red line' and your opponent crosses it and you are thus forced to carry out definitive action to back up your threats. A 'game changer' is actually a blackjack dealer in Las Vegas, Nevada. Hope you can visit, but please don't join the GSA and hold a frivolous conference there. A 'red line' is merely a line that is red. It has no other meaning.

"An 'illegal alien' is a Chinese-made bootleg Blu-ray copy of the movie *E.T.* and not ~~one of my supporters~~ ~~future Democratic voters~~ the folks slipping into America from heinous regimes – such as Mexico and Canada. These folks are merely 'undocumented workers.' If they are not working, then they are 'future food stamp recipients.' Oh, that reminds me: if you need some food, don't hesitate to sign up for food stamps. The requirements are super easy. If you can master a pen, you are, as they say, in like Flynn.

"Jihadists are not people intent on the annihilation of the gentiles. As my CIA appointee John Brennan succinctly stated: 'Jihad is a holy struggle, an effort to purify for a legitimate purpose, and there is nothing—absolutely nothing—holy or pure or legitimate or Islamic about murdering innocent men, women, and children.'

"We believe the concept of Radical Islam is as silly as balanced budgets. Speaking of balance, it is a term that means rich, fat cats should pay more in taxes. Those rich, fat cats will likely include you as everyone should pay their 'fair share.' Sorry. Fair share is whatever I determine it to be. (By the way, I am paying more than my fair share as I recently agreed to give back five percent of my pay as President. Unfortunately, we can now only afford to eat Kraft macaroni and cheese as we struggle on $400K-plus a year, but my wife won't let us eat this unhealthy gem, so I am forced to sneak away on the balcony and smoke Marlboros to curb my hunger when I am not having steak with members of Congress.)

"We do not refer to those who differ with us and want to blow up innocent Americans as terrorists, at least not initially or until pressed.

These folks are merely enemy combatants unless my Attorney General does not want to call them that in the case of the recent unfortunate 'incidents' in Boston.

"Again, welcome to America. Don't worry about getting a government-issued I.D.—I took care of that nonsense, too. Hope you are well. In November 2014, I hope you appreciate what your new President has done for you. Vote the Chicago Way (nod, nod, wink, wink)."

The "Stand Up" Administration: May 14, 2013

President Obama performed, by all accounts, a hilarious stand-up comedy routine at the recent White House Correspondents' Dinner. The problem is: he and some of his team now think the world's a comedy stage.

On May 13th, Mr. Obama, feigning anger, tore up the house with this knee-slapper about the Benghazi cover-up allegations: "It defies all logic." Yes, Mr. President, blaming the attack on a video when it was clear from the get-go it was an orchestrated terrorist attack does, as you say, "defy all logic." So, why in the world did you, Susan Rice, and Hillary Clinton do it countless times? Mr. Obama's next side-splitter was blaming Republicans for making the ever-changing Benghazi talking points a "political issue" and a "side show." Irony is often a comedian's most wicked tool, for it was Team Obama that immediately "politicized" the tragedy in Benghazi, trying to disguise the attack so that he could continue his campaign narrative of having al Qaeda "on the run."

Alas, despite all of Mr. Obama's rich laugh lines, he is not, however, the Last Comic Standing. That honor goes to the soon-to-be-fired IRS employee who oversees tax-exempt groups, Lois Lerner. Lerner brought down the house when she said that the targeting of the Tea Party and other right-wing groups was not motivated by a "political bias." (I laughed so hard at this gag that my Dr. Pepper came out my nose.) Stop it, Lois, stop it: you're killin' me!

I am certain Lerner's gem will make it on the "Best Laugh Lines in D.C. History" CD, along with Hillary's "vast right wing conspiracy," Bubba's "that depends what the definition of the word 'is' is," and Tricky Dick's "I'm not a crook."

As Eric Stratton said in *Animal House*: "What a lively sense of humor."

Administration Scandals et al.: "I Love to Count!" May 18, 2013

Okay, kiddies, it's Sesame Street, Washington-style. And today's letter is the letter "I." "I" as in those wacky non-partisan folks at the "IRS" charged with snatching as much money as they can from your wallet, by hook or by crook—literally. While Republicans in Congress foam at the mouth with this pre-2014 election gift and Democrats feign outrage while blaming an over-worked and under-staffed IRS, the real issue of this sordid affair is getting somewhat lost.

Most of last Friday's Congressional hearing focused on who knew what and when conservative groups were being harassed by the IRS (possibly at the urging of Michigan's Carl Levin and his Democratic colleagues), while their non-profit applications gathered dust in Cincinnati. Ousted IRS Chief Steve Miller proved to be a disaster of a witness, invoking the "I" word throughout his testimony as in "I don't believe so." A lawyer himself, Miller knows that phrase is merely a parlor trick in the legal profession: if later proven wrong, you can beg ignorance, confusion, or a faulty memory to cover up what you actually did. Lie.

Hysterically, one Congressman asked Miller what the IRS would do if one of its auditors, grilling an individual American taxpayer, received an "I don't know" as an answer to a question. "We would work with them," said Miller to more than a few chuckles. The IRS's idea of "work with you" is to pummel you with phony requests and financial intimidation. I know. I have had three inquiries from the IRS over the past six years. No, I am not bitter—and thus this column—as I prevailed each time and my accountant charged me nothing to fight back. But I wonder how others in my situation at the time would have reacted out of fear. The IRS claimed I overdid my charitable giving deduction. Yes, it was a large number in that particular year, but not grossly more than past giving. 501(c)(3)s Forgotten Harvest, Judson Center, Habitat for Humanity, and my church were thrilled, but the IRS was not happy.

We gathered all the receipts and fully explained the math in a letter to the geniuses in Cincinnati. I guess the IRS official who lifted the lid on the current scandal and infamously said, "I'm not good at math" may have been talking about the whole agency. Three weeks after our submission, I received four, yes four copies of the same, exact letter from the IRS informing me that I was wrong and owed $22,000. My accountant got on the phone to the IRS. After providing all the details, the agent replied: "I don't know why you got that letter. We haven't even processed your information yet. Just ignore that letter." Ahem, all four of them.

The question is how many people get such treatment from the IRS and buckle, immediately writing an unnecessary check to the government for fear of penalties or time in the hoosegow?

Back to the current scandal, or better said, the rash of scandals infecting the "most transparent administration of all time," and the letter "I." Miller pleaded that the IRS's transgressions were only "inappropriate," not "illegal." When this is all over, targeting of conservative groups most likely will not be deemed illegal, but merely "idiotic" and "immoral" and "ill-advised," as in who advised them to do it. And, the Administration will find itself "in" court losing suit after suit as a result of their behavior.

Finally, to the real issue: if it proves true that this same IRS or those connected with it (Treasury and/or The White House) gave the confidential applications of nine conservative groups to a "progressive" investigative journalists group, people are going to lose their jobs and some will go to jail, i.e. "incarceration." The group, George Soros-funded

ProPublica, has admitted that it received the applications from the IRS. Starting to smell, isn't it?

Oh, it gets fishier. The National Organization for Marriage, a group that defends the traditional family, says the IRS leaked information to *The Huffington Post* and the Human Rights Campaign (HRC) regarding a Mitt Romney donation to their group. Both used the illegally-leaked information to portray Romney as the "marriage equality denier" he is. The President of HRC, at the time, was also the co-chairman of President Obama's re-election campaign. Even a second-grader with bad vision could connect these dots.

As noted in *The Washington Times* last week: "Michael Dukakis, the Democratic presidential nominee, said it well in 1988, commenting on a scandal in a Republican administration – 'There's an old Greek saying. The fish rots from the head first. It starts at the top.'"

Even Obama's PR Machine Is Blowing It: June 1, 2013

You know the Obama Administration is on its heels when its finely-tuned PR machine throws a rod. That machine, aided by a compliant media, guided Obama first into office in the 2008 election and then ruthlessly destroyed a tone-deaf-but-correct-on-every-issue (like Benghazi) Romney in 2012, again aided fully by the MSM.

But now most—sadly not all—of the liberal media has somewhat turned on Team Obama. Check that. They have turned on his Attorney General, Eric "the lie of the be" Holder; the chief law enforcement official in our country. The Justice Department's admission regarding spying on fellow journalists was just too much for the press to take. Finally, the MSM had found their nads (oops, that was sexist) and, um, er, their ovaries. The Washington press corps is officially outraged, yet one has to wonder if that outrage would exist if FOX's James Rosen was the only one targeted and not the Associated Press as well.

Holder, supposedly "careening towards regret" for his violations of the First Amendment, decided to pivot from his usual demeanor of petulance and try his hand at damage control. He'd sit down with reporters and tell them the rationale for spying on the media (presumably, national security). There was a catch, though; it would be off-the-record.

You are accused of spying on the media, you lie about it in front a Congress, and then you want to make good by talking to reporters off-the-record? The media, for the most part, said no thank you. I don't blame Holder for this silly offer. He's got nothing to lose; he's toast as Attorney General. Even if he were to face charges (perjury and obstruction to start), Obama would pardon him in a nanosecond. No, I blame the Obama PR machine. Wasn't there at least one of the machine's minions who had the brains or guts to stand up and say an off-the-record fix was a bad idea and more?

The good news for Mr. Obama is that Americans could care less about the media spying scandal. Journalists are pretty much at an all-time low in terms of approval ratings, slightly above Congress. Most people have no sympathy for reporters—the people who stick a mike in the face of a grieving parent and ask them how they feel. The bad news for Mr. Obama is that Americans (at least half of them) do care about the IRS targeting of conservative and religious groups for harassment. The Justice Department scandal has toes while the IRS scandal has legs that are growing longer by the day. With more hearings this week on this bigger scandal, sooner or later someone is going to crack and the extent of how high in the Administration this puppy goes will be exposed.

Practice your lines, Mr. President: "I'm not a crook. I'm not a crook."

Back "to" the USSR: June 16, 2013

As part of the caboose of the Baby Boom, born in 1960, I lived more than half of my life during the Cold War, ever fearful of a nuclear showdown with the communist Soviet Union. We came kind of close a couple of times, but rational thinking took over and the only nukes we witnessed were launched in Hollywood studios, political campaign ads or underground test facilities. Thanks to Ronald Reagan's unrelenting push for the demise of the USSR and the Russians disastrous ten-year, budget-busting war in Afghanistan, the Soviet Union crumbled soon after the fall of the Berlin Wall.

Everything was peachy. America was without an enemy of equal stature in the world. Hollywood sure saw it. Well, at least Disney did. In the first installment of the movie, *The Mighty Ducks*, Emilio Estevez's team of misfit hockey kids beat the evil Russian team in the upset of all time. But by the time Disney had produced the second sequel, the big, bad team was none other than those evil-doers from, ahem, Iceland. The Icelanders wore black and, hilariously, spoke with a Russian accent. It was so sad that we didn't have a real enemy anymore.

9/11. Okay, game on again. But where's the playing field? Arab Spring. Okay, what and where. But whom? Back to the USSR.

A few years ago, automotive journalist John McElroy and I started doing a parody news show to open the SAE's annual Global Leadership Conference at the Greenbrier in West Virginia. One year, the butt of most of our jokes was GM's then-chief of global purchasing, Bo Andersson. Bo was not the most popular auto exec among the supply base. Check that: he was pretty much despised for being a hard ass. John and I "reported" that parts supplier association honcho, Neal DeKoker, had been murdered in his room at the Greenbrier; bite marks found on the neck of his lifeless body, and police in pursuit of his murderer—the evil, blood-sucking vampire, Bo Andersson. The crowd of auto execs went nuts with laughter. The folks sharing a table with Andersson at the event told me they almost peed themselves.

The prickly Andersson then did something no one ever imagined. The next night at the black tie gala, he showed up dressed in full vampire attire, including white pancake make-up and "blood" running out the sides of his mouth. Andersson decided to run with the joke and his image changed overnight. And we became friends.

Two years ago, back at the Greenbrier, Bo invited my wife and me to an after-hours party in his suite. No longer at GM, Andersson was now the head of GAZ, the Russian automotive behemoth, and somewhat chummy with Vladimir Putin. Nonchalantly, I said to him that it looks like Putin is trying to put the Soviet Union back together again. Bo didn't hesitate: "Of course, he is. And he will probably succeed."

This is why memories of the Cold War are back in my mind. As we enter the mess that is Syria—and much of the Middle East—we once again find ourselves on the "wrong side" according to the communist Russians. Russia, along with those fine folks in Iran, have been arming Syrian leader Assad to carry out the slaughter of his own people. President Obama, famously, does not want any run-ins with Putin. After all, his administration had earlier declared a "reset" in our relations and whispered for "flexibility" with Putin so that he could get re-elected and then forge a bond with the Russian who closer resembles Khrushchev with each liberty he takes away from the people of his empire and his support of human rights violators.

Up to now, whether it's Iran's pursuit of nukes or Assad's slaughter of his people, President Obama has resembled Neville Chamberlain, one of history's most notorious wusses. He said Assad's use of chemical weapons would be a "game-changer" and "cross a red line." When the French and British confirmed chemical weapons had been used, Obama initially waffled, praying the evidence was sketchy and asked the UN to check it out, hoping the UN would follow its usual pattern of ineptness. When the use of chemical weapons became an undeniable fact, Obama was begrudgingly forced to act.

But, it might be too late. Obama has promised small weapons to the rebel fighters in Syria. Bet there is nothing "small" coming from the Soviet Union, er, Putin and the Russkies.

Secretary Kerry: Welcome to Liar's Gulch: July 9, 2013

The U.S. State Department is located in the area of Washington, D.C., known as Foggy Bottom. However, considering the problems its spin doctors have with the truth, it might be best to rename the area Liar's Gulch.

By now, everybody should be aware of the mind-boggling number of half-truths and outright lies regarding the Benghazi cover up – which began at State and made their slippery way to the White House, twisting up spokesperson Jay Carney like a pretzel. State's lack of honesty eventually caused then-Secretary of State Hillary Clinton to melt down and utter that infamous phrase that will undoubtedly give her heartburn when she runs for President in 2016: "What difference, at this point, does it make?"

Fast forward to the current crisis in Egypt, where Egyptians took to the streets to depose President Morsi. The White House, as it likes to do, issued photos of President "Lead from Behind" Obama with his top national security advisors discussing options. But someone was missing: Secretary of State John Heinz Kerry. Was he in Egypt or in the air there to make sure the dismissal of the Muslim Brotherhood went through as hoped? Nope. A CBS producer vacationing in Nantucket, Massachusetts, snapped a photo of Kerry on his $7 million yacht and tweeted it.

The lying jets scrambled at State: an absolute, unqualified denial that Kerry was on his yacht. "Any report or tweet that he was on a boat is completely inaccurate," Kerry's spokesperson cried. Problem was: it was yet another lie out of Liar's Gulch. State would soon admit that Kerry was on his boat "only briefly."

Any wonder we are losing faith in our government by the minute?

Pressure Cooker Bombs from Our President: July 19, 2013

Boom!

Sadly, Boston is not the only city to see the existence of pressure cooker bombs. Tomorrow, 100 cities across the country will have them thanks to President Obama's race-baiting and rambling press conference today.

In a stunning display of hypocrisy, our President called for "calm" while stoking the fire of black-versus-white. "We're not going to stand for any violence," he said. Then he described the litany of how racist America remains. His comment that every black man has gone on an elevator with a white woman, only to have her "clutch her purse and hold her breath until she got out," was blatantly careless.

White America is racist. Black America has and continues to be victimized. That is the gospel from our Commander-in-Chief. I guess God should damn America, but I realize I just plagiarized Mr. Obama's former spiritual mentor.

George Zimmerman, the world's first "white Hispanic," should head for the border as he is now, thanks to the President, not safe in our country.

It's shameful on so many levels that I want to puke.

At one point, I thought Mr. Obama was going to be intellectually honest when he started to acknowledge that most African-American murder victims are killed by African-Americans. Nope. He said most black murder victims were killed "by their peers." He couldn't bring himself to be straightforward and decided to Clintonize his words.

Then, he did what so many on the Left have done since the Zimmerman verdict: he made up stuff. He talked about getting rid of laws like Florida's version of Stand Your Ground, despite the fact that Stand Your Ground was not used in the defense of George Zimmerman.

Had the victim in the Trayvon Martin killing been white, the outcome would have been different, said THE PRESIDENT OF THE UNITED STATES.

Good luck with calm tomorrow among the 100 planned protests. If there is just one death (Joe Biden's measure for doing something), then the blood is on the hands of the man on Pennsylvania Avenue.

President Obama: The World's Rodeo Clown: August 18, 2013

Nero fiddled while Rome burned; as the Middle East implodes, Obama putts. Ironically, the vacationing President Obama played his final round of golf in Martha's Vineyard with *Curb Your Enthusiasm* creator, Larry David. It appears that leaders and their minions the world over have lost their "enthusiasm" for Mr. Obama, his policies or lack thereof, and sadly, America as a force for good.

The Administration, according to their leaks, supposedly had a deal with the Egyptian military leaders to stop the violence against the Muslim Brotherhood that claimed 800-some dead the past week alone. Last Thursday, Mr. Obama took a break at the turn for the back nine to hold a news conference in which he pouted about the fact that America was getting the blame from both sides in the Egyptian crisis.

With growing calls for elimination of U.S. aid to the Egyptian military government—since under U.S. law, aid must be stopped in the event of a military coup—Mr. Obama decided to do what he is prolific in doing: ignoring U.S. law. To jog your memory, think Fast and Furious, the new Black Panther Party voter intimidation, NLRB appointments, ignoring provisions of Obamacare, "phony" scandals in Benghazi/IRS/ media snooping, and the NSA debacle.

The Administration's failure to acknowledge the military coup is nothing more than an admission that this gang is clueless. Mr. Obama's long-ago "Apology Tour" to the Muslim world has melted away in a mass slaughter of the Muslims in Egypt and Syria. Team Obama says the

97

Egyptian aid, including military, needs to continue so that we can "exercise our influence." Thanks to their waffling and their "lead from behind strategy," our influence exercise regime looks more like a fat kid on a couch playing Super Mario while eating a box of Twinkies and a big bag of Doritos, with a Big Gulp to wash it down.

No one is enjoying our lack of influence more than Russia's Vladimir Putin. First, he began arming Syria and continued to help Iran develop its nuke program. He then offered fugitive NSA leaker Edward Snowden asylum…and a freaking job, after no doubt extracting 100 percent of Snowden's brain contents, his computer files, and possibly his manhood. Team Obama reacted with what amounted to a hissy fit, accusing Putin of acting like we were back in the Cold War when he was "grilled" in the inquisition also known as The Tonight Show with Jay Leno. I think the Administration had harsher words for the rodeo clown who wore the Obama mask with a broom handle checking his temperature.

A return to the Cold War? But wasn't it candidate Obama who literally mocked Mitt Romney for channeling the 1980s when the Republican, in a debate, declared that Russia was our number one geopolitical foe?

Putin is getting absolutely giddy in his toying with Mr. Obama. Case in point: I really don't think Putin gives a darn about homosexuals in his homeland. Gays are inconsequential in his effort to reformulate the old Soviet Union. However, because Mr. Obama famously "evolved" on the issue of gay marriage and then personally called mediocre NBA journeyman Jason Collins a "hero" when he "came out," it was a chance to stick it in Obama's eye, knowing the President couldn't do anything more than stomp his feet and come up with the lame throwaway line that our Olympic team was stronger because of our gay athletes (with absolutely no way to prove it one way or another.) Does being gay make you a better or worse athlete? Who the hell knows that?

Perhaps that rodeo clown had it wrong, after all. It's not a broomstick stuck up the "President's" tush.

Obama: Inflictor-in-Chief: October 5, 2013

As we enter Day Eight of the Federal Government shutdown, the debate rages as to whom is to blame for this debacle. Democrats blame John Boehner, Ted Cruz, and the "loons" in the Tea Party. Republicans, me included, blame President Obama via Harry Reid. For Obama/Reid, this is all about the 2014 mid-term elections. As usual, my detractors will call me a sycophant for doing so and slam Republicans in Congress leading the charge with a variety of "civil" names – anarchists, terrorists, etc.

Okay, I give. Let's all agree the shutdown is the Republicans' fault. Oh, what an epiphany! But one thing is undeniable and undebatable: responsibility for how the shutdown is carried out falls squarely in the lap of the President and his minions. And considering how he—Barack Obama—has handled it thus far has earned him a new designation. Not merely content with being alternatingly Commander-in-Chief, Campaigner-in-Chief, and Divider-in-Chief, President Obama can now add Inflictor-in-Chief to his legacy.

The totally unnecessary pain Obama is inflicting in the name of the shutdown can be described no other way: purely vindictive. The closing of the memorials on the National Mall, including the World War II Memorial, shows the mean-spiritedness of our President. These are open-air memorials that typically have few guards policing them when they are open. Now that they are closed (barricaded and wired shut), the number of Park Police guarding them has grown exponentially.

The closing of the World War II Memorial is sick (and backfired on Mr. Obama big time), but the closing of the U.S. Cemetery at Normandy is heartless, considering pilgrimages to that hallowed site in France are planned months in advance for our aging veterans and their families. (The image of the tears generated by the movie, *Saving Private Ryan*, instantly come to mind and sum up how truly pathetic this sick and twisted decision really is.)

Oh, it gets even sillier, and meaner. The water faucets on the Mall have had their handles removed, rendering the faucets useless. The parking lot at Mount Vernon has been closed, despite the fact that the Federal Government doesn't own George Washington's home any longer and only jointly owns the parking lot with the new owner, the Mount Vernon Ladies Association.

A Park Service Ranger tasked with making sure Mount Vernon parking was on lockdown told *The Washington Times*: "It's a cheap way to deal with the situation. We've been told to make life as difficult for people as we can. It's disgusting."

On the orders of the President of the United States, our government is making life "as difficult for people as we can." That is depressing and indefensible. President Obama is treating Vladimir Putin and the new Iranian President with more respect than the citizens who elected him to a second term.

Many of my neighbors here in Alexandria, Virginia—a stone's throw from D.C.—have been furloughed since the shutdown began. All are treating it for what it is—a few more days or weeks of bonus vacation. They know once back to work they will be paid for the time off.

But not everyone impacted by the shutdown will be made whole retroactively. Saturday morning, while taking my dog Sam for his morning constitutional, I passed by the nearby school yard to find a young father and his two sons playing on the merry-go-round. It seemed odd as it was 7:30 in the morning. "Boy, those little tigers are at it early this morning," I said to the dad.

"Well, we were supposed to be fishing, but we got turned away by the Park Police," he said.

"What? The Federal Government owns the Potomac? How did they do that," I asked.

"The Government owns the land where the Belle Haven Marina and Park are located. We go there every Saturday until it gets cold."

I asked him if he ever saw Park Police in any of his previous Saturday morning fishing expeditions with his three and six-year-old sons. "Never," he laughed.

What became clear in my mind was that President Obama was using aging and—sadly—dead veterans, the women entrusted with George Washington's estate, and little kids who just want to catch fish with their dad, as human shields in his political quest while claiming the Republicans have "a gun to the heads of Americans."

So, the Inflictor-in-Chief continues his Reign of Pain as he prepares for the next major battle with those "anarchists and terrorists" in the Republican House: the debt ceiling debate. But before we start assessing blame in advance of that showdown, heed this infamous March 16, 2006 quote from then-Senator Barack Obama: "Increasing America's debt weakens us domestically and internationally. Leadership means that 'the buck stops here.' Instead, Washington is shifting the burden of bad choices today onto the backs of our children and grandchildren. America has a debt problem and a failure of leadership. Americans deserve better. I, therefore, intend to oppose the effort to increase America's debt limit."

And, no, Mr. and Mrs. Defend-Obama-Despite-the-Facts, the quote is not taken out of context; it is merely a snippet of Senator Obama's floor speech slapping around President Bush before he joined his Democratic colleagues and voted "no" on raising the debt limit. So, in a bonus for Mr. Obama, in addition to Inflictor-in-Chief, he gets to add the "honor" of Hypocrite-in-Chief to his legacy.

What a month!

Uncle Joe and #FreeCommunityCollege: Stupid Is as Stupid Does: January 28, 2015

Saw a tweet from my Uncle Joe today. My uncle is your uncle: Uncle Joe Biden, Vice President of the United States. Our, and yes, my Vice President, tweeted to showcase three mega-millionaires that were alumni of community colleges. The Axis-of-Success are stellar: Tom "Forrest, Forrest Gump" Hanks, George "Star Wars" Lucas, and Steve Wozniak, co-founder of Apple. Good message; no complaints.

Uncle Joe was tweeting with the tagline #FreeCommunityCollege, an initiative launched at his boss's State of the Union speech earlier this month. It was a hollow pitch by President Obama, knowing Republicans would, rightfully, trash it. After all, students of poor families, through the 50-year-old Pell Grant program, generally get community college free, anyway. It's been a good thing for some time. President Obama's "new idea" means that students that can afford community college, mostly from middle-class families, can get two years of "free" community college, as well.

Well, we all know that nothing in life is truly "free"; somebody has to pay for it. And, of course, at its foundation, it is a continuing theme of this Administration: redistribution of wealth. Sadly, this time, the "redistribution" TO the middle class is FROM the same middle class. The Obama Administration threw up a trial balloon filled with what I am certain was methane gas: they would tax the I.R.S. 529 Accounts in which families set aside money—pre-tax—for their kids to go to college. It has been and is a wondrous program for families—especially middle class families—to give their kids a leg up and avoid the iceberg of student loan hell this Administration has designated as a "problem." So, how did the Obama Administration propose to "fix" this fantastic "529 problem-avoidance"? Tax it. Duh.

Thankfully, the Administration quickly flushed this turd of an idea.

Uncle Joe? Mr. Vice President, who's counseling your people? It appears the left hand on Pennsylvania Avenue in Washington, D.C., doesn't know what the right hand is doing. Or, perhaps, the Left Hand doesn't know what the Left Hand is doing.

Uncle Joe, one of the community college grads you are spotlighting, Tom Hanks, said it best: "Stupid is as stupid does."

White House Should Hire Baghdad Bob; at Least He Was Entertaining: January 29, 2015

I believe in the craft of Public Relations when it is done right, which starts with telling the truth. As I wrote in chapter one of my first book, "Tell it like it is, clearly and succinctly. Natalie Wood did not die from 'excessive hydration.' She drowned. And Tupac Shakur didn't die from 'lead poisoning.' He was shot. The art of being clever or linguistically illusive will compromise the integrity of your organization."

The Obama Administration has a master's degree in linguistic illusiveness, from Benghazi to the IRS to Obamacare. But yesterday's example took the cake, at least for now. Described as a "rookie" White House spokesman, Eric Schultz embarrassed himself and, unfortunately, the craft of Public Relations. Supposedly, this White House adheres to a decades-old U.S. policy of negotiating with terrorists: we don't. At least not publicly. When asked how exchanging five Taliban operatives from Gitmo for soldier and alleged deserter, Sgt. Bowe Bergdahl, did not violate that policy, Schultz twisted like a Rold Gold pretzel in one of the most painful press conferences I have ever witnessed. It was part Anthony "Show me your" Weiner, part Baghdad Bob.

Rookie Schultz called the Taliban an "armed insurgency" as opposed to ISIS, which he said was "a terrorist group." When a befuddled ABC News reporter followed up that pathetic answer by asking Schultz why he didn't think the Taliban was a terrorist group, the young White House PR guy's head almost exploded until he attempted an answer: "I don't think that the Taliban (painfully long pause)…the Taliban is an armed insurgency." And then, when finished, I think Schultz experienced one of those annoying vomit burps.

Schultz had another painful gem while making a fool of himself. He said the prisoner swap was a "traditional end-of-conflict interaction." Think of the Japanese and Germans at the end of WWII. But obviously, Schultz had been paying more attention to ProActive zit cream ads than actually reading the news. The "conflict" with the Taliban is far from over. Just last month, the Taliban went into the Army Public School and Degree College in Peshawar, Pakistan, and slaughtered 154 people, more than 100 of which were children. Don't know about you, but that sounds a whole lot like garden variety terrorism to me.

Perhaps as a PR practitioner I should cut Schultz some slack. Hell, maybe this White House has put miniature cattle prods in the ears of its spokespeople and those talking similarly at the State Department. Say the words "terrorist" or "Radical Islam" and you get a massive jolt.

But I am not cutting any slack for Schultz or chief spokesman Josh Earnest or the spokeswomen at the State Department. They all have been a disgrace to my profession and, more importantly, the United States of America. Look for Saturday Night Live to open up their next show mocking this national embarrassment.

Queen Elizabeth: Obama Advisor: February 1, 2015

(Note: This just "might" be true. A friend of mine sent it to me this afternoon.)

A conversation between President Obama and Queen Elizabeth:

"Your Majesty, how do you run such an efficient government? Are there any tips you can give me?"

"Well," said the Queen, "the most important thing is to surround yourself with intelligent people."

Obama frowned, and then asked, "But how do I know if the people around me are really intelligent?" The Queen took a sip of champagne.

"Oh, that's easy; you just ask them to answer an intelligent riddle, watch." The Queen pushed a button on her intercom. "Please send Tony Blair in here, would you?" Tony Blair walked into the room and said, "Yes, Your Majesty?"

The Queen smiled and said, "Answer me this please, Tony. Your mother and father have a child. It is not your brother and it is not your sister. Who is it?"

Without pausing for a moment, Tony Blair answered… "That would be me."

"Yes! Very good," said the Queen.

Obama went back home to ask Joe Biden the same question. "Joe, answer this for me. "Your mother and your father have a child. It's not your brother and it's not your sister. Who is it?"

"I'm not sure," said Biden. "Let me get back to you on that one." He went to his advisors and asked everyone, but none could give him an answer. Frustrated, Biden went to work out in the congressional gym and saw Paul Ryan there. Biden went up to him and asked, "Hey Paul, see if you can answer this question. Your mother and father have a child and it's not your brother or your sister. Who is it?"

Paul Ryan answered, "That's easy, it's me!"

Biden smiled and said, "Good answer, Paul!" Biden then went back to speak with President Obama. "Say, I did some research and I have the answer to that riddle. It's Paul Ryan!"

Obama got up, stomped over to Biden, and angrily yelled into his face.

"NO, you idiot! It's Tony Blair!"

AND THAT, MY FRIENDS, IS PRECISELY WHAT'S GOING ON AT THE WHITE HOUSE.

A Look Back at the Most Lawless Week of the
Obama Administration: March 2, 2015

I wanted to reflect over the weekend before I commented on the shear lawlessness that took place in our country last week, courtesy of the Obama Administration. As they say, let's go to the video tape.

Because this Administration knows it cannot completely wipe out the Second Amendment and take all guns out of the hands of law-abiding citizens, it decided to do an end-run and unilaterally ban the sale of one of the most popular bullets used by hunters. This immediately led to a "run" on the bank of this ammo and will necessarily result in a flourishing black market for the bullets, which, by definition, is a criminal enterprise. Most likely, criminals will not be fearful of buying on the black market, while law-abiding citizens will have second thoughts. Good job, Mr. President.

Next up in our lowlight reel is the FCC, unlawfully high-jacking the Internet in a scheme called "Net Neutrality." These are the same clowns that previously thought about putting "monitors" in news stations to make sure they were being "fair and balanced." It was a blatant attempt to bottle neck and perhaps shut down FOX News and conservative talk radio. The Net Neutrality regulations were written in the dark of the night with no sharing with Congress. Obama's FCC merely said 'trust us.' Previous supporters (the big broadband providers) are now crying foul and are threatening lawsuits. Good luck with that, suckers. Already, the FCC's still-undisclosed kidnapping of the Internet has been deemed ObamaNet. Good grief. Lie to us once; shame on you. Lie to us all the time; shame on all the people that gave this President a second term. I will say, you were promised "change."

Rounding out the lowlights was an Obama town hall, sponsored by MSNBC and Telemundo, attended by a host of illegal aliens. Oh, my bad, er, illegal immigrants. Snap, I meant undocumented workers. What's that you say? We don't call them that anymore either? Oh, that's right, the

President is now referring to people who illegally gained entrance to this country and its services as "future Americans."

Whatever you call them, I remember the good ol' days when law enforcement carried out very clever sting operations to catch dead-beat dads and other law breakers by arranging a bogus job fair or some other made-up event in which the participants would get something for free, only to find that they were being busted. Never been to one of these, but it's got to be a hoot. Smile criminal, you're on Candid Camera.

For a moment I thought what an opportunity this Obama town hall would be: we could suck in all these "future Americans" and bust them for violating the laws of our land. Better yet, we'd have the evidence on tape as the two TV networks were there to record it. But NOOOOOOOOO! They were there to hear what the President of the United States, by his lonesome, was going to GIVE to them – if not now, very soon. And he made sure he let the illegal aliens (there, I said it) know that if Congress tried to make him enforce our laws, he just wasn't going to do it. That wasn't his job, dammit!

Obama and his team topped off the week by awkwardly trying to bitch-slap the prime minister of Israel, our closest ally in the Middle East, by sending out his pathetic attack dogs, the serial-lying Susan Rice and his incoherent Secretary of State John Kerry.

It was a week to behold. Actually, cry.

Hillary Clinton: Liar, Liar, Pantsuit on Fire: March 9, 2015

Back in 1978 and 1979 when America was crumbling under a massive recession, First Lady of Arkansas, Hillary Rodham Clinton, raided the cookie jar and dabbled in a series of trades considering cattle futures. Magically, her $1,000 investment soared to almost $100,000 when she stopped trading 10 months later. Then in 1994, as Hillary was planted in the White House as First Lady of the United States, her Wall Street prowess gained much notoriety although there was never an official investigation or any charges.

The rest is well, history. The White Water real estate scandal in Arkansas served as a mere speed bump for Bubba Clinton and Hillary. Hillary couldn't find key documents in that scandal, until they magically appeared too late in the White House. Or, was that the scandal surrounding the scandal of Clinton confidante and "suicide" victim, Vince Foster? Hard to keep the scandals straight.

Of course, the Whitewater scandal led to an investigation of Bubba's personal life, including multiple affairs, in which Bill and Hill tried to personally destroy the lives of two women Bubba had come on to. And of course, the world learned about Monica Lewinsky. Lewinsky was in the process of having her young, White House intern life destroyed at the hands of Hillary when there was the "little matter of a stained blue dress." Bubba was disgraced, impeached by the House of Representatives and saved by the U.S. Senate. Hillary's claim of a VAST "right-wing conspiracy" was eventually exposed as a classic Clinton ploy to harm those who were telling the truth and exposing the Clintons as habitual liars.

Americans forgave the Clintons for ONE reason—the economy was rocking and rolling. There was a chicken in every pot and 401K accounts were soaring. And, America was at relative peace with the world. Back then, Osama bin Laden was merely a pain in the ass. Bubba Clinton won re-election in a walk against too-moderate Bob Dole and the increasingly wacky Ross Perot, who stole tons of votes from Dole.

Hillary was now facing her destiny: the first female President of the U.S. She and Bubba overnight became New Yorkers—although they were "dead broke" and she walked into a Senate seat without breaking a sweat. "Presidency or bust" and 2007 provided her chance to announce a run that would, in effect, be a coronation. But along came a slick and smooth-talking community organizer from Chicago that no one knew anything

108

about and who refused to share basically anything about his life not in his autobiography. Hillary was robbed—robbed I say—of the 2008 Democratic nomination.

What to do? What to do? Become Secretary of State in the Obama Administration—a man she and Bubba loathed—in order to sit tight for 2012 or 2016. Surely Obama was ill-prepared to lead so that just maybe Hillary could ride in for the 2012 vote with a white hat and save the Democratic Party and the country. But no, Obama had too weak a candidate to face in Mitt Romney. He won re-election despite a pathetic first-term record.

And Hillary's record as head of the State Department? Admittedly, she flew a lot of miles on the public dole – ate, drank, and was mostly merry. Accomplishments leading the foreign policy of the most powerful nation on the planet? The Arab Spring which the Obama Administration and Hillary cheered on? Oh no. The Russian "Reset"? Doh! Libya "free at last" and the subsequent Benghazi murderous disaster? Wait, didn't they put someone in jail for that? Oh yeah, the filmmaker in California they blamed for the death of our Ambassador and three other brave servicemen. Iran seems to be under control, Syria is calmer than calm, and Yemen isn't being overrun by radical Islamists. Oh snap, I guess I got that wrong, too.

And now we have the email scandal in which our former Secretary of State refused to use protocol-insistent, security-proof government email and instead had her own home server for her most sensitive government emails. Wow. She now vows to turn over all her emails. Yeah, right. If you believe that, I have some river property in Arkansas I want to sell you. Care to buy some cattle futures? You can't lose. Trust Hillary: maybe, sadly, the next President of the United States.

Hillary is supposedly soon coming "clean" with an "innocent" explanation for Email-gate. Hope she doesn't wear a blue dress at the press conference. Too many bad memories.

But I guess, at this point, WHAT DIFFERENCE DOES IT MAKE!!!!!!!!!!!!!!

"Some Democrats" Slam @HillaryClinton in Sexist Rant in @nytimes: March 12, 2015

I am appalled. Appalled, I say! *The New York Times* is reporting today that "some Democrats" are saying that Hillary Clinton "is too big to fail." I find it disgusting that "some Democrats" would be commenting on Mrs. Clinton's weight or other physical state. After all, she is trying, thanks to a serious Yoga routine she recently wiped off her "convenient" private server at her home in New York.

I wonder what "some Democrats" will declare next after their sexist slap at Hillary: Bill Clinton is "too horny to fail," Al Franken is "too stupid to fail," The Reverend Al Sharpton is "too much a race hustler to fail," Harry Reid is "too clumsy to fail," Eric Holder is "too much a riot instigator to fail," and John Kerry "uses too much Botox and makeup to fail?"

Stay tuned, campers.

Chapter Five: Stupid Democrats

comics.com EMAIL: hpayne@detnews.com

Do as I Say, Not as I Do: June 15, 2010

Michigan Democratic gubernatorial candidate, Andy Dillon, is supposedly "fighting for a law to hire MICHIGAN workers first," and is telling voters just that in a new commercial produced by, ahem, an ILLINOIS-based firm.

The Chicago firm, AKPD, also has offices in New York and Washington, D.C., and was founded by David Axelrod, a senior political advisor to President Obama. When asked why the campaign didn't hire a Michigan firm—T.J. Bucholz, a spokesman for the Dillon campaign, told *The Detroit News*: "There are only a handful of companies that do this kind of work. I'm not aware of one in Michigan with that kind of caliber."

As a public service, the Wisecracker will translate Bucholz's remarks: "We want the Democratic Party Machine (i.e., Axelrod) to support us. You can count the number of firms we were told to use on your hand. Check that. You can count the number of firms we were told to use on one finger. I used the term 'caliber' because in reality we had a gun to our head. Besides, of the hundreds of ad firms in Michigan, they all suck."

Bucholz added that the Dillon campaign "is fortunate to have the unique expertise of AKPD. It's based in Chicago, which helps the (economy in) the Midwest." Wisecracker translation: "Everything is about Chicago. So please shut up, Michigan, and enjoy the dead Asian carp we just threw in your bed!"

Clinton is Back—Hide Your Daughters: October 25, 2010

Let's start this week's Wisecracker with a bit of trivia, shall we? On what network is CNN, the original cable news show, spending gobs of cash advertising its new talk show starring Kathleen Parker and Eliot "Client No. 9, No. 9, No. 9" Spitzer? If you guessed the evil empire of FOX News, you are a winner! Just drips with irony, doesn't it? On with the show.

Bubba Clinton was in Michigan this week to stump for Dems running for a variety of offices. Bubba's charm is as powerful today as it was while he was a two-term, impeachable President. However, it is not powerful enough to help "On the Virg of Defeat" (Democratic gubernatorial candidate Virg Bernero) survive a shellacking. And surely, long-term Congressman John Dingell doesn't need Bill to push him over the victory line. If John is really in that tight of a race, then the doom Democrats face November 2nd is apocalyptic.

No. The Cigar Aficionado is not here for ol' Virg or Big John. He is here for one thing: himself. Okay, he's here for himself and, what's her name? Oh yeah, Hillary. Secretary of State Hillary, to be specific. He has his eyes on the prize once again. The White House or Bust! (My bad—shouldn't put "White House" and the word "bust" in a sentence about Bubba.)

It's all part of a brilliantly planned scheme by Billy Boy, hatched once he saw President Obama's fortunes looking weaker by the minute. It started with the surgical slight of planning his daughter's wedding on a day President Obama could not attend. Incredibly unreliable sources to the Wisecracker claim that Michelle Obama was so angry at that non-invite that she went temporarily insane and downed a whole bag of Cheetos and a box of little chocolate donuts.

Step two in the Clintonian plot was to have Hillary "inadvertently" and "secretly" criticize Obama's economic performance as a "national security disaster." The "secret" part of the plan was, of course, a complete failure as Hillary criticized Obamanomics in front of roughly 743 news cameras from around the world.

And, now, finally, the grand finale: Bubba in the flesh. (Oops, not supposed to put those two words together, either.)

The Dems will lose so big, that even the Man from "Hope" can't help "Change" the results. (Lookie there: "hope" and "change" together in a sentence. What an innovator you are Wisecracker!)

But, Clinton—as he knows—will be given a bunch of "attabubbas" for at least trying. At the same time, he will remind his base just how lovable he truly is and just how well-off the country was when his finger was on the, um, er, PULSE of America.

Starting November 3, as the Dems attempt to pick up the pieces of their disaster, the calls will be swift and loud for a return to the good old days. It "only takes a village...run by the Clintons."

Democratic Cheeseheads Raise a Stink: February 17, 2011

This just in from AP: Police officers were dispatched Thursday to find Wisconsin state lawmakers who had apparently boycotted a vote on a sweeping bill that would strip most government workers of their collective bargaining rights. The lawmakers, all Democrats in the state Senate, did not show up when they were ordered to attend a midday vote on the legislation.

Wow, so much for civility. I mean, even Barack Obama had the audacity to show up for votes while a member of the Illinois State Senate. Sure, sure, he usually "punted" and voted "present," but he kind of showed up. But not the Democratic cheeseheads. They picked up their ball and bat and ran away from the playground.

What if the shoe was on the other foot in Wisconsin, and Democratic legislators were not in the minority (19 Republicans, 14 Dems) and say the Dems were pushing for a law that forces all public sector workers to join a union? What would the MSM say if the Republicans refused to attend a vote they were sure to lose? I gotta good guess: "Un-American Republican Legislators Refuse Their Sworn Duty as Democratic Majority Leader Calls for Sanctions."

But in reality, it's the Dems playing hooky, and not just the legislators. Forty percent of the teachers called in sick. What is it teachers always claim in a political battle? Oh yeah, "it's all about the kids!" Okay kiddies, next time your teacher schedules a test, stay home like the "grown-ups" in Wisconsin are doing.

Dems Need a Course in Dirty Tricks: April 18, 2011

Where's Donald Segretti when you need him? Segretti was in charge of dirty tricks for the Nixon Administration and he pulled some beauties, if you are into that sort of thing. Michigan Democrats could use him about now as their second attempted political dirty trick in the last year has blown up in their faces.

Remember, of course, last fall's debacle with high operatives in the Democratic Party "allegedly" forging signatures and committing other crimes for creating a fake tea party with "Dems in Republican clothing" as candidates. The clowns at the heart of that scandal immediately lost their jobs and now face prison terms if convicted.

Now we find the people who want to start a recall effort against Gov. Snyder, Michigan Citizens United, may be nothing more than an Astroturf front group for the Michigan Education Association teachers' union. Indeed, the necessary paperwork for Michigan Citizens United was filed March 23 by its treasurer, Gail Schmidt of Omer, Michigan. Schmidt works as a field assistant for the Michigan Education Association. When she filed, she listed the group's fax number as one that is eerily close to that of her MEA office. No, wait. It's not eerily close, it's the same number!

Enter Michigan Citizens United spokesman, Tim Kramer, with an astonishing grasp of the obvious, saying: "if Schmidt gave an MEA fax number to the state, she shouldn't have done so." Ya think, Einstein?

Kramer claimed that his group is not connected with the MEA. He also claimed that the snow falling in Michigan April 18 was proof of global warming, believes (former Detroit City Councilwoman) Monica Conyers should be released from prison, thinks Jennifer Granholm was

115

our best governor ever, and insists that Matt Millen be given a second chance with the Lions.

Kramer doesn't, however, believe Barry Bonds is innocent of juicing, so perhaps there is hope for him. Just not for his phony group.

Warren Mayor's Stunt is Getting Old: May 15, 2011

Just when you thought we had too many examples of government employees on the taxpayer dole believing they should be treated differently than their private sector counterparts, along comes that wacky Warren, Michigan, Democratic Mayor Jim Fouts refusing to share his age with the voters in his community.

As Mayor, Fouts is, in effect, the CEO of Warren, the third largest city in Michigan. Can you imagine a CEO of a business telling his or her Board of Directors to shove it when the age question is posed? Fouts claims it's nobody's business how old he is (seventy-something). And, he threw in a killer line: he doesn't want to expose his age because "he tends to date younger women."

I can just imagine Fouts arranging a date:

Woman: What movie are you taking me to tonight, Jimmy?

Fouts: The new Twilight picture.

Woman: Oh great, I just got done reading the book for English class.

Fouts: Swell, then I'll pick you up at 6:30. Same place? The Exxon station three blocks from your house?

Woman: Nah, my parents are up north so you can come right to our house and get me this time.

Fouts: Hot diggity dog!

Mayor Fouts, nobody cares if you are 60, 65 or 80 years young for crying out loud. But they may think you have a few screws loose for putting up such a fuss trying to cloak yourself in secrecy. Look at it this way, Jim: when President Obama was deep in the Trump-induced birth certificate controversy and he finally came clean with the long form, look what it did for him. The story soon went away, and surprise, surprise, he almost single-handily bagged Osama bin Laden. Just think what great things are ahead for you when you come clean, ya little whipper-snapper.

The Vagina Stupidity: June 17, 2012

I had a great Father's Day: My college kids all called me, and my wife took me out for a great dinner even though it wasn't Husband's Day. As I sat down to write my Monday Wisecracker column, I was ready to submit a "real humdinger" as they used to say in a time gone by. It was going to be a real hoot taking on the Michigan Democratic legislator who decided that her vagina was not only a talking point, but something to celebrate this week on the steps of the Capitol in Lansing.

Happily married to my wife Betsy for 26 years now, I am all-in on celebration of said, well, um, er, you know, but puhleaze. Anyway, as I sat down to write something hopefully funny and pithy, the worst thing happened: the movie, *Saving Private Ryan*, came on the screen.

I don't know about you, but I melt every time this movie is on. My uncle (of course, I never knew him) was killed by the Desert Fox in North Africa, and my dad picked up Marines coming off of Iwo Jima. A 17-year-old kid out of Arkansas, he lied and said he was 18 when he enlisted. Cripes, my generation used fake IDs to buy beer, not go to war to fight the Japanese and the Nazis and save the world.

It's Father's Day. My dad died in 2000, this month. He was truly a part of the greatest generation – as Tom Brokaw aptly named it. So was my father-in-law, a Korean War vet, who passed in 2009. These gentlemen let me know what it truly means to be a father, a dad.

No critique of the Vagina Monologues in Lansing today—just a salute to the men AND WOMEN who gave us the freedom to act so stupidly and so incredibly self-centered. To the legislator: I appreciate what is between your thighs, but I hope there is something more meaningful between your ears. Geez.

Long Johnson a Political Weiner: August 5, 2012

Everybody needs a Long Johnson. Ahem.

This is the story of political pranks that go right, and those that go wrong. Back in the days of civility, a political prank did one of two things: create an immediate guffaw or an "Is that true?" moment. Most past political pranks had some semblance of truth—sometimes just a thread, but none-the-less, there was something true in the pranksterism. Tell Senate Majority Leader Harry Reid this. (I will get to Sirhan SirHarry – the pathetic political assassin of the Left in a bit.)

Back to political pranks. I was driving through downtown Grayling, Michigan, and I saw a vandalized banner for "LONG Johnson" for Michigan State Representative. I laughed MAO. Three blocks later, I saw the real campaign signs for "LON Johnson." What a hoot. Come on, this was funny. That is a great political prank. Funny, and it does not hurt anyone. Actually, the one laughing the most is Mrs. Long Johnson, who knows the truth of the tale. Or, the tail. Ahem, again.

Enter Senator Harry Reid. He "claims" a "Bain person" told him that Mitt Romney paid no income taxes for ten years. Really? Did a "Bain" employee say: "Hey Mitt (boss), I will do your taxes." That would have to happen for anyone to "know" that Mitt paid no taxes. Didn't happen. Did Mitt brag about not paying taxes at any staff meetings? Duh. No.

So, Sirhan SirHarry's charge is bogus. And it is blowing up in his little, putrid face. It is nothing more than a cheap political prank that is neither funny nor a wow factor. It only proves that he is an amateur punk.

When we need a Long Johnson leading the U.S. Senate, we, unfortunately, have a limp dictator.

Eva Longoria and Me: August 27, 2012

Eva Longoria is speaking at the Democratic National Convention. Why? Simply put: Hot, Hispanic, and Hollywood liberal. Deep thinker?

Um, er, duh, no. Policy Wonk? No, she's tanned eye candy. This is the depth of Obama's team in North Carolina.

The Wisecracker had the honor of hiring and meeting Ms. Longoria. At Chrysler in 2005, our head of marketing cut a deal with filmmaker/producer Arnon Milchan—a former Israeli arms dealer (no die Scheiße)—to give us access to a bunch of celebs. We got Angie Harmon and her hubby—NY Giants' Jason Sehorn—to do the Detroit Auto Show, funnyman David Spade to do likewise, and Jennifer Love Handles to grace us at the LA Auto Show.

And then there was Eva. Oh, Eva. She had a small role in a press conference at the 2006 North American International Auto Show. She was flown in first class. I would have nothing less. She was given a private green room. Of course. I melted when I met her: adoring this tiny superstar sitting cross-legged on the floor eating her lunch. (My wife knows this and is okay with it—okay, BS, she hated me for two weeks but she loved the show on Wisteria Lane.)

Then, the debacle.

Eva. Ahem, Ms. Longoria had ONE LINE as she exited the Chrysler car unveiled on the stage. She couldn't deliver it and had to be prompted by then-Chrysler CEO Tom LaSorda. Total whiff.

Expect the same in North Carolina next week.

Dems Find Jesus: September 5, 2012

After initially whacking all references to God in their party platform, the Dems have found Jesus. Funny, I didn't know he was lost. In a weird twist, the move to now include God has been damned by the Reverend Jeremiah Wright.

The Dems also did an about-face in their platform, now proclaiming that Jerusalem is indeed the capital of Israel, kinda, sorta. Tomorrow, they are expected to announce that they acknowledge that Leningrad was changed back to St. Petersburg in 1991.

Tonight after her convention speech, entitled "My Vajayjay Deserves Statehood," Sandra Fluke is having celebratory, but none-the-less protected sex thanks to the un-godly expensive birth control pills that are pushing her closer to a financial cliff.

The Brothers Levin: Disgrace Under Fire: July 1, 2013
It's natural for brothers to fight, especially in their teen years, and then grow up and get past it. Apparently, the Levin brothers (U.S. Senator Carl and U.S. Congressman Sander) never got the memo. They are battling each other for, on a seemingly daily basis, the honor of being the Obama Administration's biggest lackey.

Carl set the ground for this epic battle when he constantly urged the IRS to harass conservative groups seeking non-profit tax exemption status. Yes, my friends, through the pen of Levin and several other Democrat Senators, the IRS was actually doing what they had been told by the world's "greatest deliberative body." Excuse me while I hurl.

Not to be outdone, brother Sander gabbed on the news that "progressive" groups had been targeted by the IRS and declared the IRS scandal DOA. Like his brother, Carl, Sander decided to send a letter requesting action. He wanted to know why Inspector General J. Russell George's initial report on the IRS targeting did not mention the fact that "progressive" groups were targeted as well.

Levin got his answer and he choked on it: 100 percent of conservative groups targeted (296 of them) were harassed, including illegal demands for information and other shameful antics by a "few" rogue employees in "Cincinnati." The number of "progressive" groups harassed? Six, maybe, out of a whopping 18 allegedly targeted.

And so the Brothers Levin, deep into their seventies, finally learned a valuable lesson: be careful what you ask for, you may just get it.

Chapter Six: Stupid Republicans

" GET ME A 32-OUNCE WHISKEY, BARTENDER!"

Romney Fumbles While Newt Scores "Double Dipping": January 23, 2011

Remember when Alexander Haig boldly proclaimed, "I'm in charge" following the attempted assassination of Ronald Reagan? Perhaps, President-wannabe Mitt Romney should channel the late Secretary of State. His excuses for having no control of his Super PAC ads and, more recently and more damning, his lame response to calls for release of his tax records, seem to make the case for him getting "in charge" before his candidacy goes from an inevitable nomination to a toss-up with Newt Gingrich.

It is mind-boggling that Romney is losing the recent PR battle to Gingrich. And he should blame no one other than himself. Romney is battling a "given," while Newt is deftly handling an "unforgiveable" and winning, as we see in South Carolina, thanks in part to his tremendous debate homeruns, and the evermore evident reality that Romney's base is as solid as a Yugo.

Romney's "given" is that he is rich. No, check that: filthy rich. Most of us conservatives actually find this to be a laudable attribute. Most Americans want a candidate that knows how to work an economy. Especially now. Romney's release of any and all personal financial information would only prove the obvious: rich, rich, rich—a classic "No S--- Sherlock." But Romney's fumbling on the transparency of his bounty not only makes you scratch your head, but also makes opponents wonder what "evil" is in the numbers. Romney, stumbling, and bumbling, finally told the media he would release the information and dutifully blamed his "organization" for the snafu. It's your money, Mitt; be "in charge."

Mitt's "1040gate" comes on the heels of his insincere explanation of why he could not stop his Super PAC from running the ugly ads against Gingrich in Iowa and New Hampshire. Romney claimed time and time again that if he were to contact the Super PAC and tell them what to do, he would be breaking the law. Once again, Romney claimed he is not "in

122

charge," although he could have legally come out publicly and said he was not in favor of the ads without "contacting" the Super PAC. His excuses were always followed with his signature forced chuckle, a manufactured laugh that is starting to wear thin, at least on me. You'll know what I mean the next time you see an interview in which he gets a tough question and he employs the phony guffaw.

Mitt: your PR snafus are no laughing matter and may send you to a second consecutive and final second-place finish.

Meanwhile, Gingrich survives an ugly-of-ugly "unforgivable": his second wife claiming Newt asked her to "share him" with his mistress. I don't know about you, but if I were to ask Mrs. Wisecracker to "share me" with another woman, well, let's just say there would be nothing to share. But Newt simply said he was a bad man, found Jesus (again, as I noted in previous columns, I didn't know he was lost) and is better for it. And the Evangelicals in South Carolina voted him in by "loving the sinner while hating the sin." Effectively, the Newtster said, "I'm in charge (with a little help from my friends)." And now, he's laughing all the way to the banks of Florida, site of the next debate.

Mitt-Stake...Pure and Simple: April 9, 2011

Arriving back in Detroit Tuesday, I cringed at the coverage: Mitt Romney said "I deserve a lot of the credit" for the auto industry's recovery. Yes, maybe you do if then-candidate Barack Obama read your column in *The New York Times* two months before the 2008 election. But using the "I" word is very un-presidential—just ask critics of the I-Man himself—President Obama.

I am sure that Team Romney had a plan and expected the supremely disciplined Mitt to stick with it and not go all-Biden on them. It was simple: factually point out the meat of Mitt's call for a managed bankruptcy for Chrysler and GM long before Obama actually did so, and then lay out, in their minds, how the Administration went wrong, throwing shareholders and bondholders to the wolves while giving a sweetheart deal to Obama's union base. Pretty simple, really. And while it would not be easily swallowed in Michigan and Ohio, outside the industry it was a good, conservative diet.

But then the interview.

"I deserve a lot of credit," said Mitt to a Cleveland media outlet and Team Obama pounced, calling it a "new low in dishonesty." Actually, I never knew there were levels of dishonesty. My completely unreliable sources say that Vice President Joe Biden called Romney's remarks, "a big f---ing deal of dishonesty."

Romney didn't attempt to put his sloppy quote into context in Lansing yesterday as critics, including former auto czar Steven Rattner and Team Obama blasted away; the damage was done. Outside of his speaking engagement at Lansing Community College, a group of UAW protesters was pounding the pavement. One carried a sign that included the headline of Romney's *New York Times'* piece: Romney—Let Detroit Go Bankrupt. A journalist friend of mine approached the protester and pointed out that, in fact, President Obama sent the automakers into bankruptcy. "No he didn't," he retorted, "he bailed them out." My friend argued for only a few more seconds until finally realizing one of the truths about life: never get into an argument with a clown because people watching won't be able to decide who is dumber.

Michael Bloomberg: Tone Deaf: May 3, 2011

Michael Bloomberg, you are a different kind of mayor. A day after we learned our bravest took out the terrorist scum who ordered the horror on your citizens—USA, USA, USA!—your team awards NYC's cab contract to a Japanese company. As they say, timing is everything.

Nothing against the winning firm, Nissan. I worked for them (so, I guess I am a hypocrite, but hear me out.)

124

New York, you must admit, is America's premier city—the gateway to America and first stop to the land of the free. But Japanese taxis? Really?

Wait a minute, Wisecracker, Nissan has plants in Tennessee that produce hundreds of thousands of vehicles and provide thousands of jobs. Good point, but the Nissan taxis headed for New York are coming from Mexico. So, take a dump on that point.

Nissan's profits, as with Toyota's profits from this country, go back to Japan. Nothing wrong with that, it is just factual. America's automakers' profits—two of the three we just spent taxpayer money to shore up—stay here and their reach into American communities dwarfs the Japanese, Koreans, and Germans.

Ford was in the bidding war for the NY taxi cab business. I seriously doubt they screwed the pooch on this one.

What if the mayor of Stuttgart approved a plan to make American cars the official taxi of his city? What if the mayor of Osaka made German cars the official taxi of his city? Both would be launched off the carrier ahead of bin Laden.

Support your country, Mayor Bloomberg. There are young men and women from Michigan and other U.S. states who are putting their lives on the line every day to do so. Geez, Louise.

The Donald: Firing on all Meats: May 15, 2011

"Meatloaf, you're fired." Never in the history of mankind had this phrase been uttered.

Yet there he was again, The Donald, making history. Weeks ago, he brought a sitting President to his knees demanding a copy of a long-form birth certificate unattainable for years since Hillary Clinton first broached the subject. And here he was again, giving the *Rocky Horror Picture* star and '70s music icon the heave-ho on *The Celebrity Apprentice*. Goodbye, Meatloaf, ain't no doubt about it.

Obama, so stung by his encounter with Donald Trump, got serious about fighting terrorism and had the Navy Seals keep an eye out for Osama bin Laden.

For Trump, it really is "Paradise by the Dashboard Light," as in the dashboard on his computer system monitoring his ability to get people to keep looking at him. A clown? Maybe. Been in bankruptcy more times than members of the Detroit City Council? Sure. But he is omnipresent. Bad hair? Yep, so bad that *Detroit Free Press* columnist Mitch Albom wrote a "fair" column a few weeks ago about his proposed run for President, attacking him solely on his looks.

The next few weeks should be incredibly interesting for the Republican Party as they sift through the field of possible candidates. Huckabee's not in due to a "heart problem." As he said, all the signs— support, name recognition, and money—were there, but not his heart. I think what he meant by his "heart" was knowing that the clemency award he gave to a brutal convict whilst Arkansas governor, only to have the thug go on a killing spree in the Seattle area, was going to be his Michael Dukakis/Willie Horton campaign crusher. Soft on crime is for the liberals, not a conservative.

Palin? No way. Why take the hit to family income. Bachmann? Saturday Night Live is already unfairly making her look stupid. Amazing how the liberal entertainment elite are bitch-slapping, um, er, women, and it's okay. Gingrich? The media that tried to give Bubba Clinton a pass will crucify Newt for his infidelity while his wife was ill no matter how smart this guy is. They will make his transgression so raw that John Edwards will eventually look like a choirboy in comparison. Pawlenty? He makes Ben Stein look exciting. Romney? Nice try saying Romneycare is not Obamacare. Even John Kerry sent Mitt a pair of flip-flops after that painful speech. He would have been better off to paraphrase John Belushi in *Animal House*—"You f-ed up, you trusted me."

The Donald will run. Maybe not too long. But long enough to make this the most talked about Republican primary in history and probably make Indiana's Mitch Daniels a stronger candidate in the end. A good thing.

"Meatloaf, you're fired." You're killing me.

The Great GOP Slugfest: August 7, 2011

Bottom Up: The GOP debate's Biggest Winners and Losers:

Michelle Bachmann: A total non-player spewing campaign lines that worked in Iowa but not on the national stage. Her line that "kids need jobs" was simply stupid. Adults need jobs to support their kids. Kids having jobs is a good thing to teach them the value of working—but in today's economy, kids' jobs have been taken by adults and senior adults.

Jon Huntsman: I thought Stuart Smalley died when Weird Al Franken got elected to the U.S. Senate. Blah, blah, blah. Would make Neville Chamberlain seem strong on foreign policy. Only in the race for a couple of weeks unless someone keeps bankrolling this sucker.

Rich Santorum: Tried too hard to inject his social issues platform. DOA. Out of money in a week.

Herbert Cain: Little time, but used it well. Except for the reference to the "Chilean model." What the hell was that? Funny, smart man. Secretary of Something. But please not pizza. Godfather's Pizza sucks.

Ron Paul: Earth to Ron. Earth to Ron. Smart guy who is totally bi-polar—genius to lunatic. Put him in charge of the Postal Service.

Newt Gingrich: Smartest guy in the room. Unfortunately, the most hated Republican of all time – by Republicans and Independents. Stay a consultant and get richer. And, stop calling me with recorded fundraising calls. Dammit. I want to take you SOBs out!

Mitt Romney: On the ropes. Came out swinging. Did really, really well. His line that we are acting like an "energy poor nation" was huge. He held his own. Still in it.

Rick Perry: Clear winner when he could have pooped in the bed. Huge win. His comment near the end on capital punishment was a walk-off home run. He will increase in polls by three points. Maybe more.

Bachmann and the other dwarves need to give it up, as well as Michigan's non-invited Thad McCotter. Focus on those that can beat Mr. Obama.

Ron Paul Channels Dukakis: October 2, 2011

Remember the death penalty question that neutered (or depending on your point of view, spayed) Michael Dukakis in the 1998 presidential debate with George H.W. Bush?

Moderator Bernard Shaw: Governor, if Kitty Dukakis [his wife] were raped and murdered, would you favor an irrevocable death penalty for the killer?

Dukakis: No, I don't, and I think you know that I've opposed the death penalty during all of my life.

Opa! In an instant, the son of Greek immigrants flamed out like a plate of saganaki.

Enter Ron Paul on the heels of the Obama Administration's success in taking out yet another al Qaeda operative, this time with a drone in Yemen. No, wait—make that two operatives with one shot as American-born Anwar al-Awlaki was also a terrorist.

It is known that al-Awlaki had ties to the Fort Hood Massacre and the thwarted attempt by the "Great Balls of Fire" panty bomber over Detroit Christmas Day 2009. Anwar's own videos call for the death of any and all Americans. And al-Awlaki's lackey, also rendered a crispy critter by the drone's red glare, published ways for his jihadist butt-buddies to build bombs in the comfort of their kitchens. Bon appétit sucker! Incoming!

But Paul, a Texas congressman known for libertarian views, says the killing of Anwar al-Awlaki on Yemeni soil amounts to an "assassination."

Paul warned that "We the People" should not casually accept such violence against U.S. citizens, even those with strong ties to terrorism.

Paul has seemingly forgotten that we are at war with al Qaeda—a war we did not start but one that I believe the majority of Americans hope we can end with their destruction. But Ron Paul thinks America's leaders must think hard about "assassinating American citizens without charges."

Ron, Ron, Ron. Should our troops in Afghanistan first obtain the passport of those shooting at them in order to determine their national origin before returning fire? To paraphrase the guidance counselor on South Park: "Ron Paul is nuttier than Chinese chicken salad, okay."

When presented with evidence that al-Awlaki was in our sights, I hope President Obama thought long and hard—and then point-five seconds later gave the order to blast his keister to the 77 virgins awaiting him in "his" heaven.

Ron Paul will be pummeled with his own words in the next debate, and, thankfully, his odds of winning the nomination will go from one in a million to, in the words of Buzz Lightyear: "To infinity and beyond!"

Perry's 6-6-6 Plan: October 9, 2011

It appears that Texas Governor Rick Perry—or at least one of his spiritual supporters—has a new winning strategy for his presidential bid. It's called the 6-6-6 Plan. No, it's not two-thirds of Herman Cain's 9-9-9 Plan, but rather a plan to paint Mitt Romney as an un-Christian member of that wacky "cult" called Mormons. Now, everybody knew Romney's religion would become a bigger topic sooner or later, but Romney fans hoped it would come up in a head-to-head fight with President Obama, where Mitt could remind everyone of Obama's Reverend Jeremiah Wright "GD-ing America."

Unfortunately for Mitt, his Mormon chickens have come home to roost a tad bit early. While I honestly think most Americans don't really know or care about Mormonism, it will be a reminder to the Evangelical

Christians—a huge Republican contingency—that Romney is not one of them despite his protestations.

Wisecracker, are you being judgmental of Romney and Mormons? Nay, nay. In 2008, I gave the maximum contribution to Romney over my wife's objections, including a discussion on whether or not Mormons were indeed a cult. Of course, Catholics are a cult too if you believe Jimmy Swaggart.

Rick Perry is ever-so-slightly trying to distance himself from the cult charge his pastor friend levied against Romney. But let's be honest about what Mormons are "supposed" to stand for, according to their own doctrine, which is not under lock and key and is easily found. Mormons are, in fact, Christians, but here's the rub: According to their doctrine, they are the only real Christians. That's right, you Orthodoxers, Catholics, Lutherans, Baptists, and Methodists are phony Christians. The hypocrisy of Mormons is that they plead for the "phony" Christians to accept them as real Christians only to privately believe they—the Mormons—have cornered the market on the religion. As the Church Lady would say, "Isn't that special."

Even conservative guru and converted Mormon, Glenn Beck, can't be honest about this troublesome truth about their religion. Oh sure, not all Catholics follow the Catholic doctrine hook, line, and sinker, but the exclusivity of Mormons as the only real Christians, and thus the new age "Chosen People," is the bedrock of their faith.

The bottom line is, the damage is done to both Romney and, yes, Rick Perry, whose earlier "heartfelt" comments on giving illegal immigrants a leg up went over like a pregnant pole-vaulter with conservatives resulting in a "Hail Mary" (sorry) with the ill-conceived 6-6-6 Plan. In the end, the real benefactor of this dust-up is Herman Cain, who looks smarter, more confident, and even more likable each and every day.

Cain (Hart) Trouble: October 31, 2011

Herman Cain is squirming, and his handling of allegations of past sexual harassment will strengthen or kill his presidential ambitions. After all, the smartest guy in the GOP debates—the Newtmeister—is likely unelectable for his sexual transgression some years back.

There is no in-between here for Cain. Of course, many an executive—males, and yes, females (although a cad of a man would say that an unwanted advance from a lady is an oxymoron)—have faced sexual harassment allegations over the years.

Some are already crying foul that this is Clarence Thomas, Part II. Trouble there is that Thomas-accuser Anita Hill never spoke up when it reportedly happened, while Cain's trouble is that his organization at the time, the restaurant industry's lobbying group, reportedly settled the matter(s) and made them go bye-bye, never to be known -- until now.

True, a settlement is not an acknowledgment of guilt in the court of law. It is, however, a slam-dunk acknowledgment of "guilt" in the court of public opinion. From my experience in the corporate world, legal settlements are common when the cost of litigation outweighs the benefit of winning, which in this country can be scary, regardless of the facts among a jury of peers—think O.J. Simpson. And, what's kind of wacky in settlements is that it is often the plaintiff's attorneys who demand that record of any settlement for their client be sealed (as in the case of Cain's reported settlements). Why? Two reasons actually: the plaintiff's lawyers sometimes don't want to advertise how crappy a settlement they got for their clients; and two, said plaintiff attorney often doesn't want their ex to know they just hit the mother lode.

An executive friend of mine, a few years ago, faced a sexual harassment charge after he put an arm around a female subordinate's shoulders, congratulating her on a job well done. Thank God he didn't chest bump her like he would a male colleague in the same situation. Nevertheless, he faced the charge and eventually won. It cost him tens of

131

thousands of dollars in legal fees. The same company he and I worked for had previously settled a high-profile case for a top executive and had decided to get out of the litigation business by the time it was his time in the barrel.

Back to Herman—Mr. Tell-it-like-it-is. Cain must not dance around this issue. He must come clean. Any parsing of the English language will make him look like former Democratic presidential wannabe, Gary Hart. Mr. Cain likes to sing gospel in campaign appearances. Well, the truth is the only thing that shall set him free!

Romney, Gingrich: Dumb and Dumber: January 25, 2012

Like Jim Carrey or not (personally, he deserves as many Oscars as Obama has Nobel Prizes), his classic line in the movie, *Liar, Liar* resonates more today than when he screamed it on the silver screen. Carrey, as a lawyer who cannot tell a lie, desperately leaves for the restroom where he subsequently beats the hell out of himself. A startled onlooker asks him what he is doing. Carrey's character replies: "I'm kicking my ass!"

Fast forward to the Sunshine State of Florida. Romney and Gingrich are kicking each other's ass: 15 percent income tax rate, Cayman Islands, Freddie Mac, Fannie Mae, etc. Keep it up boys and Obama walks to re-election you morons.

Is Granny on the Pill? February 20, 2012

Apparently, my 95-year-old, Catholic great-grandmother neighbor has been "gettin' busy" lately. How else can you explain Nancy Pelosi's declaration of the "universally accepted fact" that 98 percent of all Catholic women are currently using some form of birth control. Sure, sure, the survey conducted for Planned Non-Parenthood that delivered this startling revelation was a "bit" flawed and excluded as many Catholic women as it included, but why let that get in the way of the issue.

Meanwhile, the rubber has hit a bumpy road in Rick Santorum's campaign thanks to super rich Super PAC supporter, Foster "Brooks" Friess. Friess decided to jump into a time machine before his interview with NBC's Andrea Mitchell and whip out a bad joke from an episode of "Father Knows Best," implying the best form of contraception was having a woman keep her legs together. No chauvinism there, huh? (Note for Friess: If you get an invitation to go on "The View," just say no.)

Santorum quickly pooh-poohed his supporter's stupid remark, but, of course, the MSM would have none of that. (Note: this was the same MSM that completely disregarded the Rev. Jeremiah Wright's lunacy for weeks until they were forced to attempt to cover it. Obama, as you may recall, took about the same amount of time before he rejected his Spiritual Advisor's inflammatory, anti-American rants.)

Santorum's real boner for the week was his line about thinking income inequality is a "good thing." Sure, in complete context, his statement was dead-on. But also deadly. What he should have said was the "American Dream" was a good thing—we all start out equal, but those who study hard, work hard, and perhaps, produce something lots of people like will soar economically, while slackers fall behind. Rick, like Romney on far too many occasions recently, needs to preview his comments with someone of at least modest intelligence on his staff BEFORE he goes public with them. Thankfully, for Rick, Romney still leads in the "Good Idea but Poorly Explained" race to the bottom.

I mean Sunday, Romney came up with this zinger: "I very badly want to have your support."

Very badly? I very badly want to slam my hand in the car door! Geez. Meanwhile, both candidates are writing commercials for Obama to use against either.

Speaking of the Prez, he pegged the Gall Meter this week, appearing at a unionized Boeing plant in Washington State to cheer on his job creation successes and plans. Of course, many of his detractors claimed foul for his appearance at anything Boeing after the Administration's stacked NLRB tried to keep Boeing from opening a jobs-rich new Boeing plant in right-to-work South Carolina. To be fair, Obama's appearance wasn't as much galling as it was pathetic: playing to his base and proving once again that he will do anything—even if bone-headed, economically disastrous, or downright unconstitutional—to prove that "hope and change" are alive and well.

Nice Rack, Newt! February 21, 2012

Monday evening, Newt Gingrich told Sean Hannity that "you can't put a gun rack on a (Chevy) Volt" and promised to use that Obama-buster line again in the campaign. My advice to Newt: Stop before you look even more clueless in a state (Michigan) where the start of deer hunting season is a high holy day for hunters and Budweiser alike.

As a "historian," Mr. Gingrich should know that gun racks are rarely if ever seen in a sedan; whether a Volt, Honda Accord, or Chrysler 300. In addition, Mr. Gingrich should also know that, historically, one does not put a gun rack "on" a vehicle; one puts a gun rack "in" a vehicle, or takes the risk of damage or theft.

What's more, placing a gun rack in any sedan would most likely result in a rear seat passenger being, technically speaking, "bonked" by either a gun or those cute little deer hooves that often serve as the gun holder.

This is not to say that a gun rack could not be placed in a Volt. As we speak, I am certain that the brain trust at GM is contemplating the creation of a Chevy Volt Gun Rack Technology Center in Marquette, Michigan. In the meantime, most of their gun rack-loving customers will be stuck buying a pickup truck.

Come to think of it, an electric vehicle like the Volt may be the perfect hunting vehicle as it embraces the sacred words of one of history's greatest hunters, Elmer Fudd: "Be vewy, vewy quiet."

Santorum Projectile Hurls His Way into Michigan: February 27, 2012

Today's Michigan primary is reportedly too close to call. In fact, listen to any political pundit over the past few days, and not one is unequivocally predicting a winner between Mitt Romney and Rick Santorum. I will. It's Santorum, even if he loses the voter tally.

Those criticizing Santorum for saying he almost blew chunks when he reread John F. Kennedy's comments about the separation between church and state are wrongly comparing Kennedy's position back in 1960 vs. Santorum's today. Kennedy was going on the offensive against fears that Americans would never elect a Catholic President. He was running away from his Church to save his own skin. Santorum is putting his religious roots as his own skin in the game against a current President who is trampling on the First Amendment with glee at the exact same time his campaign is sending out videos to churches across our land asking them to "organize" on his behalf.

I guess a conservative who invokes the church and its teachings into politics is a right-wing nut; while a liberal, standing President doing the same thing is just "ginning up his base."

It is ironic that this Kennedy/Santorum kerfuffle is happening, considering that the issue would more logically occur between Mitt Romney and the late President. After all, according to a piece in *The Washington Post* Monday, Mormons openly worry about Romney's Mormonism hurting his chances among Evangelical Christians who make up a huge slice of conservative western Michigan, just as Kennedy was worried about his Catholicism getting in the way of the Oval Office.

Looking back, the separation Kennedy really should have worried about for his legacy is the separation between him and Marilyn Monroe, et al.

The GOP Needs to Take a Pill and Get Over It: March 3, 2012

If Republicans have any hope of retaking the White House, they'd better stop falling into the "anti-woman" trap being successfully sprung on them far too many times in this campaign. First, it appeared that President Obama had handed the GOP an enormous gift in his assault on the Catholic Church regarding mandatory contraceptive coverage. It was "supposed" to be a blatant example of this Administration's careless disregard for our Constitution. But, as they have a penchant for doing, the Right decided to ignore their sure win and took their chips to the high-stakes room where a rich Rick Santorum donor was dealing from the bottom of the deck, cracking one-liners from 1951. Freedom of Religion became "Keep Your Legs Together, Sweetie."

Thankfully for the GOP Establishment, Mitt Romney survived a Santorum upset in Michigan and all was well again. The Cadillacs we would now discuss were the union Cadillac health care plans given an exemption from Obamacare, not Ann Romney's multiple Cadillac models the couple owns. And, finally, we could talk about Obama's Achilles Heel—the economy—as gasoline continued to spike and Obama's bumbling energy secretary Chu was getting skewered for his earlier comments about wanting U.S. gas prices to resemble Europe.

Enter a Fluke and a Rush and yet another trap. Sandra Fluke, a Georgetown University law school student, was called by Nancy "Blame My Plastic Surgeon for this Smile" Pelosi to testify in front of a Congressional committee about the plight of womanhood in this new age of intolerance. Her testimony was, by itself, pitiful. Being "forced" to pay for contraceptives out of her own wallet was rendering her a pauper. Somehow, it wasn't the $35,000 in tuition to the mega-prestigious school, or the $15,000 in room and board, or the $1,250 in books—per year. Nope: it was the pill that was breaking the bank. And, she needed the pill badly—not for any health reasons, but because she was obviously

136

involved in constant extra-curricular activities between her, um, er, classes.

The spectacle seemed ridiculous on its face: if you want to show the plight of women and the need for some type of free contraception program, why not trot out a young, uneducated poor woman, where an unwanted pregnancy would be devastating for her and the child. Pelosi's miscalculation would kill her efforts, right?

This time the mouse taking the tainted cheese was none other than the Master of the Right, the guy who claims that he ties half his brain behind his back just to give his opponents a chance in any policy debate. Yes, we are talking about Rush Limbaugh. Rush tried to make a mockery of Fluke's staged performance, but in the end screwed the pooch. He invoked the terms "slut" and "prostitute" in describing the aspiring haberdasher instead of exposing the ridiculousness of her "pity party."

It was another gift for Obama, and he gladly accepted it. He realized that the latest GOP fumble was no fluke, even if in this case it was a Fluke. And he pounced. (Sorry to mix my cat and mouse analogies.) A comforting phone call from the President of the Free World to the "victim" of the vicious right-wing attack was choreographed with Broadway brilliance, and the MSM gulped it up like catnip. Republicans were forced to rebuke Limbaugh and two advertisers pulled their support for his show. And, once again, the front page of *The Washington Post* featured a debate over the pill and nothing on a U.S. economy looking more like Greece with each new day.

The GOP needs to take a pill and get over this before it's too late.

Romney Is No Dick, Nixon: July 6, 2012
The silly season of presidential campaign politics isn't supposed to start until after Labor Day. I guess Obama chief strategist David Axel "Nim" Rod didn't get the memo. Thursday, in an interview with ABC

Radio, Axelrod accused GOP candidate Mitt Romney of being "the most secretive candidate that we've seen, frankly, since Richard Nixon." Please.

Secretive candidates? President Obama didn't release a "copy" of his birth certificate until two years into his presidency. College transcripts or papers? Nope. President Obama got Obamacare through the Senate only after offering at least two bribes—the Louisiana Purchase and the Cornhusker Kickback. President Obama invoked executive privilege to protect discussions concerning the scandalous Fast and Furious gun-running operation that he supposedly knew nothing about. Domestic terrorist William Ayers was "just a guy in the neighborhood" and not a key mentor of his ideology. Rev. Wright "gd-ing" America from the pulpit at Obama's church: don't remember that at all.

The fact is—as pointed out recently by Democratic strategist Pat Caddell—it is the Obama Administration that appears to be mirroring Nixon's. Enemy lists. An Attorney General that turns his back on the rule of law. And now, a dirty tricks clown: Nixon had Donald Segretti. Obama has Axelrod.

Romney's Gaffes in London vs. Obama's Gaffes in the Universe: July 29, 2012

The Washington Post every Sunday announces its "winner" of the "Worst Week in Washington." Past winners have included the Obama operative that proclaimed Ann Romney "has never worked a day in her life." This week's winner is GOP presidential candidate, Mitt Romney. (Can we please stop calling him the presumptive candidate as if, in a week, there will be evidence that he did something really heinous that will kill his nomination.)

Mitt got the honor for his supposed gaffe concerning his criticism of London's security issues with the Olympic Games. Never mind the British press and bloggers had been criticizing the British government for said transgression for the last month, ruthlessly. Even CNN's Piers Morgan came to Romney's defense saying, "It's no secret over here that for the last three weeks the security around the Olympics has been a shambles." Mitt called it like he saw it and was crucified for it.

This is why Romney skedaddled to Jerusalem, the site of a real crucifixion. There he said nothing controversial to his crowd, but apparently, something "foreign" to Team Obama. At a fundraiser, Romney had the audacity to declare that Jerusalem WAS the capital of Israel. Oh, it is, but don't let that get in the way of today's politics.

Earlier in the week, White House press secretary Jay Carney channeled Momma Cass and pretended to choke on a pork chop when asked "what is the capital of Israel?" Before Carney's chokage, a State Department spokesperson was obviously at the same pig roast and could not bring herself to saying Jerusalem was the capital of America's closest ally in the Middle East. Heimlich Maneuver anyone?

Romney, in Israel, was applauded, profusely. Next, he's on to Poland—another ally President Obama has dissed, removing the proposed anti-missile weapons systems against Putin's communist Soviet Union, um, er, Russia. Apparently, Poland is not that important in President Obama's "flexible" policy with the Russkies.

Romney, according to *The Washington Post*, had the "worst week." Who has had the worst month, year, and administration? Geez.

Mitt: Fire Someone! September 18, 2012

This morning, I got a passionate email from a friend—a Dem—ticked that Mitt Romney is blowing it. He wrote: "Whoever runs his communications/PR needs to be fired (and Romney likes firing people as he says)! The economy is in the tank, the world is on the verge of imploding, every indicator is worse than it was in 1979 (!), and Romney continues to shoot himself in the foot. I've never seen someone blow a more winnable contest with a series of self-destructive, bone-headed gaffes...well maybe the Lions? Really confounding as Romney is clearly an incredibly smart guy with a ton of business savvy. But his campaign seems as disorganized as an Occupy protest. Meanwhile, Professor Obama with no business experience runs his campaign with the efficiency of a 1950s-era IBM."

His emailed was entitled "Wow." He's right. Here's a smart businessman—a private equity guy worth millions—and despite being a Dem, wants Romney to win but is frustrated by the pathetic campaign Mitt and his handlers are running. The former Massachusetts Governor seemingly is snatching defeat from the jaws of victory.

Mitt: your words are not "inelegant" as you say. They are stupider than stupid. Fire your PR people as there is still a lot of time left, including the VP debate, which should be like Milton Freidman arguing with Warren of *There's Something About Mary* and multiple presidential debates where you get to expose President Obama's record, or lack thereof.

Stay thirsty, my friend.

Tubby Submarined Romney: November 7, 2012

Thanks to my brilliantly unreliable sources, the Wisecracker has obtained a copy—though quite scratchy—of the telephone conversation between President Obama and New Jersey Governor and Subway candidate, Chris Christie, prior to the President's trip last month to the hurricane-ravaged East Coast.

Aide: Governor, it's the President.

Christie: Listen, Mutha F---er, I want my loaded pizza and I want it now!

Aide: No your governorship, it's not President Pizza; it's the President of the United States.

Christie: I am damn hungry and tired and need a pizza, not a President. Damn it. Hello Mr. President.

Obama: Hey, Chris, how's it goin'?

Christie: Swimmingly. Literally. Sorry, SIR, but I am a no–nonsense governor (at least I play one on TV) and I have little time for politics in the midst of this disaster.

Obama: Chris, Chris, Chris, um, er, ah, ah, ah, hear me out. I'm goin' to give you an offer you cannot refuse. Hello, hello?

(Cell phone service, due to the storm, is lost at this moment.)

Obama: Damn. Axelrod, increase the taxes on Verizon. Governor Christie, ya there?

Christie: Yeah, yeah.

Obama: So, here's the deal. I go to New Jersey tomorrow and you give me a big bear hug and I give you all the federal help you need. In turn, I get the mainstream media to do an orgasmic story on you and me crossin' the aisle, I win the election, and you are set for 2016 against an old and saggy Hillary. What ya think?

(Cell phone service lost again.)

Obama: Hello, Chris?

Christie: Thanks for calling me three times. First of all, Mr. President, stop dropping your Gs. You are not talking to Sarah Palin. Second, I love this.

Obama: Alright, deal. Can you get your buddy Bruce Springsteen to join me on the last swing states?

Christie: Deal, buddy. See you tomorrow. Hey, any way you can bring some Ben's Chili "a Washington staple" with you on Air Force One?

Obama: I'll bring a gallon.

Christie: I'm dieting. Make it two.

2012: The Lowlight: December 20, 2012

The low moment of 2012 was certainly the massacre of those little kids and staff in Connecticut. The lowlight was the Republican Party leadership—from Mitt Romney and his incompetent staff to Todd

"Legitimate Rape" Akins to Karl "Trust Me I Know What I Am Talking About" Rove to Rush Limbaugh. Let's work our way backwards.

Rush diverted attention away from Obama's economic train wreck and allowed Georgetown law student Sandra Fluke to turn her selfish views on free contraceptives into a "noble" cause when he called her a slut. Akins added fuel to Rush's fire with one of the stupidest comments ever on rape and pregnancy. Then he added arrogance to his stupidity and refused to quit a race against the most beatable Democratic senator (Claire McCaskell) in America.

The all-knowing Rove was wrong on every aspect of the presidential campaign and lulled Republicans into believing Romney would romp into the White House. His career is clearly at a Crossroads.

Finally, dear Mitt. PR 101 says you don't say or write anything you don't want to see on the front pages of *The New York Times*. His "47 percent" comment became the rallying cry that allowed Obama to snatch victory from the jaws of defeat he had so earned.

Bless you boys.

Conservatives: Remain Calm! May 26, 2013

Conservatives need to heed the advice of Kevin Bacon's character in *Animal House* in the midst of the movie-ending runaway parade: Remain calm! The runaway parade is the peeling onion of scandals enveloping the Obama Administration—Benghazigate, IRSgate, APgate, FOXNewsgate and so on.

However, calm is not what some conservatives are doing as murmurs of "Nixonian" behavior and impeachment are beginning to be thrown around. Unless Mr. Obama actually killed someone with his bare hands (not with a drone or what Mitt Romney was accused of doing to that cancer-stricken woman), impeachment ain't gonna happen.

Case in point: Sunday morning I received an email from a conservative friend who often shares with me alternatively serious,

142

outrageous, and funny items about Team Obama and their seemingly endless plan to eliminate liberty, personal responsibility, accountability, and edible school lunches in this country. I always try to check if what I am reading is true. This morning it was true, but old news.

Perhaps you too have seen the "Memorial Day Card" below:

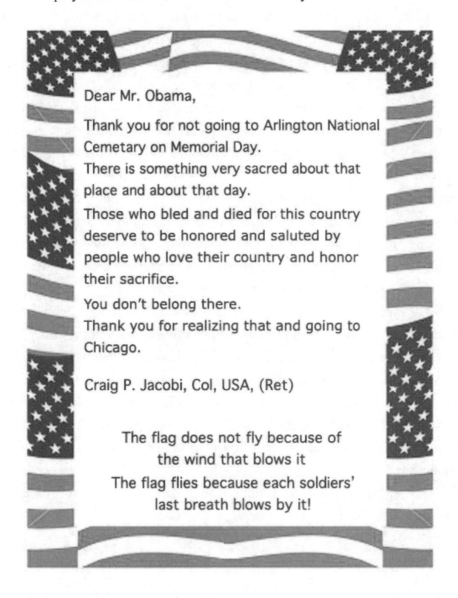

Dear Mr. Obama,

Thank you for not going to Arlington National Cemetary on Memorial Day.
There is something very sacred about that place and about that day.
Those who bled and died for this country deserve to be honored and saluted by people who love their country and honor their sacrifice.
You don't belong there.
Thank you for realizing that and going to Chicago.

Craig P. Jacobi, Col, USA, (Ret)

The flag does not fly because of
the wind that blows it
The flag flies because each soldiers'
last breath blows by it!

Problem is: President Obama will be at Arlington National Cemetery on Memorial Day 2013. He, shamefully, skipped the visit in 2010 when he was still the apple of the MSM's eye. So, when conservatives send this stuff around, it merely confirms to many that the right-wing loons are at it again.

Remain calm. Team Obama is doing a fine job of screwing everything up and finally, finally, the MSM does not have their back. Sunday's *Washington Post* is Exhibit A. A ginormous column by former executive editor Leonard Downie, Jr., assailing the administration for spying on journalists, is far better than microwaved leftovers from past Obama transgressions. And evidence that AG Eric Holder personally signed-on to bug FOX News' James Rosen, despite lying to Congress about the effort, is even better. Ironically, it was a *Washington Post* reporter, Carl Bernstein, who was most famously threatened by an Attorney General. Nixon's John Mitchell told Mr. Bernstein: "Katie Graham's gonna get her tit caught in a big fat wringer if that is published." Graham was the publisher of WaPo. Her um, er, breasts went unscathed. Not so sure about Mitchell's, as he went to prison a few years later.

Last year, Holder was found in contempt of Congress in the "Fast and Furious" gun-running scandal while apparently having nothing but contempt for the Constitution and the laws of our land. His assault on the First Amendment means he'll likely be the next one to go following IRS chief sleaze Steven Miller and co-conspirator Lois "I only love the Fifth Amendment" Lerner. White House "Misspokesperson" Jay Carney will join Holder shortly after, but will find success in the Broadway version of Pinocchio.

Again, remain calm: the Obama Administration implosion is doing just fine on its own.

Tea Party: Tweedle dee and Tweedle dumb: June 19, 2013

I hit the Mall; that is, the National Mall, on the west lawn of the Capitol for the Tea Party Rally against the liars, thugs, and various other criminals in the IRS. No racist signs or edicts. Fairly clever signs: Audit the IRS. Glenn Beck opens and rocks. (Not a fan of his theatrics on most days, but he does know how to whip up the base.) Rand Paul rocked more in a third of the time on stage.

Tweedle dee: the greatest and completely sexist quote of all time—women, can't live with 'em; can't live without 'em—plays so true here. The number of women speakers and members of the crowd was, as kids say today, amazing. These chicks have had enough. Thank God. As usual, women are smarter than men and will lead us into the Promised Land against this if-my-lips-are-moving-we-are-lying Administration. Finally, I agree with a woman's right to choose – her politicians.

Tweedle dumb: Texas freshman Senator Ted Cruz. Cruz's continuing crusade to eliminate the IRS and have tax forms reduced to a postcard is dumber than a rock. So, Teddy, how do you attach a check? Tax returns require your Social Security number. You want to put that on the outside of a postcard so that identity thieves have easy access to it?

Bottom line: you go girls and Ted, please, shut the hell up and get some experience before thinking about running for President midway through your first term; we're already suffering from that phenomenon.

Chapter Seven: Stupid Policies

"I'M OFF TO INVESTIGATE LAW ENFORCEMENT ABUSE... IN FERGUSON, MISSOURI."

Taco Bell "Runs" for the Border: January 25, 2010

There is an interesting lawsuit filed in Southern California (duh) against Taco Bell that news organizations are all labeling: "Where's the Beef?" The charge: the seasoned ground beef in many of the fast-food chain's entrees is only 36 percent actual dead cow, with the rest a variety of fillers, including wheat products. The USDA says if you are going to call it beef, it has to be at least 40 percent beef. Geez, only 40 percent? Damn. That is a pretty low threshold.

If I were 40-percent nice to my wife, I would be single and broke. That's why I'm sending my kids in college a note telling them to get at least 40 percent on their tests. The USDA says that's a passing grade. Take that Michigan State, Central Michigan, and Western Michigan!

Anyway, if the charges are true (and Taco Bell has done a really lousy early job of refuting them in the press), I and thousands of other Americans have a real problem with Taco Bell.

Not to get on the pity train, but I found out a few years ago that I have Celiac disease. I had lost a ton of weight—I thought due to stress during the dark times at Chrysler—until I had one of those "complete" tests where you ask the doctor if he had "found my dignity while he was 'up' there." Two weeks later, while test driving cars in the mountains of Arizona, my wife called with the results. The cell phone connection was spotty.

"You have silly ass disease," I thought she'd said. This made sense, considering that I had told her to buy stock in Charmin.

"Silly ass?" I said.

"No, you idiot. Celiac. C-E-L-I-A-C. You are allergic to gluten, to wheat." She said, "no more beer, no more pizza, no more pasta." Thank God, wine is safe. For the first time in my life, I turned eastward and bowed to France.

The struggle for us Celiac sufferers is finding food without wheat or other gluten products. I am sure you have seen the rise in gluten-free items, including entire sections in almost all food stores. But what my colleagues miss the most is good gluten-free junk food—a burger (doesn't exist), a pizza (they mostly suck to be honest), some crackers (more expensive than crude oil) and pies, cakes, whatever. McDonald's? Nope. Pizza Hut? Nada. Tim Hortons, Starbucks, whatever? No! No! No!

But wait! The holy grail of gluten-free goodness was sitting right in front of us and we made a run for the border. Yo Quiero Taco Bell! Corn tortillas and beef. We are safe, fat, and happy. Perhaps, until now.

Maybe the real illegal aliens are in the "beef" at your local Taco Bell.

Gored While Fishing in Los Cabos: December 28, 2010

The Wisecracker rose at the crack of 5 a.m. last Wednesday to take another stab at emptying the Sea of Cortez of yellowfin tuna bigger than a house. Last year, I landed twelve of these beauties ranging from 15 pounds to the biggest whopper I ever caught – 125 pounds. No, I did not kill them for the sport of it. I killed them for the sport and for something even more heinous. I and my family ate those suckers over the next few months. Yes, for many, many fantastic meals, I was the Hannibal Lecter to the fish world. Ah, the Silence of the Tuna.

As the El Capitan led our small boat out to sea, I roared to my sons and nephew how tired our backs and arms would be after our upcoming tuna massacre. "No señor, the tuna are not biting." What? Had I drained Baja California's beautiful ocean of tuna on my previous trip? Damn my eyes!

"No, señor, the ocean is too cold."

Too what? What about the movie, *The Day After Tomorrow*? What about those wacky Climategate "scientists"? Where was Al Gore when I really needed him? Was this MY "Inconvenient Truth"? Is Global Warming everywhere around the world except here in my Chicken-of-the-Sea wonderland?

148

El Capitan's prediction held true: not a single mouth-watering tuna would grace my line. I was stuck with a bunch of Sierra Mackerel and two Dorado. It was like expecting a hot date with Halle Berry and winding up with Roseanne Barr.

Days later, we boarded our plane back to Detroit via Houston. On arrival in Houston, we were "Gored" again and missed our connection to Motown thanks to delays in flights from the Snowmageddon on the East Coast – another victim of Global Warming's treachery.

Live From Israel: January 15, 2011
The Wisecracker has been lucky enough to join Mrs. Wisecracker and thirty-four other crazy Greek Orthodox from Bloomfield Hills on a first-ever pilgrimage to the Holy Land. No, not the Birch Run outlet mall; Israel, and in the coming days, Jordan and Egypt.

Unlike much of the images I was presented with as a tike in Sunday School decades ago, it truly is one of the most beautiful places on earth. With guide in hand, we saw everything important over the past week, from the Sea of Galilee to Jerusalem to "Stars and Bucks" Coffee. Not kidding on the latter. Or is that latte? Here are my observations.

1) After hearing time and time again about the warring history of the tribes of Israel with themselves, the Muslims and, yes, even the Crusaders over the past few millenniums, peace in the Middle East today or in the future is as close to impossible as anything I have seen. Sorry, but this is not a new phenomenon. Those that question "why can't they just get along" and call for both sides to "get back to the damned negotiating table" are ignorant of history at best and, at worst, are selling the public a hoax.

2) If the Palestinians want their own state (this conservative thinks they should have one*), then they'd better take care of what they have been given (or fought for) thus far. Palestinian-controlled Jericho – the famous city where the walls came crashing down—looks like parts of

149

Detroit on a really, really bad day. Abandoned buildings litter the city, and trash is more present than vegetation. It is appalling. Bethlehem, also Palestinian-controlled, is better but not by much.

3) Newt Gingrich's line that Palestinians are a "made-up" or "invented" people is the dumbest line of the campaign so far. It becomes even dumber when you consider that he considers himself a historian, and not just a "paid one" for Freddie Mac and Fannie Mae. The Palestinians are credited with being descendants of the Philistines, most likely near Greece. Oh crap, I used "Greece" and "credit" in the same sentence. My bad.

4) Regarding the * above: Perhaps we, as a world, maybe through the ever-efficient UN, could all agree to give the Palestinians France.

5) Funny (or not) that any Muslim can bring a Quran into Jerusalem and into any Christian church or Jewish temple, but a Christian cannot bring a Bible onto the grounds of a mosque, let alone into the mosque itself unless it goes undetected.

Detroit Gets Its NOJO Back: March 30, 2011
Like a newly-born colt taking its first wobbly steps, Detroit's automakers are slowly but surely getting their legs under them in order to fight the Feds on unrealistic and even silly regulations. Yes, my friends, the auto industry is getting its NOJO back! NO to a separate California fuel economy standard! NO to silly regulations that force automakers to spend billions designing cars that keep morbidly stupid unbelted motorists from being ejected in an accident! Think Darwinism here.

NHTSA Administrator David Strickland may be soft-peddling the battles that are just over the horizon. He recently said he was hoping for "compromise between automakers and the safety advocates." Compromise? NOJO! Perhaps Mr. Strickland does not know that these purported "safety advocates" are nothing more than shills for trial attorneys who will paint the industry as laggards as they have done for decades.

Detroit's car makers first acquired their NOJO in the early 1970s. Congress told the automakers to limit tailpipe emissions by unheard-of quantities. All, repeat, all the automakers told the lawmakers, "We don't have the technology to do it." "Just shut up and do it" was the reply. Then the clever folks at General Motors (neither Toyota nor Mercedes) went to work and invented the catalytic converter for automobiles.

Were the GM engineering geniuses, led by Dick Klimisch, heralded for their magic? Not on your life. They were ridiculed and accused of hiding it all along. (The sinister automakers had probably hidden it in an underground bunker along with the 100-miles-per-gallon carburetor, the cure for all cancers, and Viagra. The Viagra was discovered when a custodian sweeping the bunker while suffering from a migraine, mistook the pills for aspirin and "four hours later" was rushed to the hospital.)

With GM's environmental miracle, the U.S. auto industry was forever labeled as the "Can't Do" companies. Their engineering MOJO instantly turned into political NOJO.

But alas, Detroit's automakers lost their NOJO in 2008. In one of the lamest spectacles in American history, the CEOs, with the exception of Ford's Alan Mulally, played rope-a-dope in front of Congress and took an incredible beating in order to secure a lifesaving bailout. Savaged by Alabama's Dick Shelby and Massachusetts Ed "I'm not overreacting, but let's close all nuclear facilities in the U.S." Markey, Detroit's automakers limped back to Motown and basically agreed with every undoable regulation Washington threw at them. Sixty miles per gallon? Sure. In fact, why stop there, Mr. President?

Until now. Finally, Detroit's version of "Diary of a Wimpy Kid" is over. They've got their NOJO back. Yeah baby, yeah!

Nightmare (for the Greenies) on Woodward Avenue: August 19, 2011

Saturday will be a bad day for the Sierra Club. The auto industry-hating tree huggers view the Woodward Dream Cruise (of classic automobiles) as the ultimate stick-in-the-eye to environmentalists worldwide. Thousands of cars idling in bumper-to-bumper traffic along metro Detroit's most famous boulevard with no particular place to go—just being there consuming barrels of oil and spewing pollutants into the air.

But as usual, they will miss a few important points. First of which is how much science the automakers have unleashed over the last few decades with little if any credit from the greenies. They will not acknowledge the following facts:

1) What sets America apart as the world's greatest nation is our huge middle class.

2) The middle class in this country developed in great part through the proliferation of affordable modes of individual and family transportation—the automobile. The cars also helped create a greenie no-no: urban sprawl. Or, as I like to think of it: affordable and safe housing, great schools and, of course, Walmart.

3) Cars and trucks and SUVs are incredibly clean today. In fact, no other industry with a potential hazardous impact on the environment has made greater improvements over the years. Which means it's time for a Dream Cruise Fun Fact from the Cracker.

4) (Intro music for Fun Fact.) A 2011 Chevy Suburban—the "Debil" according to the Sierra Club—driving down Woodward Avenue gives off fewer emissions than a 1955 classic Corvette parked in a local Woodward eatery with ITS ENGINE SHUT OFF. No way you say? Way. Prior to emissions standards, the evaporative emissions were huge through the gas tank, fuel lines, and the engine itself. That's how clean these vehicles, even the monsters, are.

So, my dear Sierra Club friends, try to get through the Dream Cruise without a mental meltdown. Sunday everything goes back to normal. Regular traffic. Regular lives. And the MSM bashing Texas Gov. Rick Perry for having the audacity to believe that global warming is a lot of hot air.

Department of Energy Secretary Chu Is Re-Volting: March 12, 2012

The Chu Chu train officially derails in Washington, D.C. this week. Department of Energy Secretary Steven Chu walks the gauntlet at this week's Senate Lack of Energy Committee and he has no friends on either side of the aisle in our current political divide. He will have failed solar panel company Solyndra shoved up his bottom side where he will most likely hope the sun does not appear that day. He will also be skewered for giving taxpayer money to a former Ford designer to build his ultra-luxury electric Fisker Karma vehicle – in Finland. Not Findlay, Ohio. Finland. By the way, close Wisecracker sources say Consumer Reports bought a Fisker Karma and was testing it until it pooped the bed and had to be towed: So-not-good. Fisker just hired former Chrysler CEO Tom LaSorda as its new CEO. Good bye.

What Chu had absolutely nothing to do with, but will be a clear focus of the kangaroo court in the Senate, is the Chevy Volt. Perhaps no vehicle has created so much mental retardation in its critics than the Volt. Marvel of science? By all credible automotive experts: without question. Overpriced? Well, the Fisker Karma and the Tesla S coupe are $100K a pop or more; so I guess the Volt at 50 grand must be considered an entry-level vehicle.

Volt will survive – well, kinda. The plant building the vehicle is idled for a couple more weeks to get supply in line with demand. And demand, well, struggles. Heck, when you have FOX News' Eric Bolling stupidly insinuating that the Volt he was loaned ran out of a charge in the Lincoln

Tunnel (duh, it switched over to gas power without a whimper) you can figure people are questioning its doability.

I love the line of *The Wall Street Journal* reviewer when talking about the Volt: "We should suspend our rancor and savor a little American pride. A bunch of Midwestern engineers in bad haircuts and cheap wristwatches just out-engineered every other car company on the planet."

Bottom line: Take Secretary Chu to the woodshed, but stop spitting in the eye of American innovation. Please.

Chu Chu on the Tracks Again: March 20, 2012

Embattled Department of Energy Secretary Steven Chu is back on Capitol Hill again today in what has become his full-time job: getting grilled and shucking and jiving through painful-to-watch hearings. Last week he faced a Senate hearing in which Minnesota Senator Al Franken made us wish for the days when he was merely Stuart Smalley on SNL. After cheering Chu's tenure at the DoE, Franken threw out this gem: "The Bark Beetle is eating all the foliage because it is staying too cold in upper elevations and the Bark Beetle is not dying and the forests are burning."

Wait a minute!!!!!! I thought we were worried about global warming, not cooling.

Despite Franken's knee slapper, the top prize for "what is he saying" went to Secretary Chu. Chu infamously stated a few years ago that we, as a nation, need to find ways to get the price of gasoline in this country to resemble Europe—$8 or $10 bucks a gallon. But now his past comments were coming back to haunt him as gas soared to near $4 a gallon nationwide.

"Do you still feel that way, Secretary Chu?" Chu, a Nobel laureate, answered as smoothly as a Yugo driving in a Michigan orange cone zone. "U, er, ah, kill me, um, er, well." He stuttered so much I could hear BTO's "Ain't Seen Nothin' Yet" in my ears.

Then he almost made a fatal mistake, at least as far as this Administration goes. Chu intimated that the high price of gas was <u>keeping the economy from recovering</u>. As if an emergency message had been instantly sent to an undetected ear piece, Chu caught himself. Was he suggesting that the much ballyhooed Obama recovery was non-existent or stalled? In an election year? The gyrations Chu sent himself through in the next few minutes were painful theater. He finally spit out an answer that basically said: "Yep, I checked my spine at the door when I took this job."

Chu survived the hearing, even cracking himself up at the end with a line that the new $50 Philips light bulbs his agency awarded with a $10 million prize would "certainly be a part of a person's will." That's right: a joke about a homeowner having to spend $2000 to light the normal home is a real side-splitter.

Today's House hearing should provide fewer guffaws—no Al Franken, but the fiery Darrell Issa, who has replaced Charles Schumer as the most television camera-loving Pol in D.C.

Summa Chu Laude: March 20, 2012

Despite the inconvenient fact that gasoline prices in the U.S. have doubled under his watch, Energy Secretary Steven Chu has determined his performance warrants an "A" grade. Never mind he is part of an Administration that failed to hand in an assignment on the Keystone Pipeline, that failed its Solyndra Finance 101 take-home test, and has stopped given approved loan money to the companies he needs to speed up the "electrification" of our transportation sector – oh wait, they did give money to Fisker to build $100,000-plus electric sports cars in Finland. In case you missed it: while Consumer Reports was recently testing Fisker's supercar—the Karma—it literally stopped working and had to be towed. They say karma's gonna get you. What? Stranded? *Mitä helvettiä*!

Despite this reality, Chu told the House panel Tuesday that he would give himself an "A" for his handling of energy policy under the Obama

Administration. Rep. Darrell "Issa that a FOX News crew over there", the chairman of the House Committee on Oversight and Government Reform, asked President Obama's top energy official if he'd grade himself with an "A minus" on "controlling the cost of gasoline at the pump." Chu said he'd give himself a better grade than that.

"The tools we have at our disposal are limited, but I would say I would give myself a little higher than that since I became Secretary of Energy. I've been doing everything I can to get long-term solutions," Chu said.

Chu gives himself an "A" and Obama gives himself a "good solid B+" despite the fact that the economy is teetering and gas prices are soaring. This can only mean one thing: Chu is destined to take on the much-pillared Department of Education and do his handiwork there. I'm just sad this newfound grading curve wasn't available during my days in East Lansing. I wouldn't have had to study so damn hard.

The Big, "Good" Wolf Lobby: April 24, 2013

If Little Red Riding Hood has relocated to Michigan, she should be afraid; very afraid. Why? Because the Big Bad Wolf and his ever-growing family are being financially supported by a humongous Washington lobbying group that preys on the good deeds of your local Humane Society.

Here's the deal: there are too many wolves living in Michigan. Too many wolves leads to farm animals being killed, people being attacked, traffic accidents, a spread of disease among the wolf population, and the eventual starvation of wolves. Nothing about this scenario is good.

Enter three participants into the issue. First, the boys and girls in the Michigan state government who have introduced legislation—the Scientific Management Package (okay, a traditional B.S. government name, but stick with me)—building upon voter approval of Proposal G in 1996 that tells the Natural Resources Commission (NRC) to regulate the "taking of game" based on sound scientific management. In a nutshell, they want to manage the number of wolves running around Michigan before people, cows, dogs, and cats (more on them later) are the course of the day for the wolf population—importantly, while maintaining these magnificent creatures. The bill provides for the NRC to provide a specified hunting season and issue specific rules how the hunt can be carried out.

This, after all, is much like the regulated hunting of deer in Michigan. Ban hunting Bambi and the little suckers starve, spread disease, and cause turmoil on our roads. License it and tax it and the deer (that don't get shot) thrive from my old Detroit suburb in Franklin to the highest regions of the Upper Peninsula. Of course, the Michigan deer hunting season is supported by the humongous lobbying firms known as Anheuser-Busch, Miller Lite, and Jose Cuervo.

The bills, Senate Bill 288 and House Bill 4552, are thoughtful and concise. They should pass, and hopefully will despite the protestations of two groups spreading fear and misinformation so wildly it makes President Obama's "the sky is falling" sequestration look like child's play.

Enter the supposed wolf lovers trashing the bill: the Keep Michigan Wolves Protected coalition and the behemoth Humane Society of the United States. Let's explore the latter first. The Humane Society of the U.S. (HSUS), in their own words, opposes virtually all hunting while leading people to believe they humanely care for animals in pet shelters. HSUS spends very little money on pet shelters, with as little as 1 percent of their past annual $100 million budgets going toward the care of animals.

I have had a problem with HSUS for years while supporting local Humane Society branches that do phenomenal work. In 2008, I helped lead the pet march in downtown Detroit, along with former General Motors vice-chair Bob Lutz, in support of the Humane Society—that is, the local chapters. I walked with my second rescue dog Chopper along

Detroit's Woodward Avenue with hundreds of other animal lovers. (Chopper passed last year and Sammie, a weird beagle-collie mix, is my third rescue so "bite me" for my gratuitous self-congratulation.) Anyway, I asked one of the local Humane Society leaders, "What's the deal with the wacky Humane Society of the United States?" She didn't hesitate: "They are not us." Whoa.

Not to pile on the HSUS, but what the hell. A few years ago, as the Michael Vick dog scandal wound down, dear Mr. Vick, the Atlanta Falcons star QB, held a press conference and apologized for his heinous acts against dogs. After he left the podium, a senior member of the Humane Society of the United States retrieved the notes that Mr. Vick used in making his apology (for the millions in salary he was losing, oops, my bad, editorial comment). The Humane Society of the United States then decided to auction them off on eBay. Vick's apology notes sold for $10,200. Sure, the HSUS claimed the funds would be used to protect animals, but really. Thank goodness the HSUS didn't have access to Dr. Kevorkian's diary or Jeffrey Dahmer's pantry.

HSUS says: "As a matter of principle, The HSUS opposes the hunting of any living creature for fun, trophy, or sport because of the animal trauma, suffering, and death that result. A humane society should not condone the killing of any sentient creature in the name of sport." But, they seem to have no problem with large packs of wolves in Michigan hunting cattle, sheep, hogs, dogs, cats (okay, I admit I am okay with this one, so sue me), and minivans.

Finally, enter The Keep Michigan Wolves Protected coalition into the wolves' den. This group has attempted to claim that it is not an anti-hunting initiative funded by the anti-hunting Humane Society of the United States. However, as its advocacy has increased, it has been matched by the Humane Society of the United States airing save-the-wolf television ads. The Keep Michigan Wolves Protected folks claim the proposed legislation will allow aerial shooting of wolves. Problem is, any aerial hunting is completely illegal in Michigan. So, the only way a poor little wolf can get whacked from the sky is if it is sitting next to a purported terrorist—foreign or domestic—and is collateral damage when President Obama decides to nuke the dude with a drone.

Be smart: Protect Michiganders against the wolves while protecting the wolf population: They really are treasures like lions and tigers and grizzly bears; as long as you or your dog are not their lunch.

Textual Healing? April 21, 2012

The Southeast Michigan Council of Governments (SEMCOG) spokesman, Tom Bruff, said one reason why southeastern Michigan has seen an increase in traffic crashes and deaths is because the area "is a more urbanized area with more motorists than the rest of the state." No Tom, that explains why, logically, there are more accidents and deaths, but does not explain why the rate is increasing. After reaching an all-time low in 2009, numbers in both categories were up according to a report released Friday by SEMCOG.

Hmm. What could be behind this bad news after years of declining numbers? Maybe it's a new regulation that politicians began spreading around SE Michigan, the state, and, in fact, the entire country around 2009: the ban on texting while driving. Don't get me wrong, texting while driving is stupid and dangerous. *Car and Driver* magazine ran a test that concluded it was as bad as or worse than drunk driving. But like many new laws, vaccines, or drugs designed to fix an ailment, sometimes the side effects make the cure worse than the disease.

Who are the biggest violators of texting while driving? Of course, our youngest drivers whom serendipitously just happen to be the crappiest drivers to start with. Great, huh? A KPMG study released last year found that kids don't believe "texting is getting in the way of their driving"; they believe "driving is getting in the way of their texting." That's why the ban has failed. What the ban succeeded in was forcing young drivers to hold their handheld devices even lower to avoid detection, which necessarily means their eyes are now off the road longer. Good plan.

So, how do you fix this conundrum? Simple, really. Make it impossible to text when you are moving, say three miles per hour or more. Here's how that solution would be bogusly assailed.

First, the device manufacturers would claim foul saying that would make them add new technology costing gazillions of dollars. Ah, no; the necessary technology is already widely available on almost all phones today. It's called GPS.

Big Brother conspiracy theorists will come up with some stupid claim while sitting on the couch in mommy and daddy's basement. Someone would cry out "what if I am in an accident and I need to text?" If you are in an accident, chances are, your vehicle is stopped, unless, of course, you are plummeting off an enormous cliff and then, well, what exactly do you want to text? Oh, calling 911 would always work.

Some will argue that it does nothing for older phones without the technology. Those are few and far between as most Americans turn over their cell devices more often than they change their tires. (This somewhat legitimate argument is the reason you keep the ban in place and actually increase the fine to become completely nasty.)

Somewhere there has to be a sound libertarian argument that proves this solution faulty. Oh, here it is: what if you are a passenger on a train? Aha, got ya, Wisecracker! Ah, no. That's where the GPS that the system relies upon jumps into action again. It can tell you are on a train and will let you text your little heart away. If you have been on an Amtrak lately, you know that you can track your every moment on the trip.

Okay, but how about when your airplane lands and you are taxiing to the gate and you need to text? You can't wait five minutes? Nice try, Alec Baldwin.

Eric Holder Finally Cares for U.S.: March 6, 2012

I really don't like or respect AG Eric Holder. His views and actions against several of our states trying to actually fortify our laws against illegal immigration are appalling. Likewise, his agency's actions trying to allow voter fraud is shameful. I.D.? I don't need no stinkin' I.D. That's our chief law enforcement official.

But, but, but. Why are we Republicans blasting him for smoking American-born terrorists like Anwar al-Awlaki five months ago in Yemen with a drone missile? The only thing I am ticked about is we don't have it in slow-motion HD.

Libertarians, like Mars native, Ron Paul, complain that Holder's actions violate due process. Well, I DO like the process: hunt these bastards down wherever they are and light them up.

Obama Down on the Farm...Kids: April 26, 2012

The lunatics in the Obama Administration are now completely in charge, even if it means, oddly, it's going to hurt the President's re-election chances. Case in point: A proposal from the Obama Aministration to prevent farm kids from doing farm chores on their family farm. That's right; our Department of Labor wants to apply child-labor laws to children working on family farms. Under the proposed rules, children under 18 could no longer work "in the storing, marketing, and transporting of farm product raw materials."

Growing up in Iowa with my dad in the livestock feed business, I was constantly on farms with him. Heck, once we helped one of his customers castrate a couple hundred baby pigs and relished in the bounty of rocky mountain oysters that evening for dinner. (Hopefully, the reader is not getting queasy.) Anyhow, if you know anything about family farms, the "storing, marketing, and transporting" of farm raw products pretty much sums up everything that is done on a farm – by the farmer and his kids. Perhaps, this is another example of Obama's "all of the above strategy."

Obviously, Labor Secretary Hilda Solis—born in inner-city Los Angeles—is just looking after the little whippersnappers who are undoubtedly being subjected to Chinese-style sweatshop servitude by the old man. "Junior, get yer tuckus over to the barn and grab me a bucket of anthrax 'fore I beat you two sides of Sunday!" Yeah, that happens. Not.

Oh, says Solis, and no more of that silly 4H and FFA (Future Farmers of America) learnin' about the farm business; we've got a 90-hour official Federal Government training program you need to complete before you are "qualified" to be a farmer. I can just see the course work:

1) The Migrant Worker Tragedy in America in the 1930s
2) The Grapes of Wrath
3) Organic Farming 101
4) Organic Farming 202
5) Why the Farmville app is the Real Deal
6) Why We Should All Be Vegans
7) Sparing Cattle and Swine: God's Gift (if there is a god)
8) Alternative Energy Sources Farms Should Employ and How Diesel is Killing the Planet.

And the politics of this all? I am sure Obama's liberal, urban base will finally breathe a sigh of relief now that those kiddies down on the farm are safe and will feel even better as they pack their Whole Foods recycled bags with bounty from farms that are finally truly wholesome. And I am certain that farm families in Iowa, Ohio, Indiana, Nebraska, and other farming states will equally applaud this gallant measure. Right.

Courage? May 5, 2013

Official Washington was shocked Sunday when President Obama did not call Boston bombing terror suspect Dzhokhar Tsarnaev and congratulate him for his "courage" in telling the FBI that he and his dead brother were motivated by "anger at the United States over the wars in Iraq and Afghanistan" and thus finally pinning the blame on George W.

Bush for the horror in Boston. Apparently, Mr. Obama's "courage" plaudits are limited to one-a-week, and Jason Collins was the lucky recipient for having the "courage" to break the barrier (really?) of gay men playing professional basketball. (If you haven't seen the movie, *42*, do, and then ask yourself if Collins' "courage" doesn't completely cheapen the word when you see what Jackie Robinson had to put up with breaking a real barrier.)

Meanwhile, Washington, D.C. government officials were busy breaking another barrier: driver's licenses for illegal aliens, oops, undocumented workers. Yessiree, the clowns consistently in the race with Detroit for "Worst Public Servants of All Time," led by Mayor Vincent "Constantly on the FBI Radar" Gray, have introduced a bill to grant those-not-in-this-country-by-legal-means (pant!) a driver's license for "safety" reasons.

At first, I thought this was a stroke of genius. Fake out the illegals into thinking they are getting something good and then wham, busted; back to their home country. Authorities often do this to bust dead-beat dads; say they've won something and then the real jackpot is pay up or primetime in the hoosegow. But, no such luck.

The D.C. geniuses really do want to give these folks driver's licenses. Oh, there is a catch: they have to show proof of insurance to get said license. Here, however, is the beauty of the plan. If these "undocumented workers" take up the offer and first get a slip of paper that says they have insurance and then successfully get a driver's license, they will have two documents and are thus no longer "undocumented" workers. What, therefore, shall we call them? What a world! What a world!

How about LIDIAs? Legal and Insured Driving Illegal Aliens.

Abortion: Taking It to the Streets: July 9, 2013

Back here in D.C. after a glorious week in Northern Michigan, I was struck that as I walked to my office, a smattering of homeless folks and young ladies in pink shirts with clipboards were on literally every corner.

"Sir," one such pink lady cheerfully called to me, "can I talk to you a minute about women's rights?"

I normally don't engage, but with sweat dripping down the back of my neck today I decided to go for it. "Okay," I said, "if I can ask you a question first." She smiled and said sure.

"You work for Planned Parenthood, right?" (It's not that I am intuitive: her pink shirt had the organization emblazoned on the front.) "Can we talk about the rights of the little unborn girl—a woman—in her mother's womb?"

Her smile was instantly gone as she struggled to come up with a response until finally resorting to the "right to safe and affordable abortions" as a "woman's health issue."

"Really" I countered. "Isn't killing an unborn girl in the womb of an otherwise healthy woman the ultimate 'woman's health issue'?"

By now, the cheery young lady was ticked, and the clichés continued, only this time with a touch of venom. "Listen, a man shouldn't be able to determine what a woman can or can't do with her body."

"So, why then did you ask me if I wanted to talk about women's rights?"

She walked away, and I headed to the office, passing a homeless guy I see almost every day. "Hey, got any spare change?" he asked as he finished a 16-ounce can of breakfast beer. I threw him a couple of quarters (all I had) and walked on, trying to decide which encounter was sadder: A broken man with no hope and no home, or a young mind peddling misleading marketing for an organization that, by its own records, performed more than 330,000 abortions last year and almost one million over the past three years.

IRS, NSA, and Justice: The Real Vamps and Zombies! June 23, 2013

Civil war in Syria. Riots in Egypt. Riots in Libya. Riots in Turkey. Riots in Brazil. Brazil? Thought they were rocking? Occupy Wall Street. Occupy Washington, D.C. Occupy Detroit; as lame as it was. Is the world going mad? Perhaps, and Hollywood is fanning the fires.

How else can you explain that the biggest phenomenon in moviemaking over the past five or so years is supposedly real people who are actually vampires, wolves, or zombies? Cripes, even Brad Pitt has gotten into the mix with *World War Z*.

I truly miss the days of true annihilation of the world from the nuclear threat: bombs were real, and the Russkies and the Yankees hated each other to the point of extinction despite joining forces saving the world from Nazi aggression not so long ago.

But now, alas, we have to manufacture an otherworldly force to get us what? Actually, the first mention of vampires in print is reportedly around 1801, long before anyone conceived of the "bomb." But why are we so fearful or enthralled by the undead? Sorry, I haven't seen one yet. Oh wait, I watched Joan Rivers on cable the other night; my bad. Blood-sucking vampires don't really exist, do they? Oh damn, you're right; there's the IRS (who only come out at "Right"), the NSA, and our Justice League, er, Department.

Perhaps Hollywood doesn't need to make us fearful of contrived enemies when we have so many real ones. Now, I am truly scared.

Anthony Weiner Not the "Nuttiest" Person in NY After All: August 13, 2013

Two legal decisions Monday coincidentally created a new low for political correctness in this country. Not surprisingly, the decisions were handed down in two of the biggest hotbeds of liberalism – California and Weinerland. The decisions could screw up school kids in California, and

will most certainly lead to even more of the bullying it purports to stop
with the law; while the Big Apple ruling will simply lead to an increase in
murders or other crimes against, again, the people it is trying to "help." In
this case, blacks and Hispanics.

An Empire State judge ruled that New York's "Stop, Question, and
Frisk" police tactic is racially discriminatory and needs to be severely
modified or scrapped all together. This, despite the fact those reportedly
discriminated against represent the very people who the program has
spared from being victims of crimes.

Last month, New York Police Commissioner Ray Kelly wrote a jaw-
dropping op-ed in *The Wall Street Journal*. Parts of it are included below
and should be required reading for anyone offering an opinion on this
reckless ruling by the judge.

Wrote Kelly: "Since 2002, the New York Police Department has
taken tens of thousands of weapons off the street through proactive
policing strategies. The effect this has had on the murder rate is
staggering. In the eleven years before Mayor Michael Bloomberg took
office, there were thirteen thousand two hundred twelve murders in New
York City. During the eleven years of his administration, there have been
five thousand eight hundred forty-nine. That's seven thousand three
hundred eighty-three lives saved—and if history is a guide, they are
largely the lives of young men of color.

"So far this year, murders are down 29 percent from the fifty-year low
achieved in 2012, and we've seen the fewest shootings in two decades.

"To critics, none of this seems too much matter. Sidestepping the fact
that these policies work, they continue to allege that massive numbers of
minorities are stopped and questioned by police for no reason other than
their race.

"Never mind that in each of the city's seventy-six police precincts, the
race of those stopped highly correlates to descriptions provided by victims
or witnesses to crimes. Or, that in a city of eight and a half million people,

protected by nineteen thousand six hundred officers on patrol (out of a total uniformed staff of thirty-five thousand), the average number of stops we conduct is less than one per officer per week."

So, the recklessness of one judge has immediately put hundreds if not thousands of New Yorkers in harm's way, with most being blacks and Hispanics. In a rare bit of sanity, New York Mayor Michael Bloomberg assailed the ruling and promised an appeal. Here's one time we should all hope the Nanny Mayor gets his way.

Meanwhile on the left coast, Governor Jerry "Moonbeam" Brown has signed a law that permits school kids who consider themselves transgender to use whichever restroom they want. So, if tomorrow Sam feels more like a Samantha, he can relieve himself in the girls' john; or is that jill? What's more, if the new "Samantha" wants to try out for the girls' lacrosse team, he, er, "she" can. Oh, it gets worse. Sam perhaps couldn't make the boys' basketball team at five foot ten, but at that height "Samantha" would likely be one of the tallest "girls" on the team and could take the spot of a girl who actually thinks she's a girl.

The politically correct silliness in the silliest of states is "designed" in part to stop discrimination against transgendered youth and stop the bullying this huge part of the population (Not!) is facing. My guess is it will do neither and could very well backfire. Consider this plausible scenario: freshman Sam-turned-Samantha enters the girls' toilet, also being used by senior Bobby's sister Kate. Bobby sees this, confronts "Samantha" after school, and tells him, uh, her (sorry) to either knock it off (bullying in the view of the PC Police) or he beats the snot out of Samantha.

Or, what if Johnny thinks he's a boy (because he is) and goes in the girls' toilet to get some low-rent thrills. When confronted, all he needs to say is that he's a girl trapped in a boy's body and Jerry Brown's new law protects this pervert; no punishment, just "understanding."

I guess, in the end, disgraced former Congressman Anthony Weiner is just the tip (sorry, had to) of what is becoming a very deranged world. As the late Slim Pickens said in *Blazing Saddles*: "I am depressed."

Al Gore's Nightmare: September 17, 2013

The protector of the planet – no, not Vladimir Putin this time – but rather the Environmental Protection Agency, officially announced this week that the coal industry has crossed a "red line" as the agency labels coal-fired power plants, even the newest and cleanest, as WMDs, thus assuring their demise. And none-too-soon seeing what is just around the corner.

To pull off this attack, the generals at EPA have had to redefine science by declaring carbon dioxide (CO2) as a pollutant, for which EPA is all-wise and all-powerful. It's kind of like how we liked Saddam Hussein when he was helping us against the pesky Iranians, but then hated him a few years later and hung him.

For those of you who were sleeping in chemistry class, CO2 is that nasty stuff that comes out of your pie hole when you exhale, an unfortunately necessary component of breathing. It is so toxic that when plants absorb it they grow and flourish and exhale oxygen, um, for people, Fido, and Arnold the Pig. When it's added to water, it makes club soda. Our beer would be flat without it.

But trust me, at the end of the day it is a heinous and silent killer. Why? Because when it's not making our crops grow, it causes global warming. Oh, snap, we don't call it that anymore. We use the term climate change. What's that, we don't use that anymore either? Nope. Now it's "carbon pollution" thanks to the Pinocchios at the EPA.

But what's in a name. If the "scientists" in Obama's EPA say CO2 is bad, it's bad. Of course, that depends on what the definition of "is" is. And so, Mr. Obama's energy "policy" goes from "all of the above" to "ABC" or "All But Coal." (Actually, that's a misnomer too, as nuclear power is another WMD according to the Administration, we ain't never going to build the Keystone pipeline and fracking is a war crime.)

Don't get me wrong: the technology in today's newest coal-burning plants took some prodding over the years, but EPA's new mandate is unachievable according to industry experts. (If you don't believe the industry sources, and they aren't, ahem, blowing smoke, we will soon see it in either the closing of plants, the halting of new construction, or an astronomical increase in the price of electricity. Stay tuned.)

But just around the corner next week is not what will be seen by rational and intelligent people as an "inconvenient truth," but what the White House and its EPA will ignore or attempt to spin when the news hits. (I can already see the smirk on Jay Carney's face.)

A new study in the journal *Nature Climate Change*, found that of the 117 computer models used to predict climate over the past 20 years, only three correctly predicted temperature movement. That's an F-minus-minus for those keeping score at home. The average of the 114 failing models predicted an average rise of .30 degrees Celsius per decade. The actual rise was less than half of that over the two decades of the study. The journal said that "even more striking" was that over the past 15 years, the modelers overbid their warming showcases by 400 percent.

Next week, the premiere global warming/climate change/carbon pollution lunatics, the United Nations Intergovernmental Panel for Climate Change, will release their fifth assessment draft report and is reportedly ready to soften its claim that the sky is falling when it comes to the warming of Mother Earth.

Looks like the only whale in danger of a meltdown will be Al Gore.

Takata and NHTSA: Dumb and Dumber: December 15, 2014
Takata airbag modules on Honda vehicles have killed at least six people. If NHTSA has its way—demanding a nationwide recall of

Takata's faulty airbag systems—the number of dead people will most likely increase. WTF? Stay with me.

What we have here is a major automotive supplier with its head in the sand, hoping its crisis will go away, and perhaps the most-cover-your-ass U.S. government agency not only thinking stupidly, but perhaps, deadly. NHTSA is going to court to force the Japanese seat belt and airbag system company to make their recall a nationwide affair. Takata, rightfully, has refused to do so, instead focusing on those customers in harm's way in southern hot and humid states where the defective airbags seem more prone to problems.

But Takata has shamefully put its customers in harm's way. Oh, not the real driving public, but their actual customers, namely Honda and Chrysler, to name two. Honda has announced it will recall its vehicles with the nasty Takata airbag modules NATIONWIDE. Honda is in a tough spot. I understand it, but their action may actually divert Takata replacement parts for Honda vehicles where they are most needed to a Honda consumer in cold, non-humid northern Minnesota. Why?

The other day, Chrysler said it will focus on the hot, humid states in replacing Takata airbag modules in Dodge, Jeep, and Chrysler vehicles. Good for my former company. They are actually putting their customers first, but will, no doubt, receive a ration of sh-t from the plaintiff's bar and the supposed "safety advocates" that want a "nationwide" action only to load their coffers and the courtrooms.

Bottom Line: If NHTSA succeeds in court and makes Takata supply the whole country with better airbag modules before satisfying the true, scientific needs of those in the hot, humid climates, the risk of people needlessly dying will increase, as those truly in harm's way will have to wait.

It is the Ford/Firestone tire crisis, circa 2000-2001, all over again. I know. I lived it.

Sometimes, It Hertz: December 16, 2014

One bright light out of the disaster of my time at Ford Motor Company was the gift of my lifetime membership to the platinum club of Hertz rental car company (then owned by Ford). Trust me, it's cool: they bring my car to the baggage claim, and when I return to the airport, they have an associate jump in my rental and again drive me back to the gate. It is "white glove" all the way, and "almost" lets me forgive Ford for firing me.

But then, the folks at Hertz blew it. I am sure I am not the first. I rented a car in Los Angeles. I paid extra to make sure I had a navigation system in the car as LA is a spider web of freeways. Hertz's signature "Nav" system is branded "Never Lost." If you have ever used it, you will grin to know that frequent travelers call the Hertz system "Always Lost."

I entered my destination – the LA Convention Center – from my friend's driveway just south of LAX. Never Lost efficiently guided my Chevy Impala rental so efficiently, that it put me on express lanes limited to High Occupancy Vehicles despite the fact I was driving solo. As quickly as I could, I jumped my rental off the restricted lanes, but alas, not fast enough for California's highway cameras. (Oh, the government folks in California are incredibly competent in levying fines, taxes, etc.) This happened on three different occasions thanks to my Hertz Never Lost.

One month later came the message from on high: actually Hertz. Well, not actually. It came from Hertz Processing Services. I owed them $30 for "processing" the fines that were coming my way for "their" navigation system putting me on restricted lanes in Los Angeles. Naturally, I handled the news with class and calm. I called the Hertz Platinum Members line and talked with, let's just call her "LyingSackofDooDoo," or "LSD." I explained my plight. LSD had been well trained in the practice of responsibility avoidance.

"We don't own the navigation system," she said, despite the fact that it is called HERTZ NEVER LOST!!!!!!!!

171

I tried to remain calm and take her through a logical discussion of how they market the navigation feature, and how it had, ahem, steered me wrong, but ol' LSD was in a parallel universe. And then, she pulled out this gem: "Well, no one forced you to use the system."

No one forced me to use the system? Wow, a new level of customer dis-service. Of course, I remained in check (for about two seconds). Thankfully, my head did not explode (completely) and I called Hertz again and got someone on the line that actually gave a damn about customer care. They waved the "fee" that Hertz was "processing" against me thanks to their pathetic Never Lost navigation system.

I still don't know how much in fines The City of Angels is going to sock me for Hertz's mistake. I am certain the company will step up to the plate on my behalf. I'm sure ol' LSD will take care of it.

And then monkeys will fly out of my butt and it will Hertz.

The Cuban "Situation" From My Outraged Cuban Friend 52 Years "Off the Boat": December 18, 2014

The day President Obama decided part of his "Hope and Change" agenda included him single-handedly "normalizing" relations with the brutal Castro regime in Cuba, I reached out to an old friend and business colleague who escaped Cuba for the U.S. as a teenager 52 years ago. When we had talked about his experience I had remembered he had come to this country with just a few bucks in his pocket.

We had not talked in years, but we had recently connected on Facebook. My question for him was simple: what do you think about President Obama's "re-start" (Ha! Sorry, Hillary) efforts on U.S.-Cuban relations? I wanted to get the perspective of someone "who was there," instead of blowing a lot of smoke from this Iowa-born kid. Below is my Cuban friend's response. (Note: to protect my friend, I have edited out some references that make it easier to identify him. Many of my former colleagues will know in seconds who he is.)

Hi, Jason,

Great to hear from you. We are in Paris at the moment, spending the holidays with friends. Back in (Colorado) in late January.

Your recollection of my arrival in the U.S. at the tender age of 16 was pretty accurate, except for the amount of money I had with me. It was zero. I mean zero; not even loose change. If you want the short story version, I will send you a copy of an article I wrote for a (Colorado town) newspaper for their Thanksgiving Day issue in 2012 to mark the 50th anniversary of my arrival.

People always ask if I came from Cuba by myself, and my standard answer is: "No, it was worse than that; I came with my younger brother!"

With respect to the recent White House announcement on Cuba, it is hard to know where to start. I have been convinced for a long time that Obama is the worst, most inept President who ever resided in the White House, but I never expected something so moronic to come out of this Administration. First, by our government's actions today, we have announced to the world that if you want something out of us that you cannot get any other way, capture one of our citizens, put him in jail, treat him miserably and then, trade him for whatever you want.

Second, we are dealing with a country which is on the list of states that support terrorism. Just a few months ago, they were caught red-handed exporting MiGs and other weaponry to North Korea, hidden in a cargo of sugar cane.

Third, Obama says that our policy of isolation has failed to accomplish the objective of empowering Cubans to build an open and democratic country. That was never the objective of the policy. The trade embargo imposed on Cuba in 1961 by President Kennedy was in protest over the illegal expropriation of American property in Cuba. The Cuban government has always known what they had to do to get the embargo removed. Moreover, the policy of engagement announced is what every other country has been using, and they too have been unable to accomplish the "objective."

The reason? Very simple answer: the Cuban constitution forbids any efforts to "build an open and democratic country." You go to jail for that. You cannot publish a newspaper, you cannot run for office under any political party which is not the PCC (Partido Comunista de Cuba), you cannot stage a protest, and you cannot say publicly anything contrary to government policy.

Alan Gross, the fellow that was released by the Cubans today, was incarcerated and almost killed for distributing devices to connect to the Internet. And yet, Obama has the gall to say today that Cuba has one of the lowest internet penetration rates (5 percent) in the world. No kidding! It is illegal to connect to the internet in Cuba. Obama expects that "(U.S.) telecommunications providers will be allowed to set up the necessary mechanisms … to provide internet services." They already exist, set up by the Europeans. The problem is that Cubans are not allowed to use them! They are only for the government and for foreign residents.

I see this announcement as a problem for the Democrats in 2016. Hillary Clinton will lose Florida (and possibly New Jersey) while Jeb Bush's candidacy may gain from it. Already the Cuban-Americans in Congress have denounced the new policy, including my friend Senator Menendez (D-NJ), who is the Chairman of the Foreign Relations Committee.

In 1961, the embargo was imposed through executive action. In 1996, it was codified into law after the Cuban air force shot down two unarmed planes which were distributing leaflets over Havana. The leaflets, by the way, were copies of the U.N. Declaration of Human Rights which, ironically, Cuba signed in 1948 when it was adopted. Because it is now the law of the land, the so-called Helms-Burton Act cannot be changed by Obama without first getting Congress to modify or repeal it; not very likely in a Republican-dominated Congress.

Moreover, the Cuban government knows the conditions needed to suspend the application of the law: 1) No Castros in the government, 2) Freedom of the press; 3) Allow other political parties to exist with free elections. No amount of "diplomatic relations" or tourist visits will get the Castro-led Cuban government to do any of those three things.

I could go on, but it is getting late. Let me know if you want to see the story about the day I left Cuba.

Your friend (I am withholding his name for privacy purposes).

Mitt and Putin ONE; Obama and Hillary ZERO: January 30, 2015

Every PR person worth their salt knows that timing is not just everything; sometimes, it's the only thing. Consider what happened today on opposite sides of Mother Earth. In the U.S., Mitt Romney rocked the political world by abandoning what seemed like a sure run for the White House in which he was leading in every major poll of Republican hopefuls. Thousands of miles away, Russian-supported troops took over a town in Eastern Ukraine.

Two-plus years ago, President Obama cockily mocked then-candidate Mitt Romney in a debate because Romney had the "audacity" to suggest that Russia was our country's biggest geo-political threat. Earlier, of course, Obama and Obama alone had "fixed" the problem with Russia when he whispered sweet nothings into the ear of Putin's bag man, then President Dmitry "Can I buy a vowel" Medvedev: "I need space. This is my last election. After my election, I have more flexibility." Medvedev replied, "I understand. I will transmit this information to Vladimir." Transmit? Wow, spoken as only a true Russian Commie can.

Obama had every right to be confident in his ability to be the quintessential world leader. (Not!) After all, earlier he had sent his Secretary of State to Moscow where Hillary pushed a "Reset" button, ala Staples. Famously, the Russian word for reset is *perezagruzka*, but ol' Hill had a button with the word *peregruzka* on it. Russian Foreign Minister Sergey Lavrow "playfully" told the Secretary her button meant "overcharged." Mrs. Clinton then, infamously, started to cackle like a hyena on crack.

Sadly, as we all know now, Romney was right all along, despite Obama's smart-assed diss. And Putin now knows how weak we are as a global force under our President—so much so he can do what he pleases in his backyard and support all kinds of bad actors—from Iran, to Syria, to North Korea, and now to Greece. And with each new day, the world gets a lot scarier because Hillary botched a "reset," and Obama has more "flexibility." I suppose that bending over backwards to help the bad guys is a sign of flexibility…or, more likely, the lack of a spine.

I hope that, as a country, we don't make the same mistake in 2016 that too many made in 2012, even after the hope-and-change-turned-folly of 2008 was staring voters in the face.

Operation OverLOAD: No Caliphate Left Behind: February 16, 2015

Seventy-one years ago, thousands of brave American, British, and Canadian soldiers stormed the beaches of Nazi-occupied Normandy on D-Day, also known as Operation Overlord. Notice I didn't say "Germany-occupied Normandy." Germany, itself, was being occupied by fascists led by Hitler. American and Russian soldiers later freed the German people with the victory.

Well, it's time to pay back the IOU, Germany: Join the U.S., France, Egypt, Saudi Arabia, Jordan, Britain, Canada, and Australia (oh hell, maybe even the Russians) and others to stop the terror of the Islamic State (ISIS, ISIL or whatever these barbarians call themselves). Shock and Awe on Steroids.

But, some question, who is the enemy in Iraq, Syria, Libya, Nigeria, etc.? Answer: It's the "random folks" firing at you or running away. Pretty simple, especially with our intelligence capabilities. Think about it, our Smartphones and Smart TVs monitor us now.

At D-Day, we had no satellites in space or the incredible intelligence capabilities we have today. But, we had one thing: balls. Let's find the former (balls, and yes, ovaries) and use the latter (intelligence) to find these scum and wipe them off the map. If the free nations of our world get together, we can do this in months, not years. Zero tolerance. Zero prisoners.

Let's call it the T-Day Invasion. The "T" of course stands for Terrorism and let's codename it Operation OverLOAD…No Caliphate Left Behind.

Bibi Wins — NetanYAHOO! March 17, 2015

It appears now the world is a bit safer…for a few months. Despite President Obama's overt, sadly pathetic and possibly illegal covert attempts (more on this later) to cause Israeli Prime Minister Benjamin Netanyahu to lose re-election, it appears Bibi has survived. Tonight and hopefully tomorrow it is NetanYAHOO!!!!!! And payback will be a "bitch" toward this Administration. As it should.

Bibi came to the Congress of his country's most powerful friend and warned the world about a potentially nuclear Iran—a country that since 1979 has stated a chief goal is the destruction of Israel. He didn't just sway America and Congress—he MOVED us and put President Obama and the world on notice. Netanyahu warned in his address that Israel will stand alone to defend itself if it must. I felt shame when Bibi voiced those words. When should America let Israel stand alone? The answer is never.

Netanyahu has survived…maybe…but I am still not sure what "our President's Men" have up their sleeves on the ground in Tel Aviv in an ACORN-like "get out the vote and vote often" attempt in Israel against Netanyahu. I assume Team Bibi is solid when they think he has the race

177

sewed up. I sure hope we don't wake up tomorrow with a "Dewey Wins" headline in the Jewish Times.

So back to President Obama and his "negotiation partners" in Iran—ah, excuse me, I mean Secretary of State John Kerry's Iranian mullahs at the nuke table. You "folks," as the President likes to say, are on notice. America and our friends won't believe your BS. Our President has failed diplomatically and this country, the Saudis and, suddenly, our new friends in Egypt won't stand for his garbage. The gig is up, the news is out, we've finally found you—our President is the renegade.

Mr. President, your "community organization" effort in Israel failed. This is the real world and you are supposed to be the leader of it. Act like it, and Move On (oh damn, did I just say that?) And good luck with the Iranian nuke talks. You will fail miserably. Thank God. And, thank Bibi.

The Real Enemy of Autonomous Cars: The Tax Man Near You: March 19, 2015

Autonomous cars are all the rage with the media these days, especially the non-auto enthusiast media who know little if anything about automobiles and even less about transportation issues as a whole. I have not seen one aggressive and critical analysis of the downside or the unintended consequences of turning our nation's fleet of automobiles driver-less.

Don't get me wrong: the idea of autonomous cars is a great idea IF it can be pulled off. But those saying autonomous cars are right around the corner are not saying how far that "corner" is down the road. And, importantly, they are not considering who will fight tooth-and-nail to keep autonomous cars a pipe dream. More on that issue later as I see the "autonomous haters" as a major obstacle.

First, why are autonomous cars NOT right around the corner? It is wonderfully true that automobiles are becoming "autonomous" bit-by-bit. Air bags are one of the early autonomous technologies to take hold and work to near-perfection (with the exception of Takata air bags.) To work, all air bags need is a frontal or near-frontal collision. The driver does nothing else. Hell, they have done enough.

Since air bags, we have seen automatic adaptive cruise control, radar braking, lane-change warning systems and other collision-avoidance technologies like rearview, side, and frontal cameras that are working almost flawlessly—and saving lives and injuries. And heck, if you put your headlights on "auto on" you need to do nothing further to illuminate your ride.

But the holy grail of a completely autonomous car (read: self-driving) is a much, much bigger hurdle for a variety of reasons. First up: the size of the current "car park" or the number of vehicles in this country that require a driver to do the, well, driving. According to a recent article in *The Los Angeles Times*, there are around 253 million cars and trucks operating today on U.S. roads. How will autonomous cars interact with 253 million other autos? How can a passenger (in the driver's seat) react fast enough to a bonehead in non-autonomous car or semi-tractor trailer driving dangerously? Will the autonomous car be that good to overcome the non-autonomous idiot?

Completely transforming our "transportation system" has many dead soldiers scattered alongside our "roads." In the 1990s, there was a major push to make more and more vehicles capable of being fueled solely by compressed natural gas or CNG. The potential was great for economics and the environment. It fell flat with the exception of large fleets of commercial vehicles. Why? Completely revamping our fueling system (gasoline) was impractical, considering the millions of gas stations seemingly everywhere. Plus, consumers were (wrongly) concerned about having natural gas tanks strapped to their cars. Oh, and the size of the tanks took up too much passenger room and the vehicle range was limited when smaller tanks were used. Oh yeah, the oil industry didn't like it either.

With CNG's less-than-stellar success—virtually none in passenger cars—the U.S. Government, the auto industry, and, unfortunately, the buying public got suckered into an alternative – for the environment, supposedly. Bursting onto the landscape were vehicles that could run on one of the most subsidized fuels of all-time: ethanol. Soon, a vast majority of cars could run (poorly) on a combination of 85 percent ethanol and 15 percent gasoline (known as E85). But, the farmers in Iowa and other corn states (the source of ethanol) loved the new fuel as they pocketed billions. Well, Americans really didn't buy into E85 for two reasons: it was relatively costly due to its poor mileage compared with pure gasoline, and it was tough on engines. Few used E85 because their cars could more easily run on E10 or 10 percent ethanol and 85 percent gasoline. Like CNG, E85 bombed for consumers, yet to this day, E10 is virtually everywhere and continues to bolster the ethanol lobby. Shamefully.

The good news for ethanol was that you could sell it at "normal" gas stations—an infrastructure fully-developed and running smoothly. Not so much for the sweetheart fuel next up on the horizon: hydrogen via a fuel cell. Back in the late 1990s we were just "years away" from fully developing fuel cell cars. Heck, General Motors even hired a real rocket scientist to lead their program. It made sense as fuel cell had first been used by the U.S. space program in the 1950s and '60s. The rocket scientist soon departed GM, and the pipe dream of fuel cell automobiles using hydrogen soon evaporated. (Pun intended.)

Why these analogies? Completely transforming a sophisticated and mature transportation system gets people all excited quickly without much thought of the reality of the endeavor or the consequences of the change. Which brings me to perhaps the biggest hurdle against the driver-less car and why I believe it is decades, perhaps 30-to-50 years away. That hurdle, which I haven't seen discussed much up to now, are municipalities that rely heavily on driver errors and violations to fund their budgets. Last week, *Wall Street Journal* columnist Bret Stephens wrote a fascinating

180

article explaining why the recent DOJ report on racist enforcement of traffic laws in Ferguson, Missouri, was all wet. Stephens argued that Ferguson cops were acting no differently than cops all across the country in black, Hispanic, and white neighborhoods. The cops are serving as "The Tax Man" and filling the financially-struggling city and state coffers with as many traffic violations as possible.

When we drive from our home in North Carolina to see our kids in Washington, D.C., there are ALWAYS state troopers with radar guns the last two miles on I-95 in North Carolina and the first two miles inside the Virginia border. Think of it as the "last chance" and the "first chance" to collect taxes.

In Washington, D.C., this "taxation without representation" has created one of the most controversial and corrupt trafficking systems in the country, with hundreds if not thousands of remote cameras clocking motorists (often wrongly) for a variety of offenses, most of which are speeding. A study found that many, many times, the charges are flat-out bogus. But boy do the folks in D.C. government love the windfall of cash the cameras have raked in. More and more cities and towns are using these "camera cops."

Self-driving cars would presumably shut off the spigot if they become widespread. Self-driving cars won't speed, won't use the HOV lanes improperly, or make a left turn when the sign clearly says "No Left Turn." Self-driving cars won't go the wrong way on a One-Way Street and they won't drive carelessly or recklessly. Importantly, they won't collide. All these things will necessarily financially impact municipalities for the worse. Egad, they may be forced to actually develop sound, balanced budgets or cut-off funding for social needs, public safety, and other expenses under fire.

No argument these days is complete without a stupid argument against the autonomous car. I say this because as I and my companies have fought for mandatory seat belt usage for more than two decades now, we oftentimes were faced with a silly "what if." What if, the morons opined, I am driving on a bridge over a river and the bridge collapses, plunging my car into the water? I don't want to be trapped in my car thanks to the seat belt." Oh, that happens all the time, doesn't it? When it comes to self-driving cars, here's the silly argument: At 3 a.m., my wife's water breaks and we rush to the hospital but our self-driving car will only drive the speed limit and it will take too long to get there. My wife and new baby will be put in harm's way. Silly I know, but I had to share it.

In the end, the march toward autonomous cars is a great thing. Let's continue the progress made already in various technologies now almost common place. But, let's get realistic about the complete transformation that is NOT "just around the corner."

My Friend Has ALS and You Can Help #FDAhope4ALS: March 29, 2015

A friend in need is a friend indeed. Well, maybe like you, I have a friend in need and, indeed, I need your help. My friend's name is Fred Standish. He has ALS, also known as Lou Gehrig's disease. I am not asking for donations. I am asking you to go a website and sign a petition to tell the U.S. FDA to allow a promising drug call GM604 to be approved for usage in helping ALS patients like my friend Fred before it is too late.

If you read my first book (no, I am not pimping it right at this time; after all, the day is young!) you might remember the adventures of me and Fred in our days at Nissan North America. I had moved my family back to Motown because the schools stunk in SoCal, and Fred and I were the lone PR guys in our technical center out in Farmington Hills. Well, here's how the story goes in the book:

"…Back in my office, Fred Standish flew to my desk. We were the only Nissan PR guys in Detroit. A former reporter for the Associated Press, Fred had gone to the 'dark side' of PR years before to finally earn a decent living. I grabbed Fred months earlier by the scruffs. 'You are the

182

laziest PR guy I have ever seen,' I said bluntly, assessing his tenure at Nissan. 'And, I think this position is underpaid. Here's the deal: you step up your game and I will increase your salary 50 percent. Or, I fire you. Your choice.' Fred paused, 'I'll take door number one.' We laughed, and he became one of the finest, hardest working, and smartest PR guys in the industry."

My friend Fred's plight and that of hundreds of thousands of ALS patients is another reason for me to scratch my head and say WTF? It seems that states and some municipalities are falling over themselves to approve the legal use of "Rocky Mountain High" marijuana (and not just for medicinal purposes), yet promising breakthrough drugs for deadly diseases get the slow-walk or make the patients spend gobs of money flying to countries willing to let the person inflicted make their own life choices in terms of treatment. But the drug has side effects, the bureaucrats say. What, like living? Geez, watch any 60-second drug ad on TV and the narrator talks about the benefits of the drug for about seven seconds and then the disclaimer kicks in telling all the side effects for the remaining 53 seconds.

Okay, enough bellyaching. Now to the action section of this blog. Please go to www.change.org and see the ALS petition on the home page. If you sign on, you will join more than 500,000 people telling the FDA to approve GM604. And if you want to learn more about ALS, go to www.alsa.org. There are also ALS organizations in many of the states. If you send out a message to your friends, include the hashtag, #FDAhope4ALS.

In an hour, Betsy and I are off to St. Nick's in Wilmington. If you know anything about Greek Orthodox folks, we light candles the moment we enter the church. You throw down a buck, grab a skinny candle, light it, and pray for someone or something, although it doesn't work for MegaMillions or Powerball. Trust me. Or, you can pony up five bucks and get a "big ass" candle that is placed near the altar. I was GOING TO spend a Lincoln today, praying for the Spartans against Lou-ah-ville. But now that seems kind of petty. My candle is for Fred <u>and</u> the hope that you will sign the petition and send this message along to your family and friends urging them to do the same. Sorry, Izzo, you only get a dollar candle today—fair warning, have those boys ready to play! Go Spartans! Go Fred!

Wi-Fi Ya Doing That to Me? April, 19, 2015

Last week I was visiting my little brother Greg and his family in Johnston, Iowa, where I was lucky to witness the worst example of bad customer service in the history of this planet. My brother does much of his work out of his home office. All he needs is a chair, a desk, a phone, and a connection to the Internet. Unfortunately, that last essential had been quite "spotty" over the past five or six weeks and was currently "down."

Greg had had enough and called the fine folks at CenturyLink, his Internet provider, who acknowledged that, sure enough, they were having an "outage." Make that "another outage." It seems that over the past weeks, CenturyLink outages at the Vines' home had topped the 22-hour mark in total downtime. My brother remained calm, which for those folks who know the Vines boys, is a rarity in these situations. Not a single profanity was uttered, nor did Greg once raise his voice. However, he indicated that he had had enough and expected some sort of credit on his next bill for the bad performance of CenturyLink's "technology."

Unfortunately, the "customer care" person assisting my brother could not grant any credit. No, that would come from the "Loyalty Department." Greg was transferred, and for the next 17 minutes or so enjoyed a variety of uplifting elevator music. Finally, the "Loyalty" person picked up the line. Let's call her Charlotte, seeing how that was her name. Charlotte listened to my brother's tale of woe and then said she would have to talk with a supervisor in order to approve any type of credit.

So, back to elevator music it was until Charlotte returned with some "good news" for Greg. For all the hassle my brother had experienced, including the 22 hours of outage, CenturyLink was digging deep into its corporate coffers and giving Greg a <u>one dollar and twenty cent</u> credit on his next bill. My brother actually laughed out loud. He asked dear Charlotte, "One dollar and twenty cents. Do you realize how ridiculous that sounds?"

Charlotte would not answer. Perhaps she too was shocked by the putrid nature of a buck-twenty credit for a customer who had experienced repeated outages for a service that cost $150 per month. Or, maybe she just didn't give a damn and was hoping Greg's head would explode and he would offer up a profanity, which—as written in the Geneva Convention—allows frustratingly incompetent service people to hang up.

But Greg didn't take the bait and remained calm. I was in awe of his composure and was on the brink of prideful tears. He continued to speak softly and politely, yet firmly demanding that Charlotte put her supervisor on the line. This, of course, rarely if ever happens as the word "supervisor" comes from a Greek word for coward. I think.

Charlotte finally did, somehow, convince her "supervisor" that a fair settlement would be to credit Greg 10 dollars per month for the next year, thus thwarting my brother's planned action to dump the company once he got a refund. So, in order to get his due, he must experience another year of living dangerously with CenturyLink and their "Forced Loyalty Department."

The Home Depot: You Can Do It. They Can Help...in CODE: April 20, 2015

I love Home Depot. Since I got married 140 years ago—oh, crap, typo, it's been only 28 years—I have spent millions of dollars at the store. What has infuriated my wife over the years is that I go to the big ol' orange home improvement store to buy AN item—rake, hammer, whatever—and come back with a menagerie of s—t I didn't know I needed until the angels at the Home DePauw thankfully put it so conveniently in the aisles I was traveling just to get a furnace filter.

And then (dramatic pause), Home Depot violated my trust. It started out harmlessly. On my birthday, my greeting card from my wife included a Home Depot credit card. "Use this honey," she said, "Cuz you save five percent on every ridiculous purchase you make." The tears flowed. Finally, my wife had embraced my love of the Orange Shrine.

Soon (actually seconds later) I was off to buy tools and other crap I stupidly didn't know I needed to sustain my life. A hummingbird feeder? Aha, I wasn't being graced by these magnificent creatures BECAUSE I offered no incentive. I had been a bird anti-capitalist. Shame on me. A cordless drill with a seven-day charge? Oh, the pain over the years of plugging my drill into an outlet via an extension cord that created so many work hazards. A flashlight that's also a hammer…and a raft?

As I left my shrine with my bootie in tow, I glanced at my receipt. Where was any indication of my five percent discount for using my pristine Home Depot Visa? I couldn't find it, but then the Home Depot wouldn't screw me. It must be in there: I just couldn't see it.

Then, the epiphany. Days later, I was buying a fairly high-ticket item in which the five percent discount would surely keep me on the right side of bankruptcy. As I self-checked-out (a true 2015 phenomenon) I told the "associate" that I would be using MY HOME DEPOT CARD. I swiped it and completed my purchase. When the receipt was spit out, I saw no discount.

"What's the deal?" I asked.

"Oh, you have to specifically say you are using your Home Depot card IN ORDER to get the five percent discount."

"You're sh-tting me?" I classily replied. "Why?"

"Well," she started to explain, somewhat excitedly. "This is a Lowe's thing—the five percent discount when you use their card. We just decided to match it until Lowe's decides to end it."

Her honesty was breathtaking.

"Void this charge, please," I demanded. "I'm heading over to Lowe's. They don't make you talk in code to save a few bucks on a bunch of crap that I will use once and that my wife will kick my ass for buying."

Chapter Eight: Stupid Washington

DC Is Nuttier than Chinese Chicken Salad: January 29, 2012

Mrs. Wisecracker and I moved to Northern Virginia in early November in order to fully experience the indigenous political theater of the absurd. This Sunday morning offered a Metro Washington, D.C. buffet of lunacy.

It was good putting the past week behind us—a week that included a pathetic Congressional hearing featuring foolish elected officials trashing the "exploding" Chevy Volt. The hearing was led by California Congressman Darrell Issa, who has a rap sheet that would make most death row inmates envious. Look it up—including the mysterious fire that destroyed his near-bankrupt business some years ago before he got rich selling car alarms. To be fair, I guess the guy does know something about fires. So sad that a GOPer like me has to thank Maryland Democrat Elijah Cummings for being the lone sane voice on the committee while a host of Republicans embarrassed themselves with petty partisanship.

But today is a new day: just me, my coffee, and the Sunday *Washington Post*.

Let's see, there's an anti-Santorum article, six anti-Gingrich articles, and five pro-Romney articles. All in the A Section. Oh yes, the Left wants Romney in the worst way. And they may succeed.

Diverted from my favorite "Outlook" section, I am confronted with a Page One story entitled: "A debate Gingrich would lose." What piqued my interest was not the title, but rather the subtitle: "Political scientist John Pitney Jr. says against Obama, Newt would be his own worst enemy." Political scientist? I know that "political science" is a college major (my daughter is one), but is there such a thing as a political scientist? Do they have equations, theorems, slide rules, bow ties, or blazers with elbow patches?

I was an economics major. Economics is viewed as the "imperfect science." Its practitioners humbly acknowledge it's as much guess work as it is a science. Political scientist? Give me a break.

Pitney's "scientific analysis" of Gingrich vs. Obama debates is a thinly-veiled shot at everything Newt. He tries to use Newt's past quotes as "scientific evidence" of his vulnerability. But when you read these egregious quotes, you go: "Yep, I agree with that."

Setting aside this rag, I turned my eye toward the TV and Chris "Shiver up My Leg" Matthews' "political science" show, where he and his guests (including Kathleen Parker—fresh off her CNN debacle with Eliot "Client Number 9" Spitzer) called the Newtmeister "totally unelectable." Immediately, they went to a commercial break, which began with a spot for the University of Maryland University College.

University of a university of a college? Yessiree, this is one nutty place.

Washington Weakly: Truants and Killers: February 5, 2012

A Loudoun County (Northern Virginia just outside of the Looney Bin) couple is getting hauled into court for not getting their kids to school on time. The father, Mark Denicore, told *The Washington Post*, "this is the nanny state gone wild." No Marky Mark, references to the "nanny state" are for Tea Party members and others fully aligned against the real nanny state. Your kids have been late to school 30 times since September. You and your wife are idiots—and late—a lot. Go to Target and get a new alarm clock. Jesus, Mary, and Joseph.

Meanwhile in the Beltway, those stinky freaks called Occupy D.C. have been officially evicted by the U.S. Park Police after the latter got a spine transplant. I will truly miss the occupiers. Each day I walked through the formerly pristine McPherson Square on the way to my office. I thankfully inhaled the second-hand smoke from myriad doobies and bongs and usually made a bee-line for the deli once exiting the encampment. The marijuana smoke was helpfully more than just a buzz creator as it actually cloaked the stench of the occupiers as many had not seen any Ivory soap in perhaps months. Oh, and they were incoherent: stoned, stupid, and lazy—nice combo.

Washington was all abuzz about those damn Russians and Chinese. Both countries voted against the resolution at the UN to sanction Syria as it murders its own. First, think about anything that begins with "UN" – unjust, unreliable, unworthy, un f-ing believable: You get my point. I am actually cheering on the Russkies and the ChiComms for being true to their "cause." Think about it: no country has armed Syria greater than Putin's Communist Russia, and no country has murdered more of its own citizens than the criminal leaders in Red China. To chastise Syria for killing its own people would be the height of hypocrisy for these two nations. Thanks for sticking to your ideology. Ahem.

Washington Weakly: Where the Rubbers Meet the Campus: February 12, 2012

It's funny how times have changed. Back in my undergrad days, Phillip Morris used to show up and hand out free miniature packs of smokes. I knew their intent, but hell, free is free. Now, according to our President, Trojans and The Pill will soon be free whether you are Catholic or Atheist.

And insurance companies in charge of this "freedom" are dancing an Irish jig because they know a sexually-active policyholder not impregnated is a cheaper ride (um, er, so to speak). Make that a rider, as in insurance rider. And President Obama gets to save face in light of his latest assault on the U.S. Constitution.

Freedom of religion? Fuggedaboutit! Speaking of the Obama Administration, it is utterly rudderless when it comes to Syria. Last March, Obama was front and center defending his actions against the tyranny of MoMo's Libya, eventually inserting U.S. forces to stop the genocide against the Libyan people. The same thing is happening in Syria, but there is no call for action. Sure, we are getting no help from Putin's Russkies

and the ChiComms—but when did they tell us what to do? Oh, right—
now. Those pesky facts.

Finally: so much for "Miller Time" in the new, free Egypt.
Apparently, the "tolerant" Muslim Brotherhood—oh yeah, the ones that
assassinated Anwar Sadat back in the '80s—want no more of tourists
drinking alcohol while visiting the Pyramids and other sites. Nor do they
want tourist women wearing bikinis on the Egyptian beaches or tourist
couples bathing in the waters together. Talk about a beach slap.

I can't wait for the official Muslim Brotherhood-inspired tourism
advertising campaign: Come to Egypt – Party like it's 350 B.C.

Detroit City Council Loses "Stupidest" Crown: June 14, 2012

Move over Detroit City Council: you've lost it. No, not your right to
act stupidly during Detroit's financial crisis. Nope. You'll be happy to
know that despite your best efforts, you are no longer the worst city
council in America: Washington, D.C.'s gang of morons have nipped you
at the wire for that honor.

The D.C. Council has gone so mental that one member, Marion "The
Bitch Set Me Up" Barry, is lecturing his colleagues on ethics. In the past
few months, two members of the D.C. Council, including the council
leader, have been convicted of felonies and are in the hoosegow. As they
fought yesterday to name an interim "leader," the debate resulted in a
meltdown. One councilman seeking the top post repeatedly referred to
himself in the third person, while another starting sobbing. Meanwhile,
Barry—convicted of smoking crack in 1990 while Mayor of D.C. and later
prosecuted for not filing taxes for eight years—proclaimed that D.C. had
become "the laughingstock of the nation." Ya think? Barry then resorted
to planting his pie hole completely up his southern hemisphere claiming
the council crisis was so serious that "the only more serious (crisis) I can
think of is 9/11." Hmmm.

Sorry, Detroit City Council, you've lost your title, at least for now. But I am certain you'll do your best to get back the crown.

Sanity Strikes Washington, D.C. No Kidding: September 12, 2013
Sanity finally made an appearance in Washington, D.C. No, no, no, not on Capitol Hill or at 1600 Pennsylvania Avenue. It revolved around a local issue with national implications. And it came one day after complete insanity had gripped the District with a "million" Muslims holding a rally on the twelfth anniversary of 9/11.

D.C. Mayor Vince Gray vetoed an amazingly stupid bill passed by a majority of the City Council earlier this summer raising the minimum wage of big box retailers (only) in the city by 50 percent. The bill, officially known as the Large Retailer Accountability Act, had been dubbed the "Walmart Bill" as the retail giant promised to cancel construction of three of the planned six new Walmarts if the bill were signed by the mayor. How come when Democrat-led governing bodies want to stick it to businesses and actually hurt the constituents they are supposedly trying to help, they seem to almost always throw in the term "Accountability" in the name of the action?

President Obama had threatened an incredibly small missile strike on Walmart's Arkansas headquarters until Russian President Vladimir Putin jumped in and promised to take control of all Walmart's chemical cleaning products. (Oh snap, I think I got my stories mixed up.) Never mind.

Mayor Gray knew the Walmart Bill was a suicide pact that was projected to cost the city more than 4,000 jobs. It now goes back to the Council for another vote, this time to override the mayor's veto so it's not quite dead yet. Unfortunately, the D.C. City Council has a recent record of stupidity and corruption that makes the Detroit City Council look almost legitimate. Almost. D.C.'s council members, unlike Detroit's, actually show up for meetings when they are not in court, meeting with the Justice Department or in prison.

Gray is not completely sane, however. He says he is pursuing an increase in the D.C. minimum wage, which is currently one dollar higher than the national minimum wage. If successful, it will cost jobs, as it almost always does, especially in stagnant economic times. Like now.

So if an increase in the minimum wage to $12.50 was projected to cost 4,000 jobs in D.C., what would a hike in fast food workers' minimum wage to $15.00 in protest cities like Detroit and Philadelphia do for low-wage workers? Anyone paying attention and accepting Economics 101 can figure it out. Even a million Muslims marching on 9/11.

Washington Redskins: What's in a Name? September 15, 2013

While Detroit Lion fans aren't quite sure about the Lions, it's official here in Washington D.C. concerning the home team: the Washington Redskins "officially" suck, starting a season of great promise nada-and-two after a Sunday thrashing by the Green Bay Packers.

But the nation's capital football team has a far greater problem beyond a lousy defense: they are getting blitzed for having an incredibly bad offense—their nickname. The Redskins. Not a tribe like the Chippewas, Seminoles, Navajos, or Sioux, but a nickname based on the supposed color of Native American skin.

The Oneida Indians—the ones I am told from incredibly unreliable sources are the Native Americans who introduced the Pilgrims to the use of silverware—are spending big money protesting the Washington Redskins, in print and at stadiums. But, I digress.

The politically correct crowd is going nuts on Washington's team. Problem is, this is the same group that went all high-and-mighty on the major league baseball's Atlanta team for their nickname: the Braves. How is that offensive? Or Kansas City's supposed racist use of the "Chiefs."

I mentioned the "Chips" earlier. My son graduated from Central Michigan this summer and I remember the two of us going to the MSU Spartans game versus the Chippewas a few years ago in the midst of the "controversy" over CMU's nickname. The former CMU mascot, an Indian character, had been replaced by, no kidding, a co-ed housed in a giant bag of potato chips. So, we had the best mascot in all of sports—Sparty— against a bag of Lays. (Making the day even worse, CMU beat MSU in Lansing in the final seconds. I think I saw a crushed, giant bag of chips floating in the Cedar River later that night. Someone had to pay.)

Detroit, unlike Washington, is lucky. Lions, Tigers, and Pistons; who can challenge those nicknames but PETA and the National Highway Traffic Safety Administration. I guess the Oregon Ducks are safe, too, unless Ducks Unlimited gets involved. I am sure the Penn State Nittany Lions are okay, as no one I have ever known knows what a nittany lion is.

I hate political correctness for the most part. Ninety-nine times out of one hundred, it is complete BS. However, in the case of the Washington Redskins, I agree totally. Washington Redskins owner Dan Snyder has pledged to never change the name. He is a fool.

Chapter Nine: Stupid Dictators

comics.com EMAIL: hpayne@detnews.com ©10 DETROIT NEWS

Kim Jong "Ill" Is now Kim Jong Dead: December 19, 2011

I usually don't laugh or cheer when someone buys the farm. But this morning I did both. I cheered the fact that North Korean Dick, um, Dictator Kim Jong "Ill" is now officially Kim Jong Dead. This little monster starved his people and murdered countless, engaging in terrorism from time-to-time during his 25-year reign. Hey, Kim baby, say hi to Hitler and Jeffrey Dahmer.

The good news for the Kimster, who was born in Siberia and ruled a rogue nation known for its brutal winters, is that he'll never be cold again. Kind of gives new meaning to "put another shrimp on the barbie."

So what made me laugh? The state-controlled video of Korean women collectively (that's what Communists do) sobbing at the news of their fearless leader biting the dust. Were these tears of joy at his passing? Not according to the bogus video. These were young and old women allegedly crushed by Kim's death. Right. He starved a nation for decades, cut them off to the outside world, and spent gobs of money buying nukes he could never possibly use without assuring the complete destruction of all of his people. It is apparent the "crying" Koreans were either paid or forced (or both) to show their "grief."

North Korea: Not a Wet Eye in the Place: December 28, 2011

I finally figured out that the biggest threat to survival in North Korea is not a lack of food, but rather a shortage of beverages. These people are suffering from major league dehydration. How else can one explain how thousands of North Koreans lined the streets to get a glimpse of Kim Jong Dead's carcass as he made his way to Hades and collectively wailed uncontrollably, only to produce not a single tear?

The U.N. needs to act now and help avoid this atrocity before it is too late. Redirect those shipments of water to Libya, Japan, and the Sudan to North Korea as soon as possible. Drink up you crazy cryin' Koreans, because I bet your "Dear Leader" is dying for a cold beverage right now.

North Korean BBQed Rocket: April 12, 2012

Starve your people and choke them with smog while launching missiles less successfully than the beer-can cannon I built in the 1970s with duct tape. Kim Jung Dud.

It is one thing that these clowns can't build an erector set (okay, I'm old); but please look at the coverage of the failed missile launch. The air is choked with so much pollution it looks like first class on Nippon Airlines in the mid-1980s. Great strategy: can't feed your people, get them lit and kill their taste buds.

Chavez Is dead. Long Stay Dead Chavez: March 5, 2013

Hugo. You Go.

Very un-Christian of me, but glad you are eating cheeseburgers with Hitler and all those Catholics that ate meat on Friday. Sorry, just kidding on the latter: Those McDouble Catholics are merely in purgatory, which is just outside of Lubbock, Texas.

Venezuelan Dicktator, er, um, Dictator Hugo Chavez is dead. After months away getting "supreme" medical treatment in Cuba—Michael Moore's medical nirvana—the tyrant returned to the home country he has raped for two decades only to buy the farm.

Former U.S. President George W. Bush has every right to do a little jig right now on his Texas ranch; but, alas, he is too classy to do that; just as he is too classy to criticize President Obama. Chavez called Bush "Diablo," which is Spanish for the newest taco at Taco Bell. Wait: check that, it is Spanish for "devil." My bad.

In addition to worshiping Cuban killer Fidel Castro, Chavez also befriended Iran's President nut bag Mahmoud Ahmadinejad. He has— excuse me, had—an oil rich economy that is suffering from 30 percent inflation, rampant crime and upheaval, and general malaise.

Can't wait for Michael Moore's next film: My Favorite Dictator 86ed*

*Restaurant term for an item no long available.

Hugo Get an Air Freshener: March 20, 2013

If you don't believe former Venezuelan dictator Hugo Chavez was rotten to the core when he was alive (ahem, pathetic America-hater Sean Penn and on-the-CITGO-dole Joe Kennedy II), then you'll probably find it distressing that he will soon be "rotting" to the core.

It seems that those in charge of embalming Chavez so that he may perpetually remain lying in state – like Lenin, Mao, and Joan Rivers – apparently fell asleep at the switch and made the procedure impossible. Perhaps they were too busy filling out their March Madness brackets. That means Chavez's remains, if left open for the public to view, will rot like a White Castle in the back seat of a car with its windows shut on a 100-degree day. In other words, Chavez will rot in the same manner his country has suffered under his reign of personal riches.

As for Joe Kennedy, the former politician and current philanthropist and "business man," it's curious as to whether he will continue to be the paid voice of the advertisements oil-giant CITGO is running here in Washington, D.C., praising Chavez for what he has done for Venezuela and the world. Considering that Chavez was a protégée of Cuba's Fidel Castro, Joe's father (RFK) and uncle (JFK) must be rolling over in their graves. Sheesh.

Meanwhile, Chavez's handpicked successor, Nicolas Maduro, and Iranian good buddy Mahmoud Ahmadinejad are claiming that the United States poisoned Chavez with cancer and will do so to our other enemies. Yep, Maduro and the Mahster smell a rat; or perhaps, they are just standing too close to Chavez's coffin.

Chapter Ten: Stupid Media

The NY Mosque Is Greek to Me! September 7, 2010

The Wisecracker is losing his mind. Vacationing with my wife in Northern Michigan, I have been completely unable to find a conservative radio talk show. No Frank Beckmann on WJR in Detroit, no Rush, no Sean.

Then I found a talk show on You-FM with Stephanie Miller. I had never heard of her. Unlike the Left that complains about conservative talk radio or FOX News without ever actually watching it, I listened (actually stomached) her show for three days. She is so far Left she makes President Obama look like Barry Goldwater.

Now, mind you, I don't agree with everything the conservative hosts say on a daily basis, but after my time with Stephanie, they have one thing right—the Left is elitist, angry, bitter, mean, and sophomoric. They are unable to talk policy. And one more thing—they hate Christianity. Boy, do they hate Christianity. To Stephanie and her callers (all seven of them), Christians are bigots supreme. And they are stupid. They cling to their guns, hate black people (especially the President), and are stupid. I said stupid twice. Stupid me.

To Stephanie, the "occasional" black person who is anti-abortion—like Martin Luther King Jr's niece—is the "nut" that every family has. Of course, Stephanie would never do the research to discover that some of the strongest Christian denominations are African-American.

And where does Stephanie stand on the proposed mosque at Ground Zero in NYC? Gotta build that bridge! In her words, people opposed to it are un-American (and, of course, racists, bigots, morons, and probably married to their cousin.)

How about a "bridge" that was built 90 years ago in New York and was destroyed by the Islamic terrorists on 9/11. I'm talking about St. Nick's Greek Orthodox Church, which is getting the short end of the stick by NY government officials. Where are you on this issue, Mayor Bloomberg?

Full disclosure from the Wisecracker: I am Greek Orthodox. Not by birth (Baptist), but by marriage. My priest, Father Nick at St. George in Bloomfield Hills, is one of my best friends. When you want to talk about building bridges, the Greeks did more than any ethnic group in history. They were the first translators of the Bible into a language that millions could understand. They began the spread of Christianity around the world. Prior to "going Greek", the Bible was only available in scholarly versions of Aramaic, Greek, and Hebrew. The Greeks decided to translate the Bible into what was called Koine, or common Greek.

Yet the Greeks in NY cannot get the OK to rebuild a parish destroyed by the plane-bound assassins on 9/11. They have petitioned President Obama to speak up as he did in favor of the Islamic "Bridge Building" mosque last month. No comment from our President who reportedly wears his Christianity on his sleeves.

The Whine Albom: February 21, 2011

"We look like fools." So says *Detroit Free Press* columnist, author, and filmmaker, Mitch Albom, after Michigan Guv Snyder whacked the film credit that cost the state $155 million last count. No Mitch, not "we." You.

"As a person who helped create the film credits program" (his own words), Mitch is having a hard time swallowing the fact that he and a few others hoodwinked the Michigan legislature into buying their lofty "break even or better" projections.

In a tortured column this past Sunday, Albom cries about the imminent death of an industry that grew "one hundred times over from $2 million to $225 million in two years." Yes Mitch, but please do not ignore the fact that the net cost of the program for taxpayers went from zero to $155 million during that time. Oh, those doggone facts.

Don't get me wrong, it was really cool having Hugh Jackman walk around my little village of Franklin, Michigan, during his stay here. Wow, it's Hugh here, Hugh there. "Sign an autograph, Hugh?" "No problem mate!" "Oh, he is so nice!" "Did ya hear Hugh talking with Mitch Albom on his show?" "Really cool. He really, really, really likes it here."

Then, of course, Hugh left. So did George Clooney and Clint Eastwood when their lucrative temp jobs in Michigan were over. Eastwood sadly had to leave Michigan and return to awful Carmel, California, while Clooney, no doubt in tears, made his way back to Mars.

Albom not only accused the Michigan governor of misleading him, but then started his attacks on Snyder's character. He said the governor's "philosophy is built of wobbly legs." And, according to Albom, Snyder's only view of the world is that of an executive—"make it cheap for me to operate."

Note to Mitch: Snyder was elected in a landslide by the people of Michigan for this very reason: clean up this mess of overspending and entitlement and make it affordable (it will never be cheap) to operate here so full-time jobs are created—not two- or three-week filming stints. Pinning Michigan's recovery on the film industry was like counting on the notion of more and more casinos to help the little guy.

Then, of course, as is the case with most fact-less, emotional arguments, Mitch's reasoning finally jumped the shark. He wrote: "...our Michigan can't be viewed only through a CEO's lens, a budget that shows little regard for poor and elderly people, but twists like a pretzel for certain businesses." Sorry Mitch, you're just mad because Snyder didn't twist like a pretzel for the money-losing business you take credit for helping to create. What's the word I am looking for here? Oh yeah, hypocritical. And if he were to pretzel twist to support your money-losing cause, wouldn't there be even less for the poor and elderly people of Michigan who have no shot at employment or the other riches of the film industry?

The Wisecracker's usual cadre of incredibly unreliable sources has obtained an audio copy of that now infamous meeting some weeks ago between Albom and Snyder:

Albom: Governor, you've gotta save my, er, the film industry credit.

Snyder: Mitch, I'm struggling with this one. Our state is bankrupt and we have to start cutting costs or we're dead.

Albom: Governor, Governor. (Condescending sigh.) I don't want to sound disrespectful, but you are confused. The film industry is not a liability to this state, it's an asset.

Snyder: Is it costing us millions of dollars we don't have? Yes or no? (Sound of crickets.)

Snyder: That is how I have to approach this issue, Mitch. By the way, your (newspaper) industry is facing many of the very same challenges. I now have to drive down to the gas station to get my *Free Press* every morning. From my view, the film credits are a luxury we cannot afford. But I am open to you proving me wrong.

Albom: Your clever use of facts is getting in the way of my passionate and highly-personal argument. I find it despicable and Republican. What about the attention the movie industry has brought to the beauty and talent of our state?

Snyder: Mitch, don't get hurt patting yourself on the back. I saw *Gran Torino*. Except for the salty language, it was terrific. But I wouldn't say it exactly brought out the "beauty" of our state. My cousin called me after seeing the movie and asked me if it was really that bad in Detroit.

Albom: What about the fact that the incentive brought the sexiest man on the planet, Hugh Jackman, to Michigan! Now you can't argue with that Mr. CEO Governor.

Snyder: Who?

Albom: No, Hugh. The Wolverine Man.

Snyder: Good, after the Rich Rodriguez debacle, we need all the Michigan men we can get.

Albom: No, no. He starred in the movie, *Wolverine Man*. You know, the Marvel Comic character.

Snyder: Oh, fiction. Sorry Mitch, why would I want to pay to see a fictional movie when I've been watching one in this state for years?

More Bubbly from Albom's "Whine" Cellar: March 14, 2011

A tale of two journalists: one that makes you think and one that wants to think for all of us.

In the March 14th *Wall Street Journal*, L. Gordon Crovitz has a thought-provoking column concerning the recent "sting" operation that led to the dismissal of NPR's chief fundraiser, and moments later, the CEO. He did not criticize the intentions of the stingers or their methods which he said required "sophisticated planning." His viewpoint was that in this day and age of technology changing at warp speed, what we say and do is being captured and broadcast right under our noses. A private lunch? Maybe in a bunker, but that might not even be safe.

Crovitz did point out that high-tech isn't always needed. After all, all it took was a regular phone for Ian Murphy, a blogger that goes by Buffalo Beast, to call Wisconsin Governor Scott Walker and claim he was billionaire businessman and philanthropist David Koch. Although he got fooled, Walker (luckily for him) didn't get stung, nor did he say anything he hadn't already said in public. Walker came away a bit of a sucker, but without any of the inflammatory and bigoted remarks that sank the NPR folks. (Side note: Did the fake Koch alert Walker he was being taped? Isn't that unethical?)

Crovitz ends his piece with the thought: "Technology has quickly shoved aside longstanding expectations of privacy. There are enormous benefits from the information that we get from access to unscripted conversations, including a clearer understanding of what people really believe. Losing some privacy in the process seems to be a trade-off we're happy to take."

That is, unless you're Mitch Albom, who in his March 13th *Detroit Free Press* column once again showed his rage, his bias, and, this time, his selective memory. "Maybe I'm confused" was the three-word start to this Albom gem. Those words turned out to be prophetic. From there it was attack, attack, attack.

Albom wrote, "The sleaze ball behind this latest 'gotcha' (NPR) incident is James O'Keefe, who is all of 26 years old, calls himself an investigative journalist without formal training, and thinks nothing of lying and fraud as long as it perpetuates his strong conservative viewpoint." Hold the phone, Mitch. The fake caller in Wisconsin—who runs a blog that perpetuates his strong liberal viewpoint—was lying and perpetuating a fraud, but I don't remember your column on that incident.

Albom did offer at least one rich laugh line when he said, "Let's get a few things straight. I'm not here to defend or attack public broadcasting. That's a debate for another day." Stop it Mitch, my sides are hurting. Your column was all about <u>defending</u> public broadcasting and <u>attacking</u> those who don't see the world as you do.

Finally, Albom posed the question that showcased his "selective memory," and it was a beauty when he cried, "When did this become journalism?" Albom complained, "But there used to be certain rules for reporting. No matter what your opinion of a subject, you did not pretend to be a person you were not. You didn't give a fake name or a fake workplace. You didn't hide cameras and mikes during phony conversations."

Uh, Mitch, this became journalism decades ago, not just now thanks to the conservative, untrained, sleaze ball (your classy, unbiased words) guy who exposed NPR at its worst. Ever heard of *60 Minutes*? They became (and are still) a ratings juggernaut by oftentimes posing as people they were not (lying according to Albom) and using hidden cameras and mikes to catch their prey (audible gasp). Not only did they do this, but they perpetuated a fraud in trying to prove the killer nature of the Audi 5000 in 1986, paying a "safety advocate" by the name of Bryon Bloch who actually rigged a test to prove their point. That's "rigged" as in "faked." "Faked" as in "lied." Auto industry followers know that the ordeal literally put Audi all but out of business in the U.S. In fact, Audi just caught up to their previous high sales number last year! True. It took them 24 years to recover from the damage.

Years later, Mr. Bloch was hired by *Dateline NBC* to "rig" another test. Remember the side-saddle tank issue? Remember the embarrassment for NBC when the fraudulent test was exposed by GM's Harry Pearce? (Side note: Still the greatest press conference in history.) Remember Jane Pauley being forced over her dead body to apologize on the air? Well, at least it's a good thing Dateline doesn't use hidden cameras. Oh, my bad, of course they do. Silly me.

What Albom lacks in historical knowledge of his own industry (or chooses to ignore to support his cause), he more than makes up for with outrage, writing: "And yet this 'Punk'd' version of news is now so accepted, no one makes nearly the stink about O'Keefe as they do about his victim."

Someone made a stink, Mitch. You. And it smelled to high heaven.

NewsCorpse: July 20, 2011

While NewsCorp's Rupert Murdoch claimed he was at an all-time low and got the Senator Carl Levin pie-in-the-face treatment in the process, no one is hurting more today than FOX News Chief Roger Ailes. Ailes had it all it seemed. FOX News was kicking the snot out of all the other cable news shows combined. Heck, CNN can't seem to keep any of its "talent." He even did the crafty thing of dumping Glenn Beck before it was too late to say that FOX News was indeed "fair and balanced" compared to the MSM. (Every time I argued with a liberal friend about the virtues of FOX News, their only retort was, "But what about Glenn Beck? Come on!")

I can only imagine the seizures overtaking Ailes' body as he watched NBC Nightly News with Brian Williams open up Tuesday's broadcast—

not with coverage of the debt debate that could cripple the good ol' USA, impact generations to come, destroy the value of the dollar and thus lose its status as the world's core currency—but with almost ten solid minutes of the British government officials grilling Murdoch and his pie in the eye.

Think about it: with commercials deducted from the broadcast, Brian Williams shares about twenty-two minutes of news. So almost half of our country's and our world's news from NBC was thrashing News Corp and thus FOX. It got so bad that even loveable Charles Osgood got into the act today in his radio piece on CBS.

Murdoch, I believe, is mortally wounded by this sickening phone hacking affair, whether he knew of it or not. If you don't believe me, ask Brian Williams and the folks at NBC, MSNBC, CNN, CBS, ABC, and NPR who will beat this horse until it is glue.

Free Copy of *The New York Times*: I Want My Money Back: September 19, 2011

I love the Sunday *New York Times*…when I'm waiting to board a flight and someone has discarded the paper on a chair for me to grab free-of-charge. I tore through the paper looking for the political section—called Sunday Review—to read the Thomas Friedman column my friend Doron Levin said was a "must read" on the Israel-Palestinian situation.

Friedman is the most high-profile de-facto spokesperson of the Obama Administration. Let's face it, along with Paul Krugman, *The New York Times* is THE communications team for the President. Sorry, Jay Carney, you are irrelevant.

Friedman argues that while Obama is getting grief from New York's Jewish population in the surprise election of a Republican for the Congressional seat vacated by Anthony "The Left Yank" Weiner, it is not Obama's weakness on support of Israel, nor his previous Apology Tour through the Middle East, but rather the failings of Israel's Prime Minister Bibi Netanyahu. Bibi, after all, is completely at fault for the current conundrum over Palestinians demanding statehood despite the fact the Palestinians pulled away from the negotiations table more than two years ago and stood by while Hamas factions of their "people" decided to bomb innocent Israeli kids.

Not Obama's fault, according to Friedman. The President, as usual, is a victim: Like he is now the victim of the once-cheered Arab Spring, the Japanese tsunami, Ron Artest changing his name, and eight years of W and Cheney drivin' this economy into a ditch.

Yes, Friedman loves Obama. So maybe he can help him "pass this bill." Sorry, I digress.

And for those that want to replace Mr. Obama with a collegiate failure like Texas Governor Rick Perry, *The New York Times* has got you covered there, too. Columnist Gail Collins spreads her hatred of Perry from the front page of the Sunday Review to a full half-page in the middle of Pravda—I mean The Times. She castigates Perry's parents for leaving him to schooling solely in Texas while the (formerly evil) Bushes at least had the decency to send W to prep school in the civilized eastern part of America. She points out repeatedly that Perry sucked, grade-wise, in college, and that he seems to be proud of his less-than-stellar college career that he overcame to be a popular leader of the country's most successful state and on the brink of being President of the United States. I don't know about you, but if you are going to suck at something, suck best. (I'm trademarking that, um, er, sucker.)

Sadly, Collins mocks Perry's military service in the Air Force while stationed in Texas, Germany, and THE MIDDLE EAST! Finally, she questions his credentials as an elected official who went from agricultural commissioner to lieutenant governor to multi-term governor, repeatedly beating long-time political office holders. (Funny, considering that his likely opponent in November 2012 has an office-holding resume that couldn't hold the spit of Perry's—nor the success.)

But this is *The New York Times*. All the news that's fit to print? Hardly. Rather, it is showing its bias in black and white. I want my $4 back. No, wait. I got it for free. I still feel cheated.

MSM Pre-"Occupied" with "Grassroots" Nature of Protests: October 11, 2011

"Speaking of Wall Street, we thought we'd bring you up-to-date on those protesters, the Occupy Wall Street movement. As of tonight, it has spread to more than 250 American cities, more than a thousand countries—every continent but Antarctica."

■ Anchor Diane Sawyer, Oct. 10, 2011 on ABC World News Tonight

Trouble is, Ms. Sawyer forgot her name is Diane, not Tom. According to the U.S. State Department, there are only 195 nation states. So Diane is, well, exaggerating just a bit, don't ya think? But that has become the norm in covering this GRASSROOTS movement. I emphasize "grassroots" because the liberal media is desperately trying to hammer home that OWS is a real grassroots movement, unlike the phony AstroTurf movement Nancy Pelosi called the Tea Party. Pelosi called the Tea Party racist as well. More on that later.

And who better to prove Occupy Wall Street is in fact grassroots than the adorable radio talk show queen of the Left, Stephanie Miller. Once again, stuck up here in Northern Michigan, I find myself free of anything moderate or conservative when it comes to radio. Oh, I get Debt-free Dave Ramsey and Dennis Miller in the afternoon, but the morning resigns me to The Stephanie Miller Show. I patiently listened for an hour, and here is what I heard (much of which is what I hear every time I listen to her show.)

1) The Tea Party is made up of racists.

2) Republicans are racists. Sorry for the redundancy.

3) The word "lesbian" used every ten minutes. Yes, Stephanie, we get it: you are a lesbian. Moveonitstiring.ugh

4) Upstart Conservative candidate Herman Cain is not very bright and made pizzas for a living (Ah, Steph, it was one of many jobs in which he succeeded and, oh yeah, he was the CEO of the company. He rescued it from liquidity and saved thousands of jobs. Shame on you Herman!)

5) Herman Cain is proof the Republicans are racist. They might even let him win, but in the end will pull a "Trading Places" moment and tell him he's not in charge. If you don't understand this "clever" reference Miller used, let me explain. In the movie *Trading Places*, street bum and black guy, Eddie Murphy, takes control of a company owned by snooty white guys (the 1-percenters) and with the help of an insider, Dan Aykroyd, turns the tables on the elitist white dudes. The implications are that, of course, all white people are racists and think black people are stupid. The movie also includes an incredibly gratuitous topless scene with Jamie Lee Curtis, which is why I think the Academy was completely wrong in not nominating the movie for an Oscar. But I digress.

6) The Occupy Wall Street movement is real, compared to the fake Tea Party, which again, is made up of racists.

7) Unemployment and the credit downgrade are the fault of the Republicans, who, by the way, are all racists.

Remember in 2008 when the rub on Obama was that he had never done anything to qualify himself for the Presidency? That criticism— including life as a community organizer, an Illinois State Senator who voted "present" a lot, and a U.S. Senator that spent more time on the campaign trail than in the U.S. Capitol Building—was met every time with a charge against Republicans of obvious racism. Now, the Left is questioning African-American Herman Cain's intelligence and career, but the only charges of racism are still toward Republicans and the dreaded Tea Party.

Ms. Miller did have a classic moment in talking about Cain. She derided his lack of foreign policy experience by mocking his flubbed answer regarding "Right of Return" between the Israelis and Palestinians by saying something like this: "Remember when he didn't have a clue about that issue between Israel and Palestine, ah, what was it called, ah, um, er?" Miss Miller couldn't come up with the name of the policy with which she was trying to demean Cain's intelligence and experience. Ironic and sad. But, no, not racist. The Left can never be racist.

Interestingly, in the hour I listened, there was no discussion of the Rick Perry/Mitt Romney smack down on Mormonism. Oh wait, I almost forgot that on an earlier show, Miller's team—on the air—referred to Christianity as a "douchebag cloaking device." So, they really don't care about this subject anyway other than the fact that Perry and Romney are, by their standards, douchebags.

The Wisecracker's usual cadre of spectacularly unreliable sources tells me to expect Perry to issue a statement that Mitt cannot be a douchebag because he is not really a Christian. Romney will counter that he is, indeed, a douchebag and call on Perry to apologize.

Cain "Most Racist" in Campaign: October 12, 2011

Yep, she said it. I'm not quite sure if Lefty radio talk show host Stephanie Miller accused Republican and African-American Herman Cain of "being" the biggest racist in the current presidential field or "saying" the most racist things in the race, but either idea is wackier than even I expected from "these" people.

The statement by Miller was soon followed by a lambasting of FOX News' Juan Williams (black and liberal) for having the gall to correctly say that any black conservative is immediately viewed as an enemy of the Left.

Unfortunately for Racist Supremo Cain, his colleagues running for the GOP ticket did him no favors. In the latest debate, Michelle Bachmann

212

tried to tell a lame joke about turning the 999 Plan on its head (666, get it) because "the devil was in the details." Sorry Michelle, the "666" reference was already used in *The Michigan View* earlier in the day by the Wisecracker in describing the Perry/Romney smack down on Mormonism. And you thought Joe Biden had cornered the market on plagiarism. And, Romney's "side-splitter" that he thought 999 was the "price of a pizza" was not only lame, but was highly tacky and sophomoric from the man that just got a huge endorsement from Chris Christie. Huge endorsement from Chris Christie: is that redundant?

Black Knight; Pathetic Morning for Journalism: July 22, 2012

It was indeed a Black Night, minus the "K" after midnight in Aurora, Colorado, on July 21, when a psycho's lost life imploded on the lives of his tragic victims enjoying a late night out at the premiere of the latest Batman extravaganza, *The Black Knight*. The next morning, thanks to ABC News' Brian Ross, brought us a Pathetic Morning for the profession of journalism and more insight into what has become a partisan divide so great in this country that news organizations are rendering themselves completely useless. In the case of Brian Ross: not only useless, but corrupt and downright dangerous. Perhaps, even deadly.

In case you missed it, Ross, appearing on ABC's not-so *Good Morning America*, told host, George Stepandfetchalot, that the suspect in the Aurora murder spree was a member of the Colorado Tea Party. But, of course! Right wing, bigoted, racist, and now mass murderers. Ah! Victory! Problem for Ross—his deep investigation into the suspect consisted of a nanosecond Google search that uncovered that a James Holmes was a Tea Party member. The poor bugger nabbed by Ross was almost 30 years older than the real suspect. Today, the 50-something James Holmes and his wife are scared to death after receiving threats due to Ross's carelessness and, yes, blatant bias in his reporting.

Ross wanted the Black Knight Mass Murderer to be a Teabagger. He willed it until it blew up in his snide, little, sanctimonious face. Ross, who was body-slammed by then-presidential candidate Michelle Bachmann's security forces, is—to be fair—a highly awarded investigative journalist and a complete something that rhymes with "rick." I learned this from my PR days in the auto industry.

The Wisecracker, through my normal dubious sources, has gotten my hands on an alleged ABC News interview that Ross had WITH HIMSELF—of course, in an attempt to first break the story that will appear Monday night on ABC's Hurled News Tonight. Here is the transcript as best I could type while searching Google for other Brian Rosses who have committed equally heinous crimes against humanity and decency.

Investigator Brian Ross: Mr. Ross, you falsely reported that a 53-year-old man with ties to the Tea Party, with the same name as the Colorado theater shooting suspect, was, in fact, the killer.

Ross: Ah, yeah. But I apologized, kind of profusely. Well, not really. Elton John was right. For journalists, sorry seems to be the hardest word.

Investigator Brian Ross: How much investigation did you do into this, now victim, 53-year-old Jim Holmes that you initially identified as a Tea Party member and mass murderer?

Ross: Um, a couple of minutes. It would have been faster, but the Wi-Fi connection in the Starbucks was slow.

Investigator Brian Ross: Do you realize the pain you have caused for 53-year-old Jim Holmes, wrongly accused by you? After all, he's had to turn off his phone.

Ross: It's Google's fault. This huge corporate giant is leading America astray while collecting billions.

Investigator Brian Ross: Why this rush to judgment of the Tea Party?

Ross: There is never a rush to judgment of the Tea Party.

(At this point, Ross body slams Investigator Brian Ross into the wall.)

Investigator Brian Ross: Some say your apology is not enough, especially in light of the death threats received by the man you wrongly accused.

Ross: Look. I gave him his fifteen minutes of fame. He should be grateful.

Investigator Brian Ross: Do you plan to resign? By the way, I ask that of all of my interviewees.

Ross: Resign? I made an honest mistake.

Investigator Brian Ross: Honest?

Ross: I looked at myself in the mirror this morning and saw you. We have a different set of standards than those we spend our occupation accusing and exposing.

Investigator Brian Ross: Well said, my friend. Well said.

Ross: FOUR MORE YEARS FOR OBAMA!

Investigator Brian Ross: What was that?

Ross: Sorry. The stress of this situation has given me Tourette's syndrome.

The Bitchings of Eastwood: September 3, 2012

Liberals, in general, and *The Washington Post*, in particular, are obsessed with Clint Eastwood. In fact, they haven't gone this bonkers since the last time they heard Sarah Palin's name mentioned. Mr. Eastwood entered the liberal hate neighborhood last week with his kooky stand-up comedy routine at the Republican National Convention. *The Washington Post* has had something nasty to say about Eastwood's appearance and his politics in every edition of its paper since then—five straight days and counting. How dare a Hollywood legend support a Republican!

Now, according to the *Post*, Eastwood is not only a washed-up, senile hater, but also a racist and a liar. He's a racist because "he looked more like Walt Kowalski," his bigoted character in *Gran Torino*, than Dirty

215

Harry when he graced the GOP convention. To the *Post*, life imitates art. So indeed, Eastwood is a racist, just like Senator Mitch McConnell is for pointing out how much golf the President plays while Rome burns.

What, you don't get that link? See, President Obama is a man of color who plays a lot of golf, just like Tiger Woods. And America has shown their racist feelings for Tiger by making him one of the richest athletes in the history of mankind. Ahem. (Yes, it is the dumbest charge in the history of politics, but these folks are beyond desperate.)

Eastwood is a liar, too. Clint told an empty chair (representing President Obama) that he couldn't grant Obama's wish to tell Mitt Romney to "go (something) himself." "A man can't tell another man to do that," Eastwood growled.

This, apparently, is not true according to the *Post*. In a front page story September 3rd—"Exit from Bain gave Romney rare benefits in retirement"—intrepid reporter Tom Hamburger uses almost one hundred column inches to guess (yes, guess) how much Romney has stashed away in his IRA and other retirement accounts. The conclusion: Romney made sure that the company he started from scratch would reward him financially for years to come even after he left the company. The Man has screwed The Man.

That same front page of the *Post* featured a story that allowed Obama operatives to lob the claim that Republican attacks on Obama's "you didn't build that" gaffe shows the GOP's "broader pattern of dishonesty." Hmm. Team Obama has recently lied about:

- The "Fast and Furious" gun-running debacle
- Not knowing anything about the Super PAC ad accusing Romney of giving a woman deadly cancer
- Romney not paying taxes for ten years
- Raiding Medicare to fund Obamacare

And, here's the real doozie of their dishonesty: If the navy seal-turned-author is telling the truth, Team Obama even lied about how the

Osama bin Laden killing went down. This last one was completely unnecessary, as the vast majority of Americans don't give a damn if bin Laden was killed with a gun in this hand or tied up and forced to listen to non-stop Justin Bieber songs until he took his own life (although the latter would clearly violate the Geneva Convention). But, this is what pathological liars do; lie even when the truth works better.

Dying Wrong: April 8, 2013

On the day the King of Pop Michael Jackson died, one other famous celeb died as well. Remember who? It was Farrah Fawcett—the greatest pin-up of all time. Yes, I had the poster, and so did millions of other young men lusting in their bedrooms. Ahem. What was sad was, number one, that she had died, but also how it was overshadowed by the Man in the Mirror. Farrah had fought gallantly against a horrendous cancer while Jackson was drugging himself to sleep and eventually to death. Yet, Jackson got all, if not most, of the ink.

Fast forward to 2013 and history repeats itself. Dead at 87 is the Iron Lady, former British Prime Minister Margaret Thatcher. She was Ronald Reagan's co-pilot in crushing the Soviet Union. In fact, it was Soviet reporters that gave Ms. Thatcher her nickname. (Funny, because they were living under the Iron Curtain at the time.) I am sure Ronnie met her at heaven's gate and is holding a helluva, em, fantastic roast as we speak.

As the Queen of Conservatives made her way north, much like with Fawcett's death, another babe passed away with much less fanfare. Annette Funicello died at the young age of 70. Like Fawcett, the last years of Annette's life were tough, struggling through MS, which first afflicted her some 30 years ago. No, Annette did not alter the course of history like Ms. Thatcher, but she did impact many lives as the classy former Mouseketeer whom Walt Disney found and suggested wear a one-piece bathing suit in all of those silly beach movies in order to protect her reputation. I loved Annette Funicello, and would have given my left arm to be Frankie Avalon. She never succumbed to stardom; she protected her image, and eventually turned her attention to her children when the Hollywood lights faded.

Thank you, Ms. Thatcher, for making this world a better place. Thank you, Ms. Funicello, for giving a little kid from Iowa a reason to enjoy a Malibu beach. Say hi to Ronnie, both of you.

The Left's Tragedy of the Boston Bombing: April 21, 2013

Last Friday wasn't "good" for many of the political pundits on the Left. When Dzhokhar Tsarnaev was hauled into police custody "right off the boat" hours after he had supposedly run over this older brother in the midst of an intense firefight with the cops, defeat had been snatched from the jaws of victory.

The terrorists were not American-born, white rednecks ala Timothy McVeigh, but young Chechens by birth, and, oh yeah, Muslims. Young Muslims who so appreciated their access to America's finest schools that they decided to visit a school and shoot dead a 26-year-old campus cop in the back of the head.

So much for a plan: one that started almost immediately after the gruesome bombing at the end of the Boston Marathon, killing three and injuring almost 200. Merely hours after pressure cooker bombs ended lives and tore off limbs, MSNBC's Chris Matthews offered up the following incoherent gem: "Let me ask you about domestic terrorism as a category. Normally, domestic terrorists, people tend to be on the far Right, well that's not a good category, just extremists, let's call them that. Do they advertise after they do something like this? Do they try to get credit as a group, or do they just hate America so much or its politics or its government that they just want to do the damage, they don't care if they get public credit, if you will?"

Matthews and his cohorts were trying to "will" their version of "White Christmas": a gift that would keep on giving to expose the bigoted, racist cloak that hangs around the neck of Conservative Americans. Salon's David Sirota doubled down on Matthews' wager with a column titled, "Let's hope the Boston Marathon bomber is a white American," citing "white male privilege" as a reason for the bombing. (Technically, I guess he was right as the terrorists were "white" and "American" thanks to citizenship granted on September 11, 2012. Ouch.)

By then, it seemed everyone on the Left was riding the white-guy-or-bust bandwagon. NPR's Dina Temple-Raston punched her ticket with this beauty: "April is a big month for anti-government, and right wing individuals. There's the Columbine anniversary. There's the Oklahoma City bombing. There's the assault on the Branch Davidian compound in Waco. And the FBI right now is comparing this to the (Atlanta Olympics) Eric Rudolph case."

By Friday evening, Matthews, Sirota, and Temple-Raston's white dream scenario had turned flaccid. The killers weren't from Idaho, Texas, or the Michigan Militia. They weren't Bible-hugging rednecks with NRA and "Honk if you love Jesus" bumper stickers on their rusty, gun rack-equipped '95 Ford pickups.

Never one to apologize for his transgressions or outright bias (and stupidity), Matthews dug in his heels on his Sunday NBC show. During a panel discussion, he and his cohorts discussed what they thought would be the impact of the Boston Marathon bombing and outcome on us lowly Americans. CNN chief political analyst Gloria Borger summed it up brilliantly: "President Barack Obama's actions during the crisis were a reflection of what he learned from George Bush's mistakes following the September 11, 2001 attacks."

Ah, perfect. Blame it on Bush. We have a wrap.

Blame It on the Intern: It Worked for Bubba Clinton: July 15, 2013

The incredibly embarrassing snafu at San Francisco FOX affiliate KTVU regarding the fake names of the pilots of the crashed Asiana Airline 214 would be hilarious had it not been surrounded by an incident where three young lives were lost. Looking at the clip of the newscast, it looks like something out of either *Anchorman* or *Porky's*. Here it is: (http://www.youtube.com/watch?v=L1JYHNX8pdo)

The "pilots" were identified on the air by the geniuses at KTVU as:

- Captain Sum Ting Wong
- Wi Tu Lo
- Ho Lee Fuk
- Bang Ding Ow

Have the "news" gatherers at the nation's television stations become this addle? Did two eighth-graders sitting by the pool call the station and pull off this prank? Do you have Prince Albert in a can?

Of course, as usual these days, the idiots at KTVU could not give an unqualified apology. They blamed it on the National Transportation Safety Board (NTSB) in Washington. The NTSB, in fine Washington fashion, blamed it on an intern—probably an unpaid intern which is the new business model here in the District and sadly the new face of slavery among our young college students in this crappy economy. (Sorry, got off message and will discuss this unpaid intern travesty in the future.)

The Wisecracker's incredibly shaky sources tell me the suspect intern who confirmed the bogus information regarding the Asiana pilots has actually been promoted to a paying job at the U.S. State Department, reporting directly to Secretary John "I am 'yacht' on a boat while Egypt burns" Kerry. They apparently see a lot of potential in this young person. His/her code name is Pinocchio.

**Read This Column and Then Shut the F--- Up! September 29,
2013**

Washington Post columnist Alexandra Petri is applauding *Popular
Science*'s announcement last week that the magazine is eliminating the on-
line comments section attached to each article. Petri is hoping the *Post*
will follow the lead.

Pop Sci's explanation for no longer giving readers a voice? According
to its on-line content director Suzanne LaBarre: "A politically motivated,
decades-long war on expertise has eroded the popular consensus of a wide
variety of scientifically validated topics. Everything, from evolution to the
origins of climate change, is mistakenly up for grabs again. Scientific
certainty is just another thing for two people to 'debate' on television. And
because comments sections tend to be a grotesque reflection of the media
culture surrounding them, the cynical work of undermining bedrock
scientific doctrine is now being done beneath our own stories, within a
website devoted to championing science."

Translated: Buy what we are selling and then shut up.

The timing of *Pop Sci*'s diminishment of free speech is rich, coming
the same week the "premiere" United Nations Intergovernmental Panel for
Climate Change released their fifth assessment draft report in the midst of
news that "global warming" was, in fact, looking more and more like
hooey. If you remember my September 18th column, "a new study in the
journal *Nature Climate Change* found that of the 117 computer models
used to predict climate over the past 20 years, only three correctly
predicted temperature movement. That's an F-minus-minus for those
keeping score at home. The average of the 114 failing models predicted an
average rise of .30 degrees Celsius per decade. The actual rise was less
than half of that over the two decades of the study. The journal said that
"even more striking" was that over the past 15 years, the modelers overbid
their warming showcases by 400 percent."

The U.N. panel summed up its report this way: the chances of man being the cause of climate change was now "extremely likely." Wow, that's all you got? It seems like just yesterday that if you did not believe man was 100 percent to blame for climate change, you were either ignorant, or worse yet, an evil "denier," who also most likely dabbled in racism, homophobia, Islamophobia, and the War on Women.

What's more, the U.N. panel completed ignored the facts concerning the lack of warming cited in the *Nature Climate Change* report, defensively claiming that "Due to natural variability, trends based on short records are very sensitive to the beginning and end dates and do not in general reflect long-term climate trends." Oh, so now 15 straight years of little or no rise is too short a time period? Yet, these are the same clowns who were crying wolf in year-to-year differences as the climate crowd, led by academia, stoked the fires and stole the keys to the ATMs of many governments the world over.

I will admit that when I heard the U.N. panel officials use the term "extremely likely," I laughed out loud as I was immediately reminded of *Animal House*'s Dean Wormer when he put Bluto, Otter, Boon, and D-Day on "double secret probation." Apparently, the U.N.'s "little known codicil" is an "extremely likely designation", a notch above "really, really likely," yet far-stronger than "pretty sure."

So, in the end, the U.N. is having trouble with those pesky little facts, while *Popular Science*, the world's most popular monthly publication for science and technology, wants its readers to put a sock in it. But of course, that is pretty much the view of the "progressives" in general: you have a right to free speech, as long as your speech is in lock-step with theirs. Dissenters are, in the words of *Pop Sci*, "grotesque."

Saw *American Sniper* and My Wife Wants "to Kick Michael Moore's (blanking) Ass": January 27, 2015

Just saw *American Sniper* with my wife. As we walked out of the theater and she wiped away tears, her first words weren't "what a great movie." They were: "I want to kick Michael Moore's (blank) ass."

If you see it, you cannot objectively say this movie glorifies war or "defends" President W's decision to invade Iraq as many have suggested in the media. It is gritty, troubling, and graphically depicts the horror of war for the good guys, the bad guys, and those—including the kids—sadly caught in the crossfire. But one thing is undeniable: the late American sniper Chris Kyle was and is an undeniable hero in the greatest tradition of our country and the world.

For "filmmaker" Moore to call Kyle a "coward" because he was a sniper and then double-down on those cowardly comments led my wife to determine: "Michael Moore—no way—saw the movie." Or, I surmised, if he did and still believes in what he is spewing, he is more than a coward; he is a traitor, a pathetic one at best.

Perhaps Michael Moore "abandoned his post" in the theater to consult with the enemies of our country, freedom and decency. Again, he seems to be "doubling-down" in his criticism of *American Sniper*. Perhaps, he is just a cornered rat.

Fascinating in watching *American Sniper* was the lead-up, as in the mind-numbing number of previews. With the exception of a peek at the new Kevin Costner tear jerker/feel good *Black or White*, the remaining previews were for upcoming blockbuster shoot-em-and-blow-em-up "superhero" movies coming in months, including *Fast and Furious 7* or 50 (not sure), two new Marvel Comics movies and a new take on *Mad Max*— the franchise that launched Aussie Mel Gibson. All these new Hollywood films about "imagined heroes," led up to the feature film telling the life, times, woe, and tragic death of genuine American hero, Chris Kyle, directed by the Hollywood actor Hollywood loathes—Dirty Harry, Clint Eastwood.

Mr. Eastwood. Clint, if I may call you that? Once again, you made my/our day. To *American Sniper* detractors—Dinty Moore, Seth Rogen, and former Vermont Governor Howard "the Shouter" Dean—if you really believe what you have said on camera, you should be ashamed; Very, very ashamed.

Oh, the movie is great.

Universal UClick/GoComics.com/hpayne@detnews.com ©14UFS

Chapter Eleven: Stupid Occupiers

Occupiers Throw Homeless to the Curb: November 2, 2011

Oh, the irony is rich. Sitting in Amsterdam's Schiphol Airport, I picked up a copy of the *International Herald Tribune*—published by *The New York Times*—which here is by comparison akin to FOX News. And in said rag, I read that apparently the "organizers" of the Occupy Whatever don't want homeless folks infiltrating their communal gatherings.

Really? Yes, REALLY. But wait, aren't the homeless part of the 99 percent of Americans getting the shaft?

"There are a lot of them here that have mental problems and that need help. They are in the wrong place," said 22-year-old Jessica Anderson as she occupied Los Angeles and complained about one homeless gent who stayed up "all night saying all kinds of crazy stuff."

Mental problems? Staying up all night saying crazy stuff? Sounds to me like he has found his home in the Land of Occupation.

One of the "managers" of the food tent at Occupy L.A. had this beauty: "If you are hungry and are in need of a meal, we will serve you as long as you do not disrupt the occupiers."

How in the hell do you disrupt people doing absolutely nothing?

OWS to Homeless: Leggo My Eggo: November 13, 2011

There is growing evidence that those "thoughtful" Occupy Wall Street folks are having problems with those silly and ungrateful homeless people that have crashed the gates, um, er, grounds at gatherings around the country. This past week, one organizer charged with providing the food spread for the protesters offered up this gem: "We worked really hard to gather and prepare this food (sounds kinda biblical doesn't it: think loaves and fish, oh, and some fine narcotics) and these homeless people think they should get it for free."

Take another hit off your bong and read that quote slowly—some people are working hard while others want something for free? Ironic?

Hypocritical? Of course, but just part of the stench of OWS in its various misguided (make that unguided), clueless, stupid, and lazy forms.

Meanwhile, half a world away in Egypt, the OWS could actually learn something if they were to take the time to see what happens when you get what you are asking for, only to realize you really didn't know what you were asking for. *The New York Times*' Neil MacFarquhar reports that "the euphoria of Egypt's political spring has surrendered to a season of discontent." The reporter interviewed Abu Ghaneima, an entrepreneur who gave literally dozens of camel rides a day to tourists exploring the Great Pyramids. Ghaneima had—repeat had—five camels until Egypt's economy went from Arab Spring to The Winter of His Discontent. "The revolution was beautiful, but nobody imagined the consequences," he told the *Times*.

Mr. Ghaneima fired 12 of his 15 employees and had to sell three of his beastly transporters to make ends meet. They are now camel steaks and McHumppets, if you know what I mean. Not certain if any of the camel meat went to feed the growing local homeless population. But then, as we know from the OWS folks here in America, why should homeless folks get food for free.

Raid on Insipid: The Occupiers: November 21, 2011

Just returned from Cancun where the "99-percenters" there realize that if they serve the one percent all the way down to the 50-percent tourist they may get a 20 percent tip—by the way, a day's wage on a $50 dinner. While there, I sat on an incredible beach, grasping the only real U.S. newspaper available, *USA Today*. *USA Today* in Mexico is always a day late (news-wise) and more than a dollar long—it's two bucks.

The news was Paterno, Sandusky, and Paterno until I arrived at the editorial pages where I found a jewel—an Op-Ed by Caitlin MacLaren and Zoltán Glück, organizers with the New York City Student Assembly, a group "proudly" affiliated with the Occupy Wall Street "movement." If you didn't have the joy to read their silly opinion piece, please let the Wisecracker translate their absolutely pathetic rhetoric.

MacLaren/Glück: "The whole world seems to be waiting eagerly for the 'next phase' of Occupy Wall Street, or else for the entire thing to dissipate overnight."

Wisecracker Translation: No, the whole world is not eagerly waiting. Yes, it will dissipate as you surmised. You are finally intelligent. Put that on your resume and give it to your local Starbucks or McDonald's.

MacLaren/Glück: "While the RAIDS on occupations from Oakland to New York…"

Wisecracker Translation: Raids? Really? You were asked to leave weeks ago to allow officials to shovel the garbage and clean up the filth; meanwhile, officials continuously balked at throwing you out. In the end, the stench was enough already, and a couple of your comrades had bought the farm. There was a Raid on Entebbe, one on Waco. Please, get real. The cops finally took out the trash. Literally and harmlessly.

MacLaren/Glück: "By focusing America's attention on the dramatic polarization of wealth and by creating a new political identity—the 99 percent—we are already impacting politics in ways the Tea Party could only dream of."

Wisecracker Translation: No, dreamers, the Tea Party impacted politics in a way that you aspire to. Good try. Think November 2010. Your Tea Party envy is breathtaking.

MacLaren/Glück: "Of course, the question 'where do we go from here?' remains a tough one, but it will only lead us to more creative solutions."

Wisecracker Translation: Creative solutions like "Why go to a park and poop in it? Go to a landfill where the poop is already there."

MacLaren/Glück: "As fellow organizer, Manissa McCleave Maharawal, has written: 'Our movement is not contained by a park, our ideas are not contained by a park, and we will not be contained by a park'."

Wisecracker Translation: I guess their "park" is worse than their bite.

Chapter Twelve: Stupid Atheists

God Checks Out of Iowa: September 15, 2010

Heeding President Obama's directive to give Las Vegas tourism the middle digit, the American Atheists organization will hold its annual convention in my home state of Iowa next spring. My home town of Pella, Iowa (population 10,200)—like many of the small, farm communities that make up the Hawkeye State—has about one church for every ten people. I'm exaggerating a bit. However, picking Christian-intensive Iowa, specifically Des Moines, seems a bit odd—but you know those nutty, fun-loving atheists.

When I read about their upcoming convention, I asked myself: If you don't "believe" in a higher being—God, Allah, Justin Bieber, whatever—what's the point in getting together? The Dems and the GOP have conventions to establish platforms and elevate candidates. The UAW has a convention to establish collective bargaining strategies and select leaders. Our forefathers held a convention to work on the Constitution in order to protect the rights of Imam Feisal Abdul Rauf, who wants to build a mosque on the site of 9/11. . . . Oops! Got distracted there. Sorry.

Couldn't the atheists save the time, gas, jet fuel—and thus the planet—by just logging onto GotoMeeting.com, click the button saying they don't believe, and get on with their lives?

But a convention it is. Their thirty-seventh. Yippee. For those who thought the "coincidental" timing of the Glenn Beck rally in D.C. on the anniversary of MLK'S "I Have a Dream" speech smelled a bit cheesy, check this one out: the American Atheists convention is on Easter weekend, arguably the most holy of all Christian holidays. Hold your nose on that one.

One should know this is the same group that placed ironic ads on buses around the country last year that read: "Don't believe in God? You are not alone?" (Hello? Note to American Atheists President Ed Buckner:

If you don't believe in God, sooner or later you will be, in fact, "alone." That is, if you don't count the worms. Time for a new ad agency, Ed.)

The host hotel for the convention is the Embassy Suites. (According to incredibly unreliable sources to the Wisecracker, American Atheists have demanded that a local eatery not far from the Embassy Suites change their name during the convention to TNIF—Thank Nobody It's Friday.)

But seriously, the hotel has actually offered, upon request, to remove any offending Bibles from the rooms of convention-goers. But why? According to Buckner, both the Bible and the Quran are books of fiction. Sure hope there are no copies of *Moby Dick* or *Harry Potter* in the rooms.

So, the Bibles be damned. Will there be threats against America for this action? No. Will there be massive coverage in the mainstream media as the Bibles—and the Bibles only—are given a "time out"? Unlikely. But what do you think would happen and how would it be covered in the media if it was the Quran that was being removed so as not to offend the atheist party goers? Hmmm.

Atheists Get Cross: July 28, 2011

Those wacky atheists are at it again, this time filing a lawsuit in protest of the famous World Trade Center "cross" inclusion in the 9/11 Memorial and Museum. The WTC cross was found amid the rubble of the terrorist attack. The cross is actually intersecting beams from one of the lost towers that broke in such a way it mirrors a perfect cross—Christian or just your everyday run-of-the-mill cross.

The American Atheists, a non-profit as well as a non-believing group, filed the lawsuit saying the steely presence violates the separation of church and state. I think their motto is: "Tra-la-la-la-la-la live for today." I have two distinct problems with this issue and these folks. Let's start with the latter.

If you don't believe in God, then you surely cannot believe his "only begotten son," who "allegedly" made the cross THE symbol of

Christianity, was the Messiah, savior, etc. So if that's what you believe, or in this case don't believe, then the steel structure pulled out of the carnage of 9/11 is just an aberration of broken metal.

Or one could argue that it is nothing more than an eerie tribute to Mr. T, who surely deserves some type of honor for all he's done for America—"Give me your tired, your poor and pity the fool."

Wisecracker: Hey, Mr. Atheist, what's the deal? If you think the cross has meaning, you must believe in Jesus Christ, right?

Atheist: God no! Um, er, I, mean, for heaven's sake, um, er, damn.

Wisecracker: Ha! Gotcha!

Atheist: Go to hell!

Wisecracker: Oh, so that exists? Nice consistency.

Atheist: 9/11 was an attack on America, not Christianity!

Wisecracker: And the Trade Center cross is not an attack on anybody; just a factual piece of history to rise from the ashes of the tragedy. You people really need to get a life, because if you and your fellow non-believers are right, that's all you've got to look forward to.

My other problems with this issue are the decent chance that some liberal judge will agree with the atheists and the future fallout from such a decision. Will the caretakers of Arlington National Cemetery be forced to sandblast away the Christian crosses and Jewish stars on the tombstones of our fallen veterans? Will the lower case "t" be banned from all books, computers, etc.? And will all participants in Pilates be forbidden from performing any exercise in which they stand erect and put their arms out to their sides?

What I do look forward to is the trial.

Bailiff: Mr. Atheist Witness, do you swear to tell the truth, the whole truth, and nothing but the truth, so help you God?

Atheist: Damn. It's a conspiracy.

Atheists Storm Washington for a "Reason": March 25, 2012

Those wacky atheists are at it again; this time in our nation's capital. They gathered on the National Mall for the first ever Reason Rally, where they pledged to stand up for their beliefs, um, er, ah, their non-beliefs I guess. Unlike those crazy people who believe in God, they believe in "reason." Obviously, none of the protesters had ever heard Rod Stewart's classic, "Reason to Believe," although he didn't write it and it was later pimped by the Carpenter's as well. So I guess everyone involved is going to Hell—ah, if that exists.

"God is a myth," said American Atheist President Dave Silverman, before offering up this gem: "Closet atheists, you are not alone." (Note to Silverman: If you are in a closet and you are an atheist, you are the definition of "alone.")

"We're godless—get used to it" was their battle cry. Okay, used to it; now what?

As I arrived for church this morning, I remember being shocked at the church leaders whipping non-believers in shackles, forcing them into the pews. Oh, wait, that doesn't happen anywhere in this country. Sorry for that temporary delusion. Back to the "Reason" Rally in D.C.

The line of the day came from "non-believer" Dustin Taylor, a 21-year-old college student who wants to become a science teacher. Taylor told a *Washington Post* reporter that he wants future students to have a "strong grounding in science" because "too often people believe something simply because it's what they've been told." Okay, Dustin, you mean like too often students believe something simply because it's what has been told in their college class?

The Rally kicked off the American Atheists National Convention concluding today in Bethesda, Maryland, just outside D.C. One atheist protester carried a clever sign: "So many Christians, so few lions." So much for civility I guess.

Earth to Vegans: You're Killing Me: April 23, 2013

(Note: I include Vegans in the "Atheists" category because they don't believe in bacon, which, I believe is a sin.)

The shark has officially been jumped concerning the Earth Day celebration here in Washington, D.C. On April 22nd, a group of Congressional staffers and friends celebrated the holy planet day by holding a Veggie Caucus (VC), celebrating all that is good and vegan. But what does being a vegan have to do with fostering good environmental behavior towards the third rock from the sun—the noble idea behind the creation of Earth Day back in 1970? In fact, aren't the vegans actually the destructors of the planet?

The VC vegans killed the naturally-growing kale and butchered it into "kale chips." The Veggie Caucus featured grape leaves, once peacefully hanging on the vine but brutally torn away, drowned in oily water and then stuffed with spices, miso, and nuts. Oh, the humanity.

Speaking of nuts, Veggie Caucus organizer Elizabeth Kucinich brought along her wacky, former Congressman husband, Dennis Kucinich. "I'm not here as a Democrat. I'm here as a vegan," he declared as he slurped down a spoonful of cucumber chamomile soup, not knowing what cucumber patch was now mourning the loss of one of its former residents.

But what does being vegan have to do with Earth Day? Aren't I doing a greater service for the planet by eating a marauding cow whose sole purpose in life is the destruction of mother earth's vegetation, the fouling of the water supply, and the production of more than its fair share of greenhouse gases from its tailpipe? Isn't my quest to find the hidden chicken in a Chicken McNugget, a nobler act of environmental stewardship? Perhaps I should do more.

I know: next year please join my Pork Caucus on Earth Day and down a slab of ribs or devour a pulled pork sandwich to celebrate the continued health of the planet and to put those dastardly vegans on notice that their destruction must end.

Chicago's "Jesus Free" School Zone: November 3, 2013

Driving into Chicago Halloween night, WBBM radio reported that a local high-school student had been booted out of school—temporarily—for having the audacity to come to class in a costume. A Jesus costume. With it, the on-going "War on Christianity" jumped the shark.

While the MSM is all but completely ignoring the persecution of Christians in the Middle East—the burning of Christian churches, the torture and murder of Christians, yada, yada, yada—the war continues here in America, less violently, but nonetheless insidious and growing.

Highland Park High School student Marshon Sanders thought he would follow-up last year's costume—Snoop Dogg—with the Prince of Peace. Incidentally, the Mr. Dogg costume caused no kerfuffle whatsoever last Halloween. But when he donned a white robe, red sash and a crucifix around his neck, he was sent to the dean's office and ordered to disrobe or no education for young Sanders that day.

The school's PR flak, Melinda Vajdic, said "Jesus" Sanders was violating the school policy that disallows costumes that might "be offensive or perpetuate a stereotype of someone's culture, gender, sexual orientation, heritage, or religion."

What students had been offended? Apparently none as the dean told Sanders' mom that two teachers had been "offended." Typical these days. Offended by what? No reason was given. Sanders' mom had encouraged her son to dress in the image of someone who was inspirational. Mrs. Sanders is obviously a very, very bad mother.

Hopefully this is a life lesson for young Marshon Sanders: next Halloween, don't offend a couple of teachers by dressing as someone who stood for love and the redemption of mankind and womankind; find your old Snoop Dogg costume, put a "cap" in someone's bottom side and come complete with a Bob Marley "fatty." Or, more in tune with the times, dress up like hip-hop artist Chris Brown and slap a few young female classmates around to make the experience "authentic." Yeah, nothing offensive about that.

Chapter Thirteen: Stupid Christians

Florida Pulpit Fiction: September 8, 2010

The Wisecracker recently wrote about the anti-Christian mentality of the Left these days. But just when it was safe to go back in the communal water, a "Christian minister" jumps the shark. A Gainesville, Florida "Christian" minister wants to spend 9/11—nine years hence the terrible terrorist attack—burning the Quran.

The liberal radio talk show—The Stephanie Miller Show—for which I have been forced to listen to while vacationing in Northern Michigan, is having a field day with Minister Hanging Chad. But, in a case of irony that goes beyond weird, they're referencing two "enemies" of the Left to implore all to demand the Quran burning be stopped (by the way, as it should be).

The stand-in hosts for Ms. Miller this week repeatedly pointed out that former President George W. Bush urged "we cannot be at war with Islam," while General Petraeus said the Quran burning would put Americans around the world—especially our soldiers—in harm's way. These are the same two men the Left has previously called, "evil" (W) and "General Betray Us," respectively.

Of course, the hosts couldn't help themselves from exposing their hatred of Christianity while calling for a counter-protest of the idiot in Florida. They actually said, on the air, that Christianity was a "douchebag cloaking device."

The Gainesville preacher—Terry Jones—told CNN's Anderson Cooper he is now "praying" over the decision whether or not to proceed with the burning of the Quran. Here's hoping those prayers include the one Jesus Christ personally taught to his apostles—The Lord's Prayer: "Forgive us our trespasses, as we forgive those who trespass against us."

One more piece of advice to Minister Hanging Chad: We Christians are taught when we pray to bow our head, not insert it.

Praise Be to the Holy Powerball! November 15, 2010

After much "handwringing" that former Detroit Public School Board President Otis "Masturgate" Mathis had perhaps bought the winning kazillionaire Powerball ticket—but was afraid to cash it due to its origins at a Highland Park adult book store—the winner has come, well, clean. Apparently.

Farmington Hills' Mike Greer, who runs a "photography" studio, cashed in the hefty winning ticket, collecting a cool $70 million lump sum payment for him and his gang of master bettors. According to Greer, a "healthy share" of the winnings will go to his church, as he didn't believe his church would mind that the winning ticket was bought at a House o' Porn.

Using the latest in detective and reporting skills amassed over several episodes of *Law and Order* and *Castle*, the Wisecracker found the church yesterday. The sermon was breathtaking to say the least.

Minister (unnamed to protect the innocent—learned that from *Dragnet*): Brothers and Sisters, today we are at a crossroads for this church community. One of our very own has sinned. (Audible gasps.) Yet—and this is a big-ass "yet"—his sin may just be the Godsend we all have been looking for to save this church in these times of economic peril and personal bankruptcy, including my own. A parishioner, or should I say a Pa-RICH-ioner, has come into what I can only describe as BIG MONEY. I mean, really, really, BIG MONEY.

Congregation: Hallelujah! Show me the money! Show me the money!

Minister: Hold on my friends and cover your youngster's ears. The money was won from a Powerball ticket purchased at a House of Ill Repute (audible gasps). The Devil's lair. A skin shop so vile that—

Parishioner (Shouting): Which one?

Minister: Oh, uh, somewhere in Highland Park.

Parishioner: Father. He risked life and limb to buy a lotto ticket in Highland Park and you are judging him? A man in a glass house should not throw stones!

Minister: How did you know that brother Greer just bought a contemporary glass mansion for me on Cass Lake, bless his soul?

Parishioners (together): What's in it for us?

Minister: Well, let's just say that for starters, today's Communion wine is a 1994 Opus One Cabernet Sauvignon. And it is fine.

Parishioners: Praise be to the Powerball!

Return of The Three Miscue-teers: March 6, 2011

Last night I was minding my own business, watching the local news as I opened my neighbor's mail, when the most dreadful of stories came across the tube—the Return of the Three Miscue-teers to Detroit.

First came word that the ringleader of the three, former Detroit Mayor Kwame "D'Artalyin" Kilpatrick, just might get out of the hoosegow early—say July—so that he can better prepare for his trial on multiple felony counts of screwing practically everyone he has ever met. Let's see: let him out of the jail early where he is housed for lying and a probation violation so that he can be a freeman among us awaiting criminal charges that could put him in federal prison for decades? Makes sense to me.

Joining the Kwamester in this merry band of losers is none other than Charlie "Pathetichos" Sheen, who after wowing the obviously super-intelligent folks in Chicago in his second appearance on his "tour," has threatened, er, I mean promised to return to Detroit for a "make up" performance. This is like letting Charles Manson out of jail and giving him a free bus pass to the Hollywood Hills. Charlie, please: You set an all-time record here for sucking; you can't sucketh any worse. (Notice the Three Musketeers-type lingo. Sweet.)

Our final Miscue-teer is that wacky man-on-fire himself, the Rev. Terry "Hairyfaceamis" Jones. Hell-bent on supposedly preaching the word

of the lord (not mine, thus no capital L), Ol' Mutton Chops Moses thinks
he has the right to burn the holy book of Islam, the Quran. Well, thanks to
literally millions of men and women of this land who have risked their
lives to protect our freedom in this country, he certainly does have the
right. But like so many issues in this country lately, having the right
doesn't mean you are right. Or in Jones' case, righteous. The Imam in NY
has the right to build the mosque on hallowed 9/11 ground, but it's not
right.

Rev. Jones' first Quran burning last month resulted in deadly rioting
in Afghanistan. Many innocent people were killed. Wrongly, yes, but
nonetheless murdered in reaction to Rev. Jones' stupidity and self-
righteousness. So what's his next move? Why, but of course—continue
the protest against Islam in the heart of Islam in the U.S.—Dearborn,
Michigan. On Good Friday no less!

I certainly hope no physical harm comes to Rev. Jones and his
followers. I pray that our friends in Dearborn take this man for what he
is—a raging lunatic—and pay no attention to him, knowing you are all a
vital part of our community.

But, someday I hope somebody listens to the wisdom of my late
Arkansas-raised father who oftentimes said: "Sometimes, some people just
need a swift kick in the a--!" For the Rev. Jones, it would certainly result
in additional brain damage.

Reverend Terry Jones: PR Master: April 26, 2011

He may be a loon. His rhetoric may be insulting and even dangerous.
But his PR skills are stellar. Okay, maybe it's all relative: his PR skills are
stellar compared to the buffoons in the Wayne County Prosecutor's
Office, the City of Dearborn Mayor O'Reilly, and Judge Somers.

Smartly, Reverend Jones is filing an appeal of the pathetic verdict
denying his First Amendment rights. He is also wisely following the
judge's projectile vomit on the Constitution with his order not to hold a

protest on the public sidewalk in front of the Islamic Center in Dearborn, despite the fact he has every right to do so. To press the issue on where to protest would take him off the side of the, ahem, free speech "angels" he is currently on.

Here's a fun little exercise I've deployed with a couple of my liberal friends as this ordeal has unwound. Ask them their stance on the proposed mosque on the hallowed ground of 9/11 in New York City. I did. The Imam has every right to build where he wants to build they say. This is America! Then pop the question of Terry Jones's right to protest radical Islam, again on a public sidewalk outside the Dearborn Center. No way! He's a hate-monger. It's just not right.

Hypocrisy abounds as usual.

The Mayor of Dearborn, the judge, and, of course, Wayne County Prosecutor Kym Worthy have heavy-handed this situation so badly, they have put Dearborn and all-but-bankrupt Wayne County in harm's way financially. Jones will sue for his denial of a protest license, the denial of his First Amendment rights and the fact that he was thrown into a Dearborn jail—albeit for a very short time—for doing absolutely nothing wrong. You gonna burn the Quran again? Nope. You gonna be peaceful Jonesy? 10-4 good buddy! When a big fat juicy check comes his way, if he still has on his PR guru hat, he'll give it to a local charity that helps the poorest among us, further burying O' Reilly, Somers, and Worthy in the manure pile they created.

Prosecutor Worthy, meanwhile, obviously still basking in the glory of her defeat of former Mayor-turned-convict Kwame Kilpatrick, proved once again that she needs to hire someone to proofread her statements before she sends them out. "These proceedings were solely about public safety. This was never about prohibiting free speech or fearing rioting but about a situation that could potentially place the public in danger in Dearborn," Worthy said.

242

Read that beauty slowly. Jones' trial was "solely about public safety" but never about "fearing rioting." Isn't a fear of rioting all about public safety? It reminds me of a quote from heavyweight wacko Mike Tyson a few years ago (recite in high-pitched, squeaky voice): "I didn't want to hurt him, but I hit him real hard."

Reverend Terry Jones Pulls a Charlie Sheen: April 29, 2011

In the end, Reverend Terry Jones pulled a "Charlie Sheen." He had a show, but it was poorly conceived, written, and delivered. He complained that the audience wasn't listening, just like Charlie. He tried to get in the audience's face, just like Charlie. The only thing he didn't say, like Charlie, was that "I already got your money." He didn't have to.

As you looked around this spectacle at Dearborn City Hall, you could see the money being wasted—snipers on just about every building top and more cops than you could throw a shoe at. (I know it is a Muslim tradition to throw a shoe in defiance, but didn't we conclude the silliness of that gesture in the first *Austin Powers* movie?)

The "show" started fifteen minutes late. That's a bad sign in the show biz business, which is all it was. The sound system was so lame I doubt Jones' followers standing directly in front of him could hear whatever nutty things he had to say, let alone the 400 or so protesters of the protest, led by a woman with such a loud and shrill voice that many in the crowd certainly stabbed their ear drums to end the misery.

I stood off to the side behind the yellow police tape line. I didn't want to join the big group against Jones, nor did I want to be a Jones supporter and get up close. Next to me were two (I assume due to dress) young Muslim women holding a baby. They were nice. We talked a few minutes. Occasionally they conversed in Arabic (My command of their language is a bit shaky but I think they were discussing one of my latest columns on the issue, which made me proud).

And then a policeman approached. One of the young ladies asked him who was across the street yelling and who was right in front of City Hall. The cop said the former were the people against Terry Jones and the people up close were his supporters. A bit shocked, she then asked "what is the area in which we find ourselves?" The cop replied, "Oh, this is the neutral zone." Aghast, the two young ladies high-tailed it for the anti-Jones area, only briefly harmed by the stain of neutrality.

The lameness of the effort reached its crescendo when Jones tried to get up close and personal with his enemies. Some threw shoes and water bottles at him. Not rocks or Molotov cocktails, but shoes and water bottles. "They were going to kill us," Jones would later claim.

Really? Shoes and water bottles, Terry? In addition to bigot and loon, we can add "wimp" when describing Jones.

Terry, you got to do your protest after your rights were previously violated by those in government who should have known better. Now, go back and work on your lame show before hitting the road again. And give Charlie a call.

The Reverend Jesse Jackson: Open Mouth, Insert Foot: May 2, 2011

According to *The American Heritage College Dictionary*, a martyr is "one who makes great sacrifices or suffers much for a belief, cause, or principle." Common belief is that martyrs are typically the good guys who stand up for what they believe until the bitter end. We don't consider terrorists martyrs, although terrorist organizations like al Qaeda advertise martyrdom as one of their fringe benefits.

Enter The Reverend Jesse Jackson. Never one to miss an opportunity to inject himself in any issue which might get him some press, Jesse has made the killing of Osama bin Laden both a partisan political event and another chance to say something stupid.

Jackson, noting that bin Laden was whacked with President Obama in office, called the killing a victory for the President. "It happened on his watch," said Jesse. If that was all he said, probably no biggie. I guess if bin Laden had been killed earlier on George W's watch his followers would claim "victory" as well. But claiming victory for Obama over Osama wasn't enough for The Reverend Jackson.

"My concern is we don't know what it does to stop terrorism," Jackson said. "It closes a big chapter in the book. (Get ready, here's the kicker.) Osama bin Laden is a martyr."

Osama bin Laden is a martyr? That is something an al Qaeda member or supporter would say, isn't it? You would think that a Christian minister like Jesse Jackson would spit on the notion of people like bin Laden ordering or committing the murder of thousands of innocents and then achieving martyrdom when they bite the dust.

Jackson should know better. He worked alongside a true martyr, Martin Luther King, Jr. So why this bizarre statement from Jackson? Oops, pardon the redundancy.

Betting the Farm on Us Buying the Farm: May 20, 2011

While yet another wacky minister gives Christianity a bad name, Harold Camping is sure the world ends May 21st, based on his exacting calculations of the Scriptures. Camping, who got his name when a friend asked his whereabouts: Where's Harold? "Harold Camping" was the reply from his wife as she dutifully proceeded with the exorcism of three "evil" cats she had caught in a trap in the backyard of her Oakland, California home.

Camping, of course, pulled up the stakes of his earlier prophecy of the end of the world back in 1994. He had "miscalculated." But Saturday, May 21 is the date of doom without question this time. Camping is betting the farm that we are all buying the farm.

'Cept for one minor problem: Camping's savior (oh, and mine), the Lord God Jesus Christ, would NEVER pick a Saturday to smite everybody. Here are the reasons why (and if I am wrong and Camping is right, thus making me blasphemous, all I can say tomorrow night is "Pass me a porn magazine, Osama" and "Hey, Hitler, can we put the A/C on?"):

1) Christ believed in hard work (and like all good Libertarians hated tax collectors—another story, sorry) and would never penalize folks on a Saturday, their first day off.

2) Saturday is a Powerball night. Just think of all the people that evoke God's name when placing a bet: "Oh, God, let me win and I'll give half to charity." Saturday by these facts is out, so let's move on to Sunday.

3) Sunday? The Sabbath? No way. One last chance for us sinners to cleanse our wicked ways by going to church.

4) Monday? And torch all those good people who went to church just to get at the slugs who can't find it in their schedule to hit the big house. No way. Anyway, as The Carpenters said, "Rainy days and Mondays always get me down." Lord knows Mondays are tough.

5) Tuesday is MegaMillions night. See Reason No. 2.

6) Wednesday? It's Hump Day and another Powerball night. Nada.

7) Friday, as in Good Friday? Nope. (Yes, I know I skipped over Thursday.)

8) Okay, here it is. If the world's going to end, it's definitely on a Thursday. Definitely on Thursday. Definitely on Thursday. (Shut up, Rain Man!) No Powerball, no MegaMillions. No Hump Day, no weekend. No date night, no start of a new week. Let's face it, Thursdays have sucked since *Cheers* and *Hill Street Blues* went off the air.

So move over, Happy Camper, I mean Harold Camping. Jesus ain't bringing the fire and brimstone on Saturday. The end of the world is Thursday, May 26. Bet on it—a straight bet in the four-digit game—0526. Yeah, that's the ticket.

Reverend Jesse Jackson Shakedown Artist: R.I.P.: March 25, 2013

Detroiters are the victims of Jesse Jackson's last and worst shakedown. Unlike his past antics, supposedly designed to help the "little guy" in a struggle against The Man, this one is all about Jackson trying to prove his relevance in a time and place he has become completely irrelevant.

Many people—okay, me—believe the tears Mr. Jackson shed in the park in Chicago when Barack Obama accepted the Presidency were not tears of joy reflecting on America's first black President, but rather tears of jealousy that the man on the stage was not him. Obama's elevation made Rev. Jackson a moot point: The Reverend Un-necessary.

The flow of money from the con game was gone. Al Sharpton knew it and quickly got a gig on MSNBC, hosting a pathetic show—but it paid the bills earlier paid by rabble-rousing and raising money as a civil rights advocate. But, Mr. Jackson was stuck. Al Gore had sold Current TV to Al-Jazeera, so there were no outlets. Reverend Jackson needed a new shakedown.

I have personally been the victim of his games. Okay, overplayed: I have had to deal with his crap—first at Nissan, then at Ford and Chrysler. My first experience was telling. Nissan was bankrupt and their North American unit was trying to shed costs. One expense was funding jazz great Thelonious Monk's foundation for youth music in Los Angeles and the contract was up. Both organizations had screwed up—for Nissan, you don't provide 90 percent of the funding for any non-profit, and for Monk, you never rely on one funder. Nissan was out of cash. Monk was screwed, so he called Jackson and had him crank up the Race Baiting Machine with threats of nationwide boycott of all Nissan dealers.

We sat in a conference room at Nissan, plotting our "strategy." It was my first day on the job as head of PR. The new head of HR, a good ol' boy from Tennessee, boldly proclaimed, "It says right here in the contract that we have the right not to sign another deal. This is nothing but extortion."

"Yeah," I said, "So what's your point?" I then spelled out the gory details. Nissan was bankrupt. It had a 4 percent share of the U.S. market, but had an 8 percent share among African Americans. A successful boycott would do big damage at a time the ship was teetering, extortion or not.

Jesse shoots; he scores. And he would score some more down the road; a shakedown here, a shakedown there. But then the shakedown machine started to squeak—an illegitimate child, and a book detailing his less-than-pure exploits, written by a black female reporter, charging him point blank with a rumor often associated with the Reverend: when Martin Luther King Jr. was shot in Memphis, Jackson rushed to his fallen leader's side and wiped King's blood off the body and onto his own shirt. For effect, I guess.

Fast-forward to November 2008. When Barack Obama took the presidential brass ring, Jackson's Shakedown Machine was spewing smoke and with Obama's reelection in 2012, the gasket was blown. But along came the opportunity of a lifetime: a broken Detroit and a really white, multi-kazillionaire governor stealing the City from its "people." He swept into the city and promised mass civil disobedience. It was like old times again!

Thirty-five people showed up, um, er, in mass Monday, the first day of the Emergency Manager. Good bye, Jesse.

Christ as a Liberal Crutch: April 1, 2013
We in Washington just survived the March Madness at the Supreme Court. Tickets to the Supremes were going for as much as six large (line waiters charge by the hour and the lineup went on for days) in anticipation of the court's hearing regarding the same-sex marriage (ahem, wedding equality) issue. And Jesus was there.

Oh no, not at the court, but in the arguments by some on the side of legalizing "marriage equality." On his radio show Wednesday, Sean Hannity had a Christian minister that vehemently purported that if Christ were alive today, he would be for same-sex marriage. My first thought was, "you idiot," Christ is alive you numb nut – this is the basis of Christianity – crucified, resurrected, up in Heaven as God. What don't you get Mr. Minister? Oh, I forget, you are all about love.

Jesus was all about love, so the minister opined. Fine argument until Hannity's other guest asked the minister the question, "what if four or five people love each other and want to get married?"

You could hear the minister vomit ever so slightly in his mouth as his stomach did flip flops. The point is that neither Hannity, nor his other guest, brought up Jesus' purported view on same-sex marriage. It was the same-sex, liberal proponent. Liberals love to use Jesus when it behooves their cause. They believe it is a "gotcha" moment.

As I listened, I hoped for Hannity to ask the Jesus-spouting liberal minister if Jesus would be in favor of killing babies in the womb—oh, excuse me, "women's health" issues?

Yes indeed, I wonder what would Jesus do to those that use his name but have no idea what He believed and tried to teach us.

Reverend Al Sharpton's Prayers Answered: July 14, 2013
Relax George Zimmerman, your nightmare is over. Or not. You think you won your second degree murder case, um, er, manslaughter case, but the real winner was on *Meet the Press* Sunday morning: the Reverend Al Sharpton. The reverend, I believe, was literally praying for a not guilty verdict so that he could continue his relentless crusade to find racism where it does not exist.

Sharpton is promising pressure on the Justice Department to go after Zimmerman for a civil rights violation despite his acquittal in a trial Sharpton and his gang demanded, despite the evidence, aided and abetted by our President ("If I had a son, he'd look like Trayvon"). On NBC Sunday he laid out his rhetorical strategy: something is wrong when a kid can be killed for doing "nothing wrong" and the killer is exonerated.

Nothing wrong? If you only watched the highlights of the trial, you saw the evidence that Trayvon Martin was beating George Zimmerman silly, including breaking his nose. Martin had not a scratch, except, of course, for a bruised hand that Zimmerman was obviously beating with his face and the gunshot wound for which a jury of six women said he received in Zimmerman's legal self-defense. The latter is indeed a tragedy, a young life snuffed out, but would there be such outrage had Martin beat Zimmerman to death? Doubt it.

So the show must go on, George. Even Senator Majority Leader Harry Reid took a dump on the verdict. And, those lunatics in America's cesspool city—no, not Detroit—Oakland, California, rioted while Florida and the rest of the country remained calm.

In some respects, this polarizing verdict reminded me a bit of the O.J. Simpson verdict. I was in Chrysler's Washington Office at the time. We all—black and white colleagues—gathered in the conference room in front of the television. When O.J. was acquitted, my white colleagues stood there in utter silence while the black colleagues literally cheered. That same scenario played out all across America. You remember. Everybody, I mean, everybody, knew O.J. was guilty. But, to some, that wasn't the point.

But the Zimmerman case is slightly different. It isn't necessarily a black/white thing. It's very much like seemingly everything is today: liberal vs. conservative. Every conservative person or media I talked to or watched believed Zimmerman was not guilty; every liberal friend I talked with believed he was guilty. The MSM of course sadly fed this beast. *The New York Times* constantly referred to Zimmerman as a "white Hispanic." In the hundreds of forms I have filled out over the years, I have seen white, Caucasian, non-white and Hispanic ethnicity boxes to check. But I have never seen a box for "white Hispanic." Zimmerman lawyer Mark O'Mara (who was great) summed it best when he blamed the media for their enormous role in this near travesty of justice.

George Zimmerman is not guilty; but to some, that isn't the point.

So, strap on your flak jacket, Mr. Zimmerman. It was bad enough that while being found not guilty in the trial of the year, you were consistently portrayed as a big, fat, wimpy, soft, wanna-be-cop liar. Now you've got to deal with Sharpton, likely Jesse Jackson, and the rest of the race-baiters trying to relive their glory years

Following the verdict, the Martin family's personal lawyer declared "Trayvon Martin will remain in the anals of history." Um, dude, the term is "annals" of history. The former is where the Reverend Al Sharpton remains.

Chapter Fourteen: Stupid Sports Figures

Universal Uclick/gocomics.com/EMAIL: hpayne@detnews.com

University of Michigan Hiring Assange as Football Coach?: December 7, 2010

In a surprise move uncovered by the Wisecracker's staff on crack—um, er, crack staff—U of M Athletic Director Dave "Selling Domino's Pizzas was Easier" Brandon has offered to trade unwanted football coach Rich Rodriquez for WikiLeaks alleged-pervert and threat-to-national-security Julian Assange.

Brandon, in an email to President Mary Sue Coleman, said, "We want to be number one in everything we do at this university, from academics to football. Unfortunately, our football coach has now fallen to the SECOND most-hated person behind Mr. Assange. We need to be at the top again. That's why I took this job."

"Think about it Madam President," continued the ex-Domino's CEO, "Julian could steal the plays of all of our competition. (Ohio State head coach) Tressel would be toast and (Michigan State's) Dantonio would be crying his eyes out. Besides, Assange may be a creepy little dude, but I don't think we'll catch him quoting scripture and singing "You Lift Me Up." (As Rich Rodriguez did as his tenure crumbled.)

No word yet on Coleman's response but a press conference is planned for 10 a.m. tomorrow in Ann Arbor.

Ban Tobacco in Baseball? Why Stop There? October 19, 2011

Baseball's Nanny—er—Commish Bud Selig wants to ban tobacco. Really?

Why stop there? Ban sugary bubble gum (tooth decay), tattoos (potential infection), balls scratching (perverts), spitting (gross), crossing one's self or pointing up to heaven (offends atheists), the national anthem (glorifies imperialistic killing machine that is the USA), hot dogs (full of nitrates and pig lips), soda pop (obesity among youth), beer (duh) and peanuts (to save those with nut allergies).

253

Also, ban scoring as we want "scoring equality" and—oh my—you must get rid of stealing.

Akin "Akin" to Penn State's Ex-President: August 23, 2012

Missouri U.S. Senate candidate Todd Akin is not the only high-profile moron making stupid comments about rape; enter ousted Penn State President Graham Spanier. Spanier and his lawyers attacked a university-backed report on the Jerry Sandusky sex abuse (rape) scandal, claiming it was nothing more than a "blundering and indefensible indictment." Spanier is awaiting whether or not charges will be filed against him.

Spanier's lawyer Timothy Lewis called Louis Freeh, the former FBI director and federal judge who compiled the scathing report of Sandusky, Joe Paterno, Spanier, and the other cowards, a "biased investigator."

He is, of course, right, as Freeh is biased against rapists and the people who condone the behavior.

"The Freeh report, as it pertains to Dr. Spanier, is a myth. And that myth ... ends today," Lewis said in a news conference.

No, numb nuts: the myth was that Jerry Sandusky cared for all these unfortunate boys. The myth was that Joe Paterno cared about young people when in truth he was only concerned about being the winningest coach in college football history; that's why he coached until he was 105 years old and ignored his sidekick raping young boys. "Hey Jerry, could ya stop the buggery for a few minutes? I've got to beat Ohio State this weekend to get the big one."

The myth is that Spanier and the rest of these creeps didn't know what was going on. It's a lot like giving a pass to Joe Biden and all of his stupid gaffes, but this time it was "Good Ol' Jerry."

Spanier told ABC News's *Nightline* that he was told only that Sandusky had been seen engaging in "horseplay" in a campus shower with a boy and he assumed that meant "throwing water around, snapping towels." Okay, Spanier: did ya ever think to tell Sandusky that grown men don't take showers with little boys...ever?!? Coaches shower with football players, perhaps. But kids? And, come to think of it, don't the coaches at big time universities like Penn State have separate shower facilities? I, for one, wouldn't have wanted to see Joe Pa naked.

I scratch my head every time I hear someone caught up in this scandal speak—from the Paterno family to the assistant coach that saw Sandusky raping a kid and walked away, to Spanier. I mean, who is giving them PR advice? (In the case of the Paterno family, I know; and I only hope they are not listening to him. If they are following his advice, he should be ashamed of himself.)

Enjoy your life, Mr. Spanier. When it's over, get ready for your dorm room with Paterno, Sandusky (eventually), Hitler, and bin Laden.

Pennsylvania Gov. Tom Corb-idiot: January 3, 2013

John Boehner can finally give a sigh of relief. The day after a fraud was perpetuated on the American people by our then-lame duck Congress, Pennsylvania Governor Tom Corbett has taken the early lead in "Stupidest Politician in America Sweepstakes." And despite this being only the first week of the New Year, he appears to have a stranglehold on the award. Why? He flunked the first rule of PR 101: Get the bad news behind you fast.

In this case, of course, it's the horrible Jerry Sandusky pedophile scandal at Penn State University. Sandusky is in prison for life, and his former boss, Joe Paterno, quickly bought the farm—most likely in connection with the scandal. Poor Joe Pa even had his statue taken down ala Saddam Hussein. The NCAA came down hard on Penn State, stopping short of "capital punishment" on the football program and Penn State, in general. Sure, the news would not completely go away as the coming lawsuits hit the courts or are settled, but Corbett's announcement of a federal suit against the NCAA was a self-inflicted blow. Or, make that a selfish-inflicted blow.

By the time this stupid suit is thrown out, the Nittany Lions' four-year bowl ban and recruiting restrictions (boo hoo hoo) will most likely be over and the football team can play in ONE or a few extra games each year if they qualify. The scars of the young men (then boys) that were sodomized by Sandusky may never heal no matter how much money they force Penn State to part with.

Governor Corbett: You are talking about a GAME for crying out loud. The victims are trying to figure out their LIVES, you creep!

Corbett's stupidity gets stupider when you consider that while Attorney General of Pennsylvania, there are allegations that he heard rumors about Sandusky and sat on them. Meanwhile, the rapes of boys by a fat, old man continued.

The good people of Pennsylvania should recall or the legislature should impeach this clown. What a disgrace.

Is the Whole World Juicing? March 17, 2013

This is the story of chicken you-know-what and chickens. Let's start with the former.

Mark McGwire, Sammy Sosa, Rafael Palmeiro, and the biggest horse's rear end in the history of Major League Baseball, Barry Bonds—okay, Ty Cobb was reportedly the biggest arse of all time—ruined our nation's pastime when it was just coming back from the strike/lockout/whatever-it-was in the '80s. They all juiced with extra pulp and lied like Nixon when confronted. McGwire's Congressional testimony may go down as the most pathetic in the history of that pathetic institution—he was a sleazy rat in a dysfunctional kangaroo court.

Then, in the hormone enhancing world, we saw the NFL go down. These sudden giants soon fell apart upon retirement and experienced early deaths—Lyle Alzado dead-dead at 43 years old and MSU's Tony Mandarich career-dead after a scant few years in the NFL after being the second round draft pick in the 1989 draft, just behind Troy Aikman.

The pinnacle of the scandal came late last year when Lance "I Will Destroy Anyone in My Path" Armstrong finally had the, um, er, "dignity" to admit he was the biggest liar in the history of sports. Live Strong? No, Live Wrong! Hope the subsequent lawsuits bankrupt him, considering all the lives he attempted or succeeded in destroying.

But now, perhaps the most onerous juicing is upon us, and it doesn't involved humans. Personally, it is so hideous because I never kissed any of those aforementioned players; BUT I have had Kentucky Fried Chicken (KFC) in my mouth. Yes, the Colonel Sanders' creation is accused of buying chickens using growth hormones. The chickens, in the spirit of McGwire, Bonds, and Armstrong are, not surprisingly, claiming fowl, er, foul.

"I used a salve I was given because I had chicken pox, seriously," said plumpy hen, Alfreda, moments before her head was separated from her body at the Osceola, Iowa chicken processing plant. (Aren't you glad we humans don't call funeral homes "processing plants"?)

"I only use vitamins I purchased at GNC," said Shaquille O'Chicken, the world's first 30-pound chicken who recently agreed to a $20-signing deal with KFC. "Well, to be honest, I didn't purchase them. But, there was a guy who sold them to me and he was legit."

KFC's biggest competitor, Popeye's Chicken, has called for a federal investigation. A spokesperson for the Cajun-influenced chicken purveyor claims KFC is cheating saying,

"Oh dat ze comin da tah convict."

You can't make this chicken (stuff) up.

A Twisted Tale in Happy Valley Gets More Twisted: January 17, 2015

All is good in Happy Valley, home of Penn State University. The NCAA has cried "uncle" and the late Joe Paterno is once again the winningest coach in college football history after the league "restored" some 111 wins tossed aside in the most hideous scandal in collegiate sports history. The Paterno family, through its spokesperson (I know him) is proclaiming a "great victory." Welcome back to the Top 40 Twisted Sister.

Joe Paterno, and other "leaders" at Penn State, ignored glaring, eyewitness accounts that former assistant coach Jerry Sandusky was RAPING boys over an extended period. Sandusky is in prison for the rest of his pathetic life, luckily out of gunshot range of his victims' fathers. Yet, if you read the pages of *USA Today*, PSU and Paterno were somehow the victims of an overly aggressive NCAA. Hell, I would have used a butter knife and salt on Sandusky's weapon of mass destruction.

Penn State's football program did not get the "death penalty" that was supposedly on the table a few years ago. That's because the money-grubbing collegiate athletic system really doesn't believe in the death penalty, no matter how heinous a program has acted. Boys were raped. Sorry for repeating myself.

Two Pennsylvania politicians sued the college and the NCAA to make sure the 60 million dollar fine against the school is spent exclusively in the state to "fight child abuse." I say give the ten young men molested by Sandusky, and ignored by Paterno and others, 6 million each, and stop the charade that Penn State and the Paterno family are somehow victims.

That would be a "great victory," but as a father of two boys it would still not be enough.

Super Bowl Announcer Al Michaels Is a Fugitive: January 31, 2015

Do you believe in criminals? Yes!

If you read the interview of sports broadcasting legend, Al Michaels, in today's *Wall Street Journal*, you'll, like I was, be surprised to learn that the voice of this year's Super Bowl is a petty thief. It's actually a great story.

Back in 2000 on the night of the presidential election, Michaels found himself in the same Nashville hotel as THE Al Gore. That evening Al Gore called "President-elect" George W. Bush to concede. Then, hours later, Al Gore picked up the phone in his hotel room and called back W, withdrawing his concession to begin the most contentious election in American political history.

Al Michaels made his way down the hall to Al Gore's hotel suite and strangely found the door ajar. Michaels entered the room and noticed no one was around. But, there in all its glory was the phone Al Gore had used to call W. twice. Like any sane man raking in millions every year in a broadcast booth, Michaels decided it was "finders, keepers" and snatched the phone, returning to his room.

The concession/non-concession phone today resides in storage in Michaels' garage. And the fugitive thief remains on the run, trying to hide from authorities as roughly 115 million people listen to and see him tomorrow night. Book 'em Danno, ah, er, Glendale (Arizona) Police.

The "Possible" Pete Carroll-Reggie Bush Pre-Game Call: February 1, 2015

The pre-game phone call I imagine between Seattle Seahawks coach, Pete Carroll, and his former USC running back star, Reggie Bush:

Bush: Hey Coach, good luck today against those cheating New England Patriots in the Super Bowl.

Carroll: Ah, Reggie. Don't mention "cheating" on the phone. The NSA is listening.

Bush: You mean the NCAA? Hate those bastards.

Carroll: No, our spies.

Bush: Spice? Like millions of Americans, I'm making some fine spice for my wings for the game.

Carroll: No, spies, as in our government spying on us.

Bush: You mean the a-holes that took away my Heisman Trophy.

Carroll: No, that was the NCAA. Anyway, we both made out okay. I left a corrupt program at USC and am getting paid millions to coach in the most popular sport on the planet and you are doing great, as well.

Bush: I play for the Detroit Lions.

Carroll: Um, (pause) that's what I am talking about Reggie. You get to be home on Super Bowl Sunday.

Bush: Do you ever feel guilty about what we did at USC?

Carroll: Hello? Hello? I can't hear you. Reggie? Reggie?

Bush: Coach? You hear me know?

Carroll: Yeah.

Bush: I asked if you felt guilty about the crap we pulled at USC.

Carroll: Hello? Hello? It's breaking up again.

Bush: Coach. Ya hear me?

Carroll: Of course, I hear you, but I got a game to coach, and a boatload of money to make. I hope the Pats have the balls…that are inflated. I hate cheaters.

Bush: Yeah. Me, too.

The Brady "Hunch": May 7, 2015

Tom Brady: Cheater and Liar according to the NFL's investigation into "Soggy Ballsgate." Yep, a guy who is considered one of the greatest quarterbacks in NFL history is a cheater and a liar: Two, two, two mints in one. Actually those two traits seem to go together more and more these days, don't they? Brady cannot cry foul for anything the NFL does to him in the coming weeks as he refused to cooperate with the investigation. So, all we have from Brady is his pathetic post-game denial of anything to do with the soggy balls he had his hand around in the first half of the AFC Title Game earlier this year.

I could go all-partisan, put on my Michigan State alumnus jersey and say, "What do you expect from a Michigan Wolverine? Cheating is second nature." But I will not do that. I repeat I will not accuse Brady of being a cheater because that is how they roll in Ann Arbor. I am staying classy, San Diego.

So what will Roger "I didn't know Ray Rice beat up his girlfriend even though he told me in a face-to-face meeting" Goodell end up doing to Brady, the "ball boys," and the New Cheating Patriots? Fines? Of course, but what's a few bucks to people like Tom Brady who has about as much money as Bill and The Woman Formerly Known as Hillary Clinton. Suspensions? Doubt it. Maybe: a game or two at the most. Draft pick? Again, maybe, but one draft pick is meaningless in the grand scheme. This is what I think will happen.

What should happen? Hammurabi baby! As in, Hammurabi's Code of Laws. You remember: an eye for an eye, a tooth for a tooth. Brady ordered his ball boys to deflate the game balls to gain an advantage and therefore, he should have his, um, er, you get my drift.

Chapter Fifteen: Stupid Predictions (on my part)

"Their T-shirts are both made in China."

Obama Gets Nailed by *The Washington Post*: June 10, 2011

Unless they can prove Mitt Romney not only bullied that poor soul at Cranbrook prep school a half century ago, but also drowned some cats, called Detroit Tiger Hall of Famer Al Kaline a wussy, and put a flaming bag of dog poop on Rosa Parks' front door, the Mittster is a walk as our next President. Why? Astonishingly, *The Washington Post*.

This Sunday's *Post* at my front door was destined to be a collector's item: a full section dedicated to the fortieth anniversary of Watergate and the *Post*'s, and journalism's, single greatest accomplishment – the bringing down of the most powerful and corrupt man in the world. But wait, the geniuses at the *Post* outdid themselves. Page two in the A section—the filet mignon of the Sunday WaPo was an article with the headline: "A bad week for the Democrats." Bad enough for Team Obama, but what was the killer and game-changer was the photograph. It was of our President in "full frown." A picture tells a thousand words? No. A picture tells the story of the next election.

Think for yourself the last time you saw a less than complimentary photo of Mr. Obama. Really, think hard. Typically the photos are of our Prez, chin up, looking as confident as LeBron James in his home arena. Geez, remember the mag cover with a halo over Obama's head just last month. Christ-like? No, Christ. But here—in *The Washington Post*—was the first pathetic picture of President Obama. Oh, the *Post* knows a pathetic picture, mind you. Study their photo gallery—along with *The New York Times* and every other liberal rag—and you will see more contorted faces of George W that by any measure seem un reasonable. Smiling George? No. Confident George? Nada. Smirking W? Yessiree. Everytime. Looks like a buffoon; must be one.

I am certain Team Obama threw a hissy fit with the *Post*. How dare they portray OUR President this way? Perhaps, the lens is on the other foot and the country may be in line with the voters of Wisconsin, Michigan, and a landslide in the making.

Here's to you, Mr. Bully, Mitt Romney. Try not to say something stupid this week about firing people, Cadillacs, or NASCAR owners; you are finally winning.

A Little Town Called Hope…in Iowa: October 7, 2012

There is hope. Trust me. I wasn't so sure until the first presidential debate. But then, one debate doesn't make a master debater. Ahem. No, I was assured there is indeed hope when I went back home to Iowa to celebrate my little brother's 50th.

One of the Hawkeyes in attendance was a 22-year-old who is a legislator in Iowa. His name is Jake Highfill. Scheez. He's a Republican and 22, sorry for repeating that. You can find more leprechauns than that. He is not out of college yet (Iowa, of which the Hawkeyes totally suck this year, getting beaten by Central Michigan University in Iowa City.). Yet, he is with the good guys. I wept when I met him. (Yes, I had had several Guinnesses with my birthday-boy brother, but golldarnit (that is Iowa speak so we don't rot in hell).

We sat along a fire pit as the night went on. I was vigorously trying to convince my wonderful, leftist niece of voting age why it was a big deal whom she voted for. At one point I turned to the young congressman and asked "how am I doing?" Keep going, he said, you're smoking. We'll see on November 6.

All is not lost. Remember when Obi-Wan Kenobi told Yoda that Luke is our last hope? Yoda replied: "Hmm, hmm, there is another." There are young people out there who understand.

There is hope, after all, in Iowa and perhaps in the country.

The Tour de Mitt: October 20, 2012

The presidential campaign now looks more like a Tour de France race—a series of legs in which if you get an early, big win, and hold your own over the following legs, you win. The first leg of the Tour de Mitt was rather odd as it started with a high altitude leg in Denver. A winded Barack Obama sputtered through this leg and when Romney crossed the finish line, the President was nowhere in sight.

The second leg was on flat land and resulted in a vicious sprint in which we saw the lead change hands over and over. The MSM gave the race to Obama for simply peddling this time and for a better-tuned bicycle thanks to CNN's Candy Crowley, while most honest judges saw it as a draw. But, importantly, in Tour de Mitt scoring, Romney still held his overall lead and perhaps even enhanced it based on the post-debate polls.

The final leg of Tour de Mitt comes Monday night. The subject is foreign policy. Months, heck, weeks ago, Team Obama would be licking their chops thinking about this leg. After all, President Obama "personally" whacked Osama bin Laden, and Mitt Romney's only foreign policy was as the "Outsourcer in Chief" in his days at Bain Capital. It was going to be an uphill leg for Romney and a downhill cruise for Obama.

But then the shift hit the man. Obama, that is. The Libya where Obama had "led from behind" in killing Gaddafi had turned ugly on him: for the first time in 30 years, an American ambassador was murdered. Oh, not just murdered, but raped as well, along with the murders of three other Americans. The subsequent cover-up by team Obama, blaming the whole affair on a wacky video, and failing to acknowledge they knew it was a terrorist attack on 9/11 for weeks, now is the umbrella under which Romney can smoke Obama in the final leg.

Here is the narrative for Romney Monday night. Obama's foreign policy disasters began at the start of his term with his infamous apology tour in the Arab world. He should have stayed home and sent out Sally Fields to speak for him. He has only wanted to "talk" with the scoundrels in Iran and has given them four years of freedom to advance their nuclear weapon program. He has turned a cold shoulder to Israel. Last month, he said Israel was "one of our most important allies" in the region. One of?

That's like asking a guy if his wife is "one of his best friends." The wrong answer gets you the couch.

Then we have that little problem with the "reset button" with the Soviets, um, er, the Russians. Romney was blasted as a foreign policy Neanderthal for calling the Russkies one of our biggest threats. Meanwhile, Obama was whispering in the Russians' ears that he needed a little "flexibility" until he got re-elected. The Russians translated flexibility into thwarting the free world's attempts to stop Syria's Assad from killing his own people and helping Iran in any way they can.

The final nail in Obama's foreign policy coffin keeps getting hammered further with each new day. The Administration ignored pleas for more security for our people in Libya. The day after the murders, Obama stepped in as Commander-in-Chief and flew to Las Vegas for a fundraiser. Appearing on a comedy show—a comedy show—he referred to the killings as less than "optimal."

This last leg of the Tour de Mitt is one in which Romney merely needs to do what he did in the previous two legs: talk about Obama's horrible record. Osama bin Laden is dead. And, thanks to this President's performance, radical Islam is alive and deadly, Israel is in peril and Putin's determination to regain Russia's status as a super power is on track. Monday you'll hear more "ahs" out of Obama than you have ever heard before.

Bring on the Hanging Chad: October 23, 2012

There is talk now in the American political world that the November 6th presidential vote could come down to recounts much like in 2000. That infamous election (thank you Ralph Nader) resulted in a fight all the way to the Supreme Court. Bush Won. Dems Puked. The decision eventually came down to a few hundred or a thousand Floridians who couldn't successfully punch their voter cards, although they had a prowess for punching their bingo and keno cards without much controversy.

I, for one, was a supreme beneficiary of the incompetence in Florida in 2000. You see, prior to the election, I was the PR chief for Ford Motor Company, and we were the top news EVERY night: Firestone tires on Ford Explorers disintegrating and killing people in roll-over accidents.

Come November 3rd, 2000, we—me and Ford—were relegated to the back pages. From then on, every morning I awoke and bowed down southward to the morons in Florida who had the hand strength of a gnat. I promised in several speeches that if I had another child, I would name him Chad.

Go ahead, Florida or Ohio. Make our day. Again.

Iowa: Obama's Field of Screams: October 28, 2012

I grew up in the small town of Pella, Iowa. Our house was four blocks from the town square and one block from a farm field. Like all Iowans, I acquired a discerning nose for cows, pigs, and yes, bulls---. This is why endorsement of Republican Mitt Romney by the behemoth newspaper in Iowa, the very liberal *The Des Moines Register*, is a wake-up call for the Obama campaign and America.

Iowans, in general, are pretty easy to stereotype—they go to school in a great educational environment, they work hard, they are honest, and they are kind. I remember going home in 1982 from graduate school at Michigan State for a Fourth of July weekend. I was in tow with two classmates-one a New Yorker. When we exited I-80 to take the secondary roads to Pella, my NY friend was blown away that every car coming the other way waved at us. "You know them," he asked time and time again. "No, we're 30 miles from my home." "Why are they waving?" "That's what friendly people do."

The people of Iowa were friendly to Barack Obama in 2008. They saw a fresh face on the American political scene. They accepted his rhetoric as real. And, like all Americans, they all wanted hope and change. The nation was tired, depressed, and war-weary. Iowa, with one of the lowest percentages of black folks in the country, didn't give a damn about the color of Barack Obama's skin. They liked his energy and his message and they rewarded him.

But, not anymore. Like a good Iowa farmer, they expect you to get up every morning and do your chores. Iowans abhor blaming others for your own mistakes. So, when the liberal *Des Moines Register* did the unthinkable Sunday and endorsed Mr. Bain Capital, it was for a reason: Iowans will give everyone a chance, but you better be prepared to earn their endorsement. And if your only reason for a second term centers around tearing down your opponent—almost always falsely—well, our mommas always told us "if you can't say something nice about the other person, say nothing at all."

Yes, indeed, salt of the earth. And salt in the wound of Obama's crumbling campaign. Is this heaven, Mitt? No, it's Iowa. Make one more trip there to cement the deal. It won't mean a whole lot of Electoral College votes, but it will close the deal with America.

Chapter Sixteen: Finally

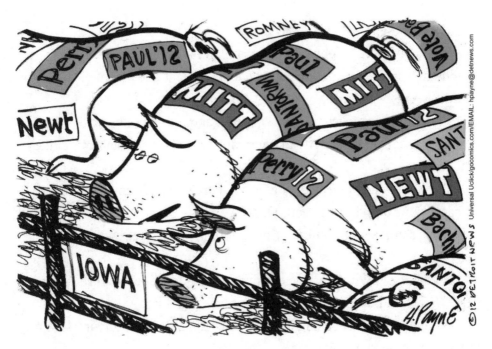

"Are they gone yet?"

(Note: Sorry if the past few chapters might have depressed you. There is hope. Maybe. Anyway, over the years I received tons of comments on my columns. Some angry, some supportive, and some just plain funny, clever, and inspired. I did not write these, but they are my favorites, and I am thrilled to pass them along to end this book.)

Energy: September 26, 2012

If you yelled for eight years, seven months, and seven days, you would have produced enough sound energy to heat one cup of coffee. (Hardly seems worth it.)

If you farted consistently for six years and nine months, enough gas is produced to create the energy of an atomic bomb. (Now that's more like it!)

The human heart creates enough pressure when it pumps out to the body to squirt blood thirty feet. (OMG!)

A pig's orgasm lasts thirty minutes. (In my next life, I want to be a pig!)

A cockroach will live nine days without its head before it starves to death. (Creepy, but then I'm still not over the pig thing.)

Banging your head against a wall uses 150 calories an hour. (Don't try this at home; maybe at work.)

The male praying mantis cannot copulate while its head is attached to its body. The female initiates sex by ripping the male's head off. (Honey, I'm home. WTF?)

The flea can jump 350 times its body length. It's like a human jumping the length of a football field. (Thirty minutes? Lucky pig! Can you imagine?)

The catfish has over 27,000 taste buds. (What could be so tasty on the bottom of a pond?)

Some lions mate over 50 times a day. (I still want to be a pig in my next life .... quality over quantity!)

Butterflies taste with their feet. (Something I always wanted to know.)

The strongest muscle in the body is the tongue. (Hmm...)

Right-handed people live, on average, 9 years longer than left-handed people. (If you're ambidextrous, do you split the difference?)

Elephants are the only animals that cannot jump. (Okay, so that would be a good thing.)

A cat's urine glows under a black light. (I wonder how much the government paid to figure that out.)

An ostrich's eye is bigger than its brain. (I know some people like that.)

Starfish have no brains. (I know some people like that, too. I didn't know they were Starfish.)

Polar bears are left-handed. (If they switch, they'll live a lot longer.)

Humans and dolphins are the only species that have sex for pleasure. (What about that pig? Do the dolphins know about the pig?!)

I Want to "Live Life Backwards": January 10, 2015

Again, I didn't write it, but feel compelled to share it. A friend told me it's "like 10 years old" but I only heard about it a couple of weeks ago. It's entitled "Live Life Backwards." Here goes:

I want to live my next life backwards. You start out dead and get that out of the way.

Then you wake up in an old-age home feeling better every day.

Then, you get kicked out for being too healthy. You enjoy your retirement and collect your pension.

Then, when you start work, you get a gold watch on your first day. You work 40 years until you're too young to work.

You get ready for high school: drink alcohol, party, and you are generally promiscuous.

Then you go to primary school, you become a kid; you play and have no responsibilities.

Then you become a baby. You spend your last nine months floating peacefully in luxury, in spa-like conditions with central heating and room service on tap.

And then…you finish off as an orgasm.

God Bless You…and God Bless America. And please, God, TAKE THE SONS OF BITCHES OUT!

Jason Vines
Bio

Jason Vines, 55, is an independent communications consultant and author. In late 2014 Waldorf Publishing released his first book *"What Did Jesus Drive? -- Crisis PR in Cars, Computers and Christianity"* to critical acclaim.

Vines served as the top communications professional for three automakers – Nissan North America, Ford Motor Company, and Chrysler Group between 1998 and 2007. He was named "Top PR Professional" in the automotive industry in 1999, 2005, and 2006 by *Automotive News*, the auto industry's lead trade publication. He is credited with leading some of the most memorable product launches in the automotive industry, including the Chrysler 300, Jeep Grand Cherokee, Dodge Viper, and the reborn Nissan 350Z. Vines also was the communications chief during some of the biggest crises in automotive history, including claims of sudden unintended acceleration in Jeep vehicles, kids getting killed by front-seat air bags, a Nissan Motor Corporation on the brink of bankruptcy, and, the granddaddy of perhaps all business crises, the Ford/Firestone tire crisis in 2000 and 2001.

Despite consistently being in the hottest-of-hot seats, Vines never lost his sense of humor. A stand-up comic during the comedy club explosion of the '80s and early '90s (all the while working as an aspiring automotive executive), Vines was recruited by the late *Detroit Free Press* Publisher Neal Shine to serve as a key writer and performer for the Detroit Press Club's annual parody show – **The Detroit Press Club Steakout** – where local and national politicians and other public figures had been skewered in an "off-the-record" and very non-PC laugh riot for more than 30 years.

Sadly, when the U.S. economy fell into crisis in 2007 and 2008, the Steakout was dead due to a lack of funding (the Detroit Press Club, like almost all press clubs across the country, had shuttered its doors several years before). But, Vines' wit lived on.

In the spring of 2010, **Detroit News'** political cartoonist Henry Payne called Vines and asked him to bring the spirit, humor, and rawness of the Steakout to a new, conservative political website he was creating sponsored by *The Detroit News* – **The Michigan View**. Vines jumped at the chance to bring his satire and (hopefully) humor to the craziness that is politics in the United States of America. A few years later, *The Michigan View* was fully incorporated as the **Politics Blog** of *The Detroit News*. The rest is, well, sometimes hysterical.

Vines is Director-Emeritus of the Automotive Hall of Fame, an organization he served as Chairman for two years, and one he hopes to be inducted in someday. But, he is not holding his breath. (Actually he is, as you basically have to be dead to get inducted.)

Vines received a Master's Degree in Labor and Industrial Relations from Michigan State University in 1984 and a B.A. with a double major in Economics and Communications/Theater from Central College in Pella, Iowa in 1982. He has been married to his wife Betsy for more than 28 years and has three college graduates that thankfully are employed and have their own health insurance, cell phone contracts, and auto insurance policies. They live in Wilmington, North Carolina, and Lewiston, Michigan (Yes, like the Clintons they have more than one home despite earlier being "dead broke").

Acknowledgments

Thank you first to **The Detroit News'** Henry Payne, syndicated editorial cartoonist genius, who not only gave me the opportunity to spew on his early political website, but later in the actual paper. Henry is a champion of conservative thought and one funny, funny man. And, he, like me, loves cars. Thanks, Henry, for the fantastic cover of this book and the use of your past editorial cartoons throughout.

Of course, thank you to Al Gore, Reverends Al Sharpton, Jesse Jackson, and "Muslim-hater" Terry Jones for being complete and utterly reliable douchebags. Thank you, President Obama and Attorney General Eric Holder, for all of your hypocritical activities. And, thank you to a host of Republican leaders for being totally clueless. A huge attaboy goes out to former Detroit Mayor and now-convict, Kwame Kilpatrick, and his moronic handlers, for giving me, and all journalists, a treasure-trove of great things to chastise.

My greatest praise goes to my lovely wife Betsy, who sometimes read my columns and said: "You're not going to print with that are you?" When she voiced those words, I knew I was on to something. Thanks, too, to my daughter Lane, who echoed Betsy's "thoughtful" admonitions of my words in print. I knew, if they were worried, I was good-to-go.

Reference Pages

Abdulmutallab, Umar Farouk   27
Ackroyd, Dan   211
Ahmadinejad, Mahmoud   45, 51, 199
Aikman, Troy   256
Ailes, Roger   207
Aikin, Clay   50
Akin, Congressman Todd   26, 50, 142, 254
al-Assad, Bashar   94
al-Awaki, Anwar   128-129, 161
Albom, Mitch   202-207
Alito, Justice Samuel   64
Allen, Senator George   77
Allred, Gloria   74
Alzado, Lyle   256
Anderson, Jessica   226
Anderson, Congressman John   76
Anderson, Pamela   14
Andersson, Bo   93-94
Armstrong, Lance   257
Artest, Ron   209
Assange, Julian   253
Avalon, Frankie   218
Ayers, William   138
Axelrod, David   75, 82, 112, 137-138, 141
Backmann, Congresswoman Michelle   6, 126-128, 212-214
Bob, Baghdad   17, 103
Bacon, Kevin   142
Barr, Rosanne   50, 149
Barry, Mayor Marion   192
Bashara, Jane   44
Bashara, Robert   44
Baucas, Senator Max   86
Beatty, Christine   21
Beck, Glenn   130, 145, 207, 230
Beckmann, Frank   200
Belushi, John   126

Bergdahl, Sgt. Bowe   103
Berman, Laura   2
Bernero, Mayor Virg   113
Bernstein, Carl   144
Berra, Yogi   19
Berry, Halle   149
Biden, Vice President Joe   26, 44-45, 65-66, 70, 97, 102-105, 123, 213
Bieber, Justin   217, 230
Bing, Mayor Dave   23
bin Laden, Osama   40, 65, 73, 108, 117, 217, 244-245, 255, 265-
                               266

Blair, Prime Minister Tony   105
Bloch, Byron   206-207
Bloomberg, Mayor Michael   46, 121, 124-125, 167
Bob, Baghdad   19, 103
Bobb, Robert   16-17
Bobbit, Lorena   51
Bobbit, John   51
Boehner, Congressman John   99, 255
Boitano, Brian   33
Bolling, Eric   153
Bonds, Barry   116, 256
Borger, Gloria   219
Brady, Tom   260-261
Brandon, Dave   253
Bratton, Bill   28
Breivik, Anders Behring   25-26
Brennan, John   87
Brokaw, Tom   117
Brown, Chris   235
Brown, Governor Jerry   167
Brown, Michael   28
Brown, Senator Scott   47
Brown, Senator Sherrod   73
Bruff, Tom   159
Byrne, Ashley   48
Bucholz, T.J.   112
Buckner, Ed   230-231
Bush, President George H.W.   128

Bush, President George W.   6, 34, 41, 54, 59, 61, 69, 74, 101, 162, 198, 219, 223, 238, 245, 263
Bush, Governor Jeb   174
Bush, Reggie   259-260
Byrd, Senator Robert   53
Cain, Herman   127, 129, 130-132, 211-212
Caddell, Pat   138
Camping, Reverend Harold   245-246
Capone, Al   68
Card, Secretary Andrew   51
Carney, Jay   45, 95, 139, 144
Carrey, Jim   132
Carroll, Pete   259-260
Carter, President Jimmy   54
Cass, Momma   139
Castro, Fidel   198-199
Chamberlain, Neville   94
Chavez, President Hugo   198-199
Cheney, Vice President Dick   6, 209
Christie, Governor Chris   75-76, 140-141, 213
Chu, Secretary Steven   136, 153-156
Clay, Andrew Dice   20
Clinton, President Bill   13, 45, 54, 68-71, 108-114, 126, 220
Clinton, Secretary Hillary   44-45, 53-55, 66, 70-71, 88-89, 95, 107-110, 113, 125, 141, 172, 175-176, 261
Clooney, George   203
Close, Glenn   51
Cobb, Ty   256
Coleman, Mary Sue   253
Collins, Gail   209
Collins, Jason   98, 163
Conyers, Councilwoman Monica   20, 115
Cooper, Anderson   238
Corbett, Governor Tom   255-256
Costner, Kevin   223
Crane, Bob   8
Cronkite, Walter   19
Crowitz, L. Gordon   205
Crowley, Candy   265

Cruz, Senator Ted · 99, 145
Cummings, Congressman Elijah · 189
Curtis, Jamie Lee · 211
Dahmer, Jeffrey · 82, 158
Dangerfield, Rodney · 8
Daniels, Governor Mitch · 127
Dantonio, Mark · 253
David, Larry · 97
Davies, Brandon · 38
Davis, Bob · 42
Dean, Senator Howard · 224
de Blasio, Mayor Bill · 27-28
DeKoker, Neal · 93
Denicore, Mark · 190
Dillon, State Treasurer Andy · 112
Dingell, Congressman John · 113
Disney, Walt · 93, 217
Dogg, Snoop · 235
Dole, Senator Bob · 108
Downie Jr., Leonard · 144
Dukakis, Kitty · 128
Dukakis, Governor Michael · 91, 126, 128
Earnest, Josh · 104
Eastwood, Clint · 203, 215-216, 224
Edwards, Senator John · 126
Emmanuel, Mayor Rahm · 33, 59
Estevez, Emilio · 93
Fawcett, Farrah · 217
Fields, Sally · 265
Fluke, Sandra · 74-75, 77, 120, 136-137, 142
Flynt, Larry · 8
Foster, Vince · 108
Fouts, Mayor Jim · 116
Fox, Nickole · 40-41
Frank, Congressman Barney · 50
Franken, Senator Al · 110, 127, 154
Franklin, Aretha · 5
Freeh, Louis · 254
Friedman, Milton · 140

Friedman, Thomas   208-209
Friess, Foster   133
Funicello, Annette   217-218
Garner, Eric   28
Geronimo   40
Gentz, Joseph   43-44
George, Inspector General J. Russell   120
Ghaneima, Abu   227
Ghosn, Carlos   83-84
Gibson, Mel   223
Giffords, Congresswoman Gabby   3
Gingrich, Speaker Newt   122-123, 126-127, 131-134, 150, 189
Giraudo, James   73
Gleason, State Senator John   40
Gluck, Zoltain   227-228
Goodell, Roger   261
Goldwater, Senator Barry   201
Gore, Vice President Al   3, 9-10, 148, 168, 247, 259
Gosnell, Dr. Kermit   82
Graham, Katherine   144
Granholm, Governor Jennifer   115
Gray, Mayor Vincent   163, 193-194
Greer, Mike   239
Gross, Alan   174
Gueyser, Teresa   16
Haig, General Alexander   122
Hall, Arsenio   50
Hamburger, Tom   216
Hanks, Tom   102-103
Hannity, Sean   134, 249
Harbaugh, Jim   54-55
Harmon, Angie   119
Hart, Senator Gary   132
Highfill, State Representative Jake   264
Hill, Anita   131
Hilton, Paris   15
Hitler, Adolf   176, 255
Hoffa Jr., James P.   3-5, 61, 146
Holder, Attorney General Eric   62, 67, 88, 91-92, 110, 144, 146, 161, 255

Holmes, James   213
Horton, Willie   126
Huckabee, Governor Mike   126
Huntsman Jr., Governor Jon   127
Hussein, Saddam   168
Igharishi, Megumi   29
Ike   54
Ill, Kim Jong   197-198
Illitch, Mike   40
Issa, Congressman Darrell   62, 155-156, 189
Jackman, Hugh   202-204
Jackson, The Reverend Jesse   244-245, 247
Jackson, Michael   217
Jackson, Rayford   10
James, LeBron   263
Jarrett, Valerie   45, 70-71
Jealous, Benjamin Todd   49
Johnson, State Representative Lon   118
Jones, Reverend Terry   238, 240-244
Kaddafi (Gaddafi), Muamar   265
Kaline, Al   263
Kelly, Commissioner Ray   166
Kennedy, President John F.   54, 135, 199
Kennedy, Congressman Joseph II   199
Kennedy, Senator Robert F.   199
Kerry, Secretary John   95, 107, 110, 126, 178, 220
Kevorkian, Dr. Jack   40, 42-43, 158
Kilpatrick, Bernard   20
Kilpatrick, Mayor Kwame   2, 19, 21-22, 24-26, 240, 242
King, Bob   33-34
King Jr., Dr. Martin Luther   201, 245, 248
Koch, David   205
Khrushchev, Nikita   94
Klimisch, Dr. Dick   151
Kramer, Tim   115-116
Krugman, Paul   208
Kucinich, Congressman Dennis   234
Kucinich, Elizabeth   234
Kyle, Chris   55, 223

LaBarre, Suzanne   221
LaSorda, Tom   119, 153
Lavrow, Foreign Minister Sergey   176
LeBlanc, State Representative Richard   40
Lee, Tommy   14
Lenin, Vladimir   199
Leno, Jay   85, 98
Lerner, Lois   88-89, 144
Levin, Senator Carl   89, 120, 207
Levin, Doron   208
Levin, Congressman Sander   120
Lewinsky, Monica   108
Lewis, Timothy   254
Limbaugh, Rush   71, 136-137, 142
Long, Bishop Eddie   11-13
Longoria, Eva   118-119
Love-Hewitt, Jennifer   119
Lucas, George   102
Lugar, Richard   49
Lutz, Bob   157
MacFarquhar, Neil   227
MacLaren, Caitlin   227-228
Mandarich, Tony   256
Madonna   29
Maduro, Nicolas   199
Manson, Charles   240
Marchionne, Sergio   32, 69
Markey, Senator Ed   151
Marley, Bob   24, 35, 235
Martin, Trayvon   97, 250-251
Mathis, Otis   2-3, 8-17, 20, 239
Matthews, Chris   75-77, 190, 218-219
McCain, Senator John   45, 49
McCaskell, Senator Claire   142
McCleave, Manissa   228
McConnell, Senator Mitch   216
McCotter, Representative Thaddeus   46, 128
McElroy, John   93
McEnroe, John   64

McGuire, Mark   256
McVeigh, Timothy   218
Meatloaf   125, 127
Medvedev, President Dmitry   63, 175
Menendez, Senator Robert   174
Michaels, Al   258-259
Milchon, Arnon   119
Millen, Matt   116
Miller, Dennis   210
Miller, Dr. Norman   22
Miller, Stephanie   5, 201, 210-212, 238
Miller, Steve   89-90, 144
Mitchell, Andrea   133
Mitchell, Attorney General John   144
Monroe, Marilyn   135
Moore, Michael   198, 200, 223-224
Morgan, Piers   138
Morsi, President Muhammed   95
Mulally, Alan   151
Murdoch, Rupert   207-208
Murphy, Eddie   211
Murray, Rev. David   8
Nader, Ralph   266
Nelson, Senator Ben   65
Netanyahu, Prime Minister Benjamin   60, 177-178, 208
Nixon, President Richard   68, 79, 138
Obama, President Barack   3-6, 16, 21, 24, 33-35, 39, 44-45, 51, 58-109,
                                  112-116, 120, 124, 126, 129, 132-144, 156-163,
                                  168, 172-178, 191, 193, 201, 208-211, 216, 219,
                                  230, 245, 247-248, 263-268
Obama, Michelle   82-83, 113
O'Keefe, James   206-207
O'Mara, Mark   251
O'Reilly, Mayor John   241-242
Osgood, Charles   208
Pawlenty, Governor Tim   126
Palin, Sarah   58, 141, 215
Palmeiro, Rafael   256
Parks, Rosa   263

Parker, Kathleen   112, 190
Paterno, Joe   227, 252, 254-255, 257-258
Pathenos, Father Nick   202
Paul, Senator Rand   145
Paul, Congressman Ron   127-129, 161
Paul, Mike   19, 24-25
Pauley, Jane   207
Payne, Henry   2, 13
Pearce, Harry   207
Pelosi, Congresswoman Nancy   79, 132, 136-137, 210
Penn, Sean   199
Penske, Roger   36-37
Perot, Ross   108
Perry, Governor Rick   5, 58, 128-129, 153, 209, 212-213
Pesci, Joe   51
Petraeus, General David   51, 238
Petri, Alexandra   221
Pickens, Slim   168
Pitney Jr., John   189-190
Pitt, Brad   165
Plouffe, David   60-61
Polanski, Roman   10
Putin, President Vladimir   45, 63, 94, 98, 100, 191, 266
Queen Elizabeth   104-105
Ramsay, Gordan   64
Ramsey, Dave   210
Rattner, Steven   33
Rauf, Imam Feisal Abdul   55, 230
Reagan, President Ronald   54, 58, 63, 93, 122, 217-218
Redford, Robert   80
Reed, Arnold   19
Reid, Senator Harry   76, 99, 110, 118, 250
Riddle, Sam   10
Rice, Ray   261
Rice, Susan   88
Rivers, Joan   165, 199
Roberts, Chief Justice John   64
Robinson, Jackie   163
Rodriguez, Rich   204, 253

Rogen, Seth   224
Romney, Ann   136, 138
Romney, Governor Mitt   26, 45, 47, 67-68, 72-78, 91, 98, 118, 122-142,
                                   175-176, 189, 212-213, 216, 263-268

Rosen, James   91, 144
Ross, Brian   213-215
Rove, Carl   142
Rudolph, Eric   219
Ryan, Congressman Paul   45, 67, 105
Sanders, Colonel   257
Sanders, Marshon   235
Sandusky, Jerry   227, 254-256, 258
Sanford, Governor Mark   51
Santorum, Senator Rick   127, 133, 135-136, 189
Saslow, Eli   63
Sawyer, Diane   210
Scalia, Justice Antonin   64
Schmidt, Gail   115
Schultz, Eric   103-104
Schultz, Howard   52-53
Schumer, Senator Charles   155
Segretti, Donald   115, 138
Sehorn, Jason   119
Selig, Bud   253
Shakur, Tupac   103
Sharpton, The Reverend Al   27-28, 110, 237, 249, 251
Shaw, Bernard   128
Sheen, Charlie   37, 39, 240, 243-244
Shelby, Senator Richard   151
Silverman, David   233
Simpson, O.J.   131, 250
Sirota, David   219
Solis, Secretary Hilda   162
Somers, Judge   241-242
Smith, Joseph   38-39
Snowden, Edward   98
Snyder, Dan   195
Snyder, Governor Rick   115, 203-205
Soros, George   90

Sosa, Sammy   256
Spade, David   119
Spanier, Graham   254-255
Spitzer, Eliot   13, 16, 112, 190
Springsteen, Bruce   141
Stallkamp, Tom   36-37
Standish, Fred   182-184
Stephanopoulos, George   213
Stein, Ben   126
Stephens, Bret   180-181
Strickland, Administrator David   150
Studdard, Reuben   50
Stupak, Congressman Bart   65
Swaggert, Reverend Jimmy   130
Taylor, Dustin   233
Temple-Raston, Dina   219
Thatcher, Prime Minister Margaret   217-218
Thomas, Justice Clarence   64, 131
Tressel, Jim   253
Trumka, Richard   5
Trump, Donald   75, 125-127
Tsarnaev, Dzhokhar   162, 218
Turner, Khary Kimani   24
Tyson, Mike   243
Vajdic, Melinda   235
Vick, Michael   158
Vines, Betsy   66, 117, 147, 149, 183, 189
Vines, Greg   184-185
Waldinger, Marcel   13
Walker, Governor Scott   205
Wallace, Chris   39, 60-61
Warren, Senator Elizabeth   47
Wasko, Steve   17
Wasserman-Schultz, Congresswoman Debbie   28, 81
Weiner, Congressman Anthony 14-16, 165, 168, 208
White, Chris   16
Wilder, Governor Doug   44
Williams, Brian   207-208
Williams, Juan   212

Williams, Pharrell   53
Wilson, Congressman Joe   81
Wood, Natalie   103
Woods, Tiger   216
Woodward, Bob   80
Worthy, Prosecutor Kim   242
Wozniak, Steve   102
Wright, Reverend Jeremy   119, 129, 133
Young, Brigham   38
Zedong, Mao   199
Zetsche, Dieter   36
Zimmerman, George   96, 249-251